I0092240

Hyperlocal Organizing

Environmental Communication and Nature: Conflict and Ecoculture in the Anthropocene

Series Editor: C. Vail Fletcher, University of Portland

This interdisciplinary book series seeks original proposals that examine environmental communication scholarship. In the Anthropocene era, the period during which human activity has become the dominant influence on climate and the environment, the need for highlighting and re-centering nature in our worldviews and policies is urgent, as collapsing ecosystems across the globe struggle to survive. Topics might include climate change, land use conflict, water rights, natural disasters, non-human animals, the culture of nature, ecotourism, wildlife management, human/nature relationships, food studies, sustainability, eco-pedagogy, mediated nature, eco-terrorism, environmental education, ecofeminism, international development, and environmental conflict. Ultimately, scholarship that addresses the general overarching question "how do individuals and societies make sense of and act against/within/out of nature?" is welcomed. This series is open to contributions from authors in environmental communication, environmental studies, media studies, rhetoric, political science, critical geography, critical/ cultural studies, and other related fields. We also seek diverse and creative epistemological and methodological framings that might include ethnography, content analysis, narrative and/ or rhetorical analysis, participant observation, and community-based participatory research, among others. Successful proposals will be accessible to a multidisciplinary audience.

Recent Titles in This Series

Hyperlocal Organizing: Collaborating for Recovery Over Time
By Jack L. Harris
Communities and the Clean Energy Revolution: Public Health, Economics, Design, and Transformation
By Melanie J. La Rosa
Fracking and the Rhetoric of Place
By Justin Mando
Water, Rhetoric, and Social Justice: A Critical Confluence
Edited by Casey R. Schmitt, Theresa R. Castor, and Christopher S. Thomas
Environmental Activism, Social Media, and Protest in China: Becoming Activists over Wild Public Networks
By Elizabeth Brunner
Natural Disasters and Risk Communication: Implications of the Cascadia Subduction Zone Megaquake
Edited by C. Vail Fletcher and Jennette Lovejoy
Critical Environmental Communication: How Does Critique Respond to the Urgency of Environmental Crisis?
By Murdoch Stephens
Natural Disasters and Risk Communication: Implications of the Cascadia Subduction Zone Megaquake
Edited by C. Vail Fletcher and Jennette Lovejoy
Communicating in the Anthropocene: Intimate Relations
Edited by C. Vail Fletcher and Alexa Dare
Communicating the Climate Crisis: New Directions for Facing What Lies Ahead
By Julia B. Corbett

Hyperlocal Organizing

Collaborating for Recovery Over Time

Jack L. Harris

LEXINGTON BOOKS

Lanham • Boulder • New York • London

Published by Lexington Books
An imprint of The Rowman & Littlefield Publishing Group, Inc.
4501 Forbes Boulevard, Suite 200, Lanham, Maryland 20706
www.rowman.com

86-90 Paul Street, London EC2A 4NE

Copyright © 2022 by The Rowman & Littlefield Publishing Group, Inc.

All rights reserved. No part of this book may be reproduced in any form or by any electronic or mechanical means, including information storage and retrieval systems, without written permission from the publisher, except by a reviewer who may quote passages in a review.

British Library Cataloguing in Publication Information Available

Library of Congress Cataloging-in-Publication Data

Names: Harris, Jack L., author.
Title: Hyperlocal organizing : collaborating for recovery over time / Jack L. Harris.
Description: Lanham : Lexington Books, [2022] | Series: Environmental communication and nature : conflict and ecoculture in the anthropocene | Includes bibliographical references and index.
Identifiers: LCCN 2022034656 (print) | LCCN 2022034657 (ebook) | ISBN 9781666927238 (cloth) | ISBN 9781666927252 (paperback) | ISBN 9781666927245 (ebook)
Subjects: LCSH: Disaster relief. | Community organization. | Community development. | Interorganizational relations.
Classification: LCC HV553 .H433 2022 (print) | LCC HV553 (ebook) | DDC 363.34—dc23/eng/20220916
LC record available at https://lccn.loc.gov/2022034656
LC ebook record available at https://lccn.loc.gov/2022034657

To Laura Greenstone.
In memory of our many WTF moments
during Sandy Response and Recovery.
Always.

Contents

Acknowledgments   ix

Introduction: Perpetual Disaster Response and Recovery: The New Normal?   1

1   Communicating and Organizing after Disaster   17

2   How Public Policy Shapes the Organizational Landscape of Recovery   33

3   Writing Community Back into Disaster Recovery: Hyperlocal Organizing and Interorganizational Relationships   53

4   Using Stakeholder Theory to Build Theories of Hyperlocal Organizing   73

5   Hyperlocal Organizing after Hurricane Sandy: The View from Coastal New Jersey and Staten Island, New York   87

6   Hyperlocal Organizing: Implications for Democratic Governance and Resilience   103

Appendix A   113

Appendix B   127

References   133

Index   149

About the Author   159

Acknowledgments

Like long-term recovery, writing a book is a collaborative effort wrapped around a long and often-times solitary slog. It is those collaborations that bring new perspectives, knowledge, and support to the task of creation and reconstruction. This book would not have been possible without the many people who gave generously of their time and insights even while enmeshed in the complexity and chaos of recovery. Those who committed time to interviews, made documents available, provided access to meetings and events, and connected me to other people and organizations made the five years of field research and three years of post-field research observation at the center of this book possible. Their work, commitment, passion, empathy, and commitment to the collective well-being of their communities is what makes post-disaster recovery possible.

Laura Greenstone, my friend, partner, and wife, embodied all of these traits, and we lost her much too soon in the summer of 2018. She spent her career helping those impacted by trauma and violence as an art therapist and counselor and was one of the first Disaster Response Crisis Counselors certified in New Jersey after 9/11. She worked extensively with families who had lost loved ones on 9/11 and lent her expertise in art and phototherapy to writers and scholars trying to make sense of the disaster through the tremendous amount of visual materials generated on 9/11 and in the aftermath. Laura was recognized nationally and internationally for her work, receiving the American Art Therapy Association's (AATA) Lifetime Achievement Award posthumously. She had previously received awards from AATA for her exhaustive work in government affairs, working tirelessly to integrate the creative arts therapies and more broadly, the arts, into our healthcare system. Laura was gifted clinically as well working for more than twenty years with children and families whose lives were upended through violence and abuse. She also gave lectures in the United States and Europe on the therapeutic, clinical, and systems dimensions of art therapy while generously sharing her own experiences as a double-organ transplant recipient who used art in her own healing and wellness journeys. My own career in disaster scholarship and the genesis of this book owe much to her influence and support, and her love continues to surround me and propel me forward across even the boggiest terrain.

On October 30, the day after Hurricane Sandy made landfall, Laura and I drove to the microshelter in our town. The middle school gym, kitchen, and library had been converted into a gathering space where residents could charge their phones, get warm, and receive information on impacts and next steps. With communication systems, both technical and human, compromised after the storm, she wanted to check in physically with the local incident commander rather than driving directly to the nearest mass shelter to volunteer. Volunteering in a congregate care operation would put her at risk as someone immune compromised from a double-organ transplant, so she wanted to stay local and avoid the mass shelters and gathering points. There we met Buzzy Baldanza, Wendy Baggot, and Chrissy Ellam. Buzzy was our town's OEM director and our incident commander during Sandy response.

Wendy approached me in the hall as I was charging our mobile phones and asked me what I did. After I said I was a Boy Scout a long time ago and now worked in communications, she said come with me and put me to work reorganizing the intake desk and recruiting new volunteers. Chrissy joined me soon after, and we began putting systems in place to track impacted residents, recruit and connect volunteers, identify resources, and connect people to those resources. Chrissy is a meticulous record keeper, and her documentation of systems and resources as days turned into weeks and weeks turned into months provided the first set of documents through which I was able to begin reconstructing the phased and rhythmic processes of long-term recovery beyond the three-month timeframe most commonly utilized for analysis of post-disaster recovery. Wendy is a connector with boundless energy and was an immensely helpful sounding board as I began conceptualizing and framing recovery processes as a people-oriented process of organizational collaboration through which resource constraints could be mitigated, managed, and sometimes even overcome. Buzzy is a master of logistics, operations, and grant development. Our small town has been immensely lucky to have him serve as our OEM director over the past decades. Throughout the research process, whenever I went to interview someone, attended a workshop, or gave a talk, people at state, regional, and national levels would sing Buzzy's praises after learning that I knew Buzzy and lived in Oceanport. Buzzy, Wendy, and Chrissy contributed immensely to my development as a disaster researcher.

Also instrumental to the development of this book are my colleagues past and present on the executive committee of the Monmouth Community Organizations Active in Disaster (the Monmouth COAD). These include the past chair Tim Hearne, the current chair Anthony Pluchino, Kevin McGee, and our county OEM director, Mike Oppegaard. Mike has done a terrific job as OEM director and has specifically made space for community organizations and nonprofits both in our county emergency plan and in the physical space of the county Emergency

Operations Center, the EOC. He has created a plan and partnerships that make our county more self-reliant and less dependent on outside institutional partners the next time a crisis or disaster of the magnitude of Hurricane Sandy takes place. Tim, now retired, was a former president of our local United Way, worked tirelessly to stand-up recovery organizations and provided fiscal assistance and oversight to community organizations across Monmouth and Ocean counties after the storm. Anthony has deep institutional knowledge of disaster recovery and case management through his work with Catholic Charities, the St. Vincent DePaul Society, and the National VOAD and provided perspective on the changing dynamics of long-term recovery. I hope we can eventually secure funding for the comparative analysis of different pro-grammatic and geographic approaches to post-disaster recovery that we've discussed over the years. Kevin McGee is someone who every community needs. A skilled professional in operations and management, Kevin has worked in both human services and post-disaster recovery organizations in our county and brings a much-needed depth of experience and expertise to the Monmouth County plural sector. Our COAD meetings and side conversations over the years have greatly enriched my perspective on the dynamics and processes of long-term recovery.

Keith Adams, NJVOAD's executive director, gave generously of his time and provided opportunities to present early versions of this work at conferences and workshops. Kelly Higgs, who currently works for FEMA, is a past executive direc-tor of NJVOAD and was also instrumental in making space for me to discuss and workshop this research over the years. New Jersey could not have better champions of the plural sector.

This book began many years ago in Chip Clarke's Graduate Seminar in Organiza-tional Sociology. Chip gave me plenty of latitude to explore the ever-accumulating data I was compiling and room to think about disasters and organizing in new and novel ways. It is in this seminar that I first began to develop and articulate the idea of hyperlocal organizing and connect it to the processes of long-term recovery.

Marya Doerfel has been an adviser, friend, and colleague and a constant, support-ive presence during a decade of turbulence and change. She knows all too well the long and tortuous journey that has accompanied the development of this book and has been steadfast in her support and encouragement of my academic, professional, and personal journeys over the last several years. Her insights and support have been and continue to be invaluable.

Mark Aakhus, Amy O'Connor, and Jorge Schement were all amazing members of my dissertation committee and indispensable parts of my intellectual and meth-odological development. *Hyperlocal Organizing* has taken a very different shape from that dissertation and explores a broader set of organizing processes, but their contributions to the development of my overall theoretical framework have been immense. Michelle Shumate made sure I had a safe harbor at Northwestern's Net-work for Nonprofit and Social Impact after Laura died in 2018. From there I was able to start the still-ongoing journey of sorting out my personal and professional life in a world without Laura's corporeal presence. Michelle and Amy interestingly enough had provided my very first professional feedback on a research poster at one of the annual Organizational Communication Mini Conferences (OCMC). I have been immensely fortunate to have such steady, ongoing professional and intellectual mentorship.

On a different note, Bruce Springsteen and the E Street Band provided much of the soundtrack that accompanied the creation and development of this book. It would be remiss to not acknowledge the influence on my thinking of an artist who understands the power of place more profoundly than most. Longtime and long-term quiet supporters of many of the vital community, grassroots, and neighborhood institutions of coastal and central New Jersey, Springsteen and his wife and collaborator Patti Scialfa implicitly understand the power that entanglements of people, organizations, and communities bring to the places we call home.

Andrew Schrock provided invaluable advice, insights, and corrections in the final stages of this manuscript through his editing services at Indelible Voice. He is an excellent editor and partner in moving a manuscript to publication.

The Department of Communication at the University of Illinois Urbana-Champaign has provided a wonderful home over the last year as I finalized the book and moved it to publication. It has been a welcoming and very supportive environment in which to further develop these ideas and move them to press.

Finally, and quite importantly, Heather Saylor and I began swimming together just a short couple of years ago as I began the development of this manuscript. She has helped me to keep the shore in sight and time and again has given me shelter from the storm.

All errors, omissions, and mistakes are mine, of course. The perspectives developed in this book are not reflective of any one person or group's ideas or opinions, especially those ideas of institutional failures and limitations in disaster response and recovery explored in this book and its related research. The disagreements and controversy that some of these ideas are sure to engender are a result of my analysis and synthesis of the research, observations, and academic literature that underly the concept of hyperlocal organizing, and not of any people, groups, or organization's perspectives, ideas, or opinions.

Jack L. Harris
Urbana, Illinois

Introduction

Perpetual Disaster Response and Recovery: The New Normal?

"I wanted to tell them what was coming, but I just couldn't," he said. "I wanted to tell them the hurricane is the easy part. That their lives were going to be miserable, pure hell for the next five years. That 'recovery' is like slow and grinding . . . it's like watching a car crash in slow motion, over and over again."

Doug Quinn Toms River, *The Star-Ledger*, September 21, 2017

Organizing for disaster recovery is a complex, time-consuming process with many moving parts. How people, communities, and organizations solve complex public problems such as recovery after disaster is of increasing importance to social, political, and economic life, not just in the United States, but globally as well. This book builds a theory of hyperlocal organizing using primarily U.S.-based data, particularly five-plus years of field research on post-disaster recovery in the mid-Atlantic following 2012's Hurricane Sandy. However, the processes outlined here and the activities of communities and organizations to recover from disaster have implications for response and recovery globally as the scope, frequency, intensity, and severity of weather-related and natural hazards events grow. Record flooding in Western Europe, wildfires in Australia, typhoons in South and East Asia all require hyperlocal as well as institutional response to disaster.

Over the past decade, there has been a significant increase in the number of billion-dollar-plus natural hazards events (disasters) in the United States. On average, the United States averaged 4.8 one-billion-dollar disasters ("billion-dollar disasters") per year between 1980 and 2010, increasing dramatically to an average of 12.3-billion-dollar weather events per year between 2010 and 2019. From 2019-2021, the U.S. averaged 18.7 billion-dollar disasters per year. 2021 saw 20-billion-dollar-plus natural hazards events in the United States. For the five-year period from 2017 to 2021, the total cost of these natural hazards events has totaled $742.1 billion dollars. Since 1980, the total cost of billion-dollar disasters has totaled a CPI adjusted $2.156 billion dollars. Over the last 5-years 5,412 California wildfires have burned 1,17,888 million acres of land. At the end of 2019, in Australia's New South Wales, 136 wildfires had killed 24 people and 480 million animals, destroyed 1,300 homes, and burned up 8.9 million acres of land. Three earthquakes in Haiti since 2010, two of magnitude 7.0 or greater, and one of 5.9 magnitude have displaced thousands of people and wrecked infrastructure, homes, and communities in some of Haiti's remotest and poorest regions. In 2017, Hurricanes Irma (Category 5) and Maria (Category 4) created catastrophic failures in infrastructure, governance, emergency response, and recovery in Puerto Rico. The yearly compounding effects of these disasters have created a need for multiple long-term recovery processes, often drawing from the same funding sources, organizational infrastructure, and interorganizational recovery networks that are required for disaster relief and long-term recovery from disaster. The role of grassroots organizing in citizen and community response takes on added urgency with the increasing frequency and intensity of natural hazards events over the past decade. Through a book, articles, congressional testimony, and tweets Montano forcefully argues for a revisioned federal disaster planning process that connects disaster response and recovery with climate change actions to address the increasing threat from the increasing frequency of billion-dollar-plus disasters.[1]

DEFINING DISASTER AND RECOVERY

"Disaster" is an increasingly contested term as the number and frequency of disasters lay bare our frayed social fabric, institutional failures, historic inequalities, and collapsing governance. How we understand disaster changes over time and reflects a witches brew of academic and professional definitions, type of disaster(s), and personal experience of disaster(s). Quarantelli frames disaster as belonging to a category of families that (a) involve physical impacts from natural hazards or weather events, (b) involve the social impact or social effects from a physical event, or (c) are linguistically or socially constructed to reflect actual or perceived danger, risk, or hazard. Linguistic and social definitions of disaster require an agreement or "consensus" around the nature and severity of the danger, risk, or hazard present.[2]

Foreshadowing more recent research on the effects of race and class on disaster response and recovery, Quarantelli's work explored how both the perception and the impact of crisis and disaster on families, communities, and organizations may have different starting and stopping points based on perception, impact from, or role in the unfolding crisis or disaster. In his history of Hurricane Katrina from 1915 to 2015, Horowitz (2020) emphasizes how the same events impacting disaster preparedness, response, and recovery were perceived very differently by African American, black, and white residents of New Orleans and the Gulf Coast parishes.

The rumors, myths, and stories of blown levees that circulated among New Orleans's black and African American communities after Katrina date back to decisions by the New Orleans elite in 1927 to sacrifice communities, wetlands, and poor and working-class homes in St. Bernard Parish to protect the City of New Orleans from the Great Mississippi River Flood. These stories were also prevalent after Hurricane Betsy in 1965. Stark differences in recovery between white middle-class neighborhoods in Lakeview and black neighborhoods in Gentilly and the abandonment and destruction of New Orleans' well-built public housing all contributed to different perceptions and interpretations of the extent and effectiveness of post-Katrina recovery among black and white residents of New Orleans. Horowitz's extensive history of Katrina makes clear that disasters are inherently political, regardless of whether a geophysical, hydrological, meteorological, or climatological event manifests specific social impacts. Perceptions of a disaster's cause manifest in communities as the extent of the disaster and the inadequacy of the response become clear and stories become repeated over time regardless of their veracity. These stories finally become perceived as facts demonstrating racial and social inequities in disaster response and recovery regardless of the geologic or hydrological factors shaping the disaster impact and government response. That is not to say that underlying political, racial, and socioeconomic factors do not result in disproportionate impacts, but rather what may seem like failure or abandonment often have historic roots that predate the physical impact of the disaster.[3]

Whether disaster is defined as physical impacts, social impact, or a linguistic construction of perceived reality may ultimately reflect differences between professional emergency managers and academic researchers' areas of concern and responsibility. For professional emergency managers seeing disaster as a specific physical event with measurable social impacts creates a framework in which specific response and recovery actions can take place. For academic researchers, debates over the true nature of disaster itself can illuminate blindspots in our work and foster cross-disciplinary engagement over problems of disaster and recovery. Quarantelli explains disaster as a series of social and behavioral processes that exist across different types of physical events, both natural and manufactured (earthquake, flood hurricane, tornado, tsunami, wildfire; chemical explosions or releases, nuclear accidents, derailments of trains carrying hazardous chemicals, and toxic waste seepage from dumps or warehouses). For the purposes of this book, I define disaster as disruptive social and organizational impacts from a physical, natural event such as an earthquake, flood, hurricane, tornado, tsunami, or wildfire. I refer to disaster, singularly, as opposed to disasters, plural, throughout the book as each disaster is geographically and temporally unique despite common and well-documented social and behavioral responses across different communities impacted by disaster at different points in time.

Framing Long-Term Recovery

While the definitions and concepts of disaster have been wrestled with for fifty years and can be categorized along a continuum of physical, social, and linguistic understandings, frameworks of long-term recovery remain elusive. Long-term recovery occurs one year after the physical impact of a disaster and can last decades, especially in regions repeatedly impacted by significant weather and climate events. It relies on interorganizational relationships that leverage civic networks and institutional response to rebuild peoples' lives, homes, and communities.[4]

While long-term recovery, or post-disaster recovery, is typically seen as part of the four phases of disaster recovery; preparedness, response, recovery, and mitigation, long-term recovery should be distinguished as its own phase of recovery. Post-disaster recovery should be divided into a fourth phase of short-term recovery and a fifth phase of long-term recovery, with mitigation as the sixth and final phase that transitions us from recovery back to planning and preparedness. There are many common rhythms to disaster response and recovery that become highly visible when we dive deep into problems of long-term recovery.

In the first seventy-two hours after disaster, individuals, families, neighborhoods, and communities are mostly on their own as emergency management protocols are executed and the institutions of response mobilized and positioned for response. In the next three weeks, as the parameters of the disaster become clear, physical safety, shelter, and food are the primary concerns of both the communities impacted by the disaster and the institutional response. Physical safety is not just a law and order response, however, but more importantly includes restoration of utilities, the resumption or relocation of public services such as hospitals and clinics, the clearing of roads, the stop gapping of breaches in levees and shorelines, the tarping of roofs to protect buildings from further weather damage, and the removal of the dangerous debris from homes and public spaces. After these three weeks, sensemaking continues for at least another three months as the impacts of the disaster and the needs of people and communities impacted by that disaster becomes clearer. It is during this time period that the shape of long-term recovery begins to come into focus. From about week three to the third month, emergent and grassroots organizations are active filling in the gaps of institutional response while national and international nonprofits and faith-based organizations begin to make longer-term commitments of people and resources. Long-term recovery groups (LTRGs) begin to form while state and county Voluntary Organizations Active in Disaster (VOAD) and Community Organizations Active in Disaster (COAD) may begin to take on coordinating activities for both short-term and long-term recovery.

Long-term recovery begins to operationalize in the three to fifteen months after the initial physical impacts of disaster. In coastal New Jersey and Staten Island after Hurricane Sandy (impact date of October 29), long-term recovery began to take shape between December 2012 and early 2014 as institutions mobilized, grassroots organizations acted, and Congress fought over funding the recovery. Sue Marticek, the former director of the Ocean County LTRG and current Executive Director of the post-disaster recovery nonprofit Compass 82, describes the start of long-term recovery as "when the adrenaline rush is over and the paperwork begins." The deskwork of long-term recovery is tedious and often more difficult than mucking out a damaged home, tarping a roof, feeding people in a shelter, or helping out with kids and teens while their parents try to figure out how to put their lives back together.

Long-term recovery is a slog with complex processes, arcane and complicated bureaucratic procedures, and uncertain funding. It involves endless meetings, close attention to detail, highly routinized work, compassion, and empathy as caseworkers grapple with bureaucrats and bureaucrats wrestle with laws, policies, and regulations that may not meet the needs of the people and communities impacted by disaster. It is no wonder that "long-term recovery is the neglected component of emergency management" (Rubin 2009) as it requires grit, resilience, and fortitude by impacted residents and communities, organizational agility and adaptability by community organizations, and a commitment to a multi-year process with dwindling funding streams.[5]

SBP, formerly the "St. Bernard Project" was founded in March 2006, seven months after Katrina's impact on Louisiana and the adjacent Gulf Coast. Traditionally, SBP entered a disaster zone a year after the physical impacts and focused on rebuilding homes through corporate partnerships and volunteer labor. In 2018, they were one of four remaining organizations (all nonprofits) still engaged in post-Sandy recovery in coastal New Jersey. The predecessor to Compass 82, the Ocean County LTRG or OCLTRG, was also one of the last participating organizations active in the coastal New Jersey recovery. What the founders of SBP (Zack Rosenberg and Liz McCartney) and Compass 82 (Sue Marticek and the team of Bridget Holmes, Cathy Farley, and Melissa Luckman), all recognized is that the size, scope, and scale of long-term disaster recovery requires organizational infrastructure and the ability of singular organizations to collaborate with multiple partners, across time.

Organizations committed to the slog of short- and long-term recovery are indispensable. However, long-term recovery is about much more than the actions of single organizations or individuals. Long-term recovery requires multiple organizations with different missions, purpose, size, scope, and capacity who engage with each other to help people and communities rebuild after the disaster. For the purposes of this book, I frame long-term recovery as a process of interorganizational communication to facilitate physical rebuilding and social and behavioral recovery beginning three months after the disaster and ending ten years after the initial physical impacts of the disaster. While this framing is admittedly somewhat arbitrary, it reflects the most recent academic research on post-disaster recovery from Hurricanes Katrina and Sandy. At the time of this writing, we are almost ten years post-Sandy and over fifteen years post-Katrina making these two meteorological and hydrological events the best-in-class cases for studying long-term recovery in the early twenty-first century.

Hyperlocal Organizing in Disaster Response and Recovery

If, as Rubin has consistently and forcefully argued, long-term recovery is "the neglected component of emergency management," hyperlocal organizing is the invisible process of disaster response, even though it is crucial to long-term recovery and related processes like resilience. Hyperlocal organizing blends emergent organizing activities after disaster with the actions of existing community organizations to fill in the gaps of institutional response and to access needed resources for people and communities impacted by disaster. Hyperlocal organizing is not simply synonymous with emergent organizing and spontaneous volunteering, frequent and important as these disaster response and recovery activities are. Instead, hyperlocal organizing is a series of collaborative activities that organize both existing and emergent responses to disaster and recovery. Hyperlocal organizing is a civic network (Diani 2015) and a social impact network (Shumate and Cooper 2022) that connect place-based communities and institutions together to solve problems of economic and social well-being. It is collaborative in nature and to be effective requires the widespread participation of local organizations and community members.[6]

Hyperlocal Organizing: Collaborating for Recovery Over Time

Hyperlocal organizing is fundamentally about participation and collaboration. Theories of stakeholders and civic media provide the scaffolding from which theories of hyperlocal organizing may be constructed. Stakeholder theory is important for understanding hyperlocal organizing because it provides a way to understand the interconnections and interdependence of organizations with joint interests or shared goals. Hyperlocal organizing takes place in a disaster-impacted community and is accomplished through communication and organizing activities that shape its response and recovery processes.

Hyperlocal organizing is a relational process involving communication and work practices that connect people, organizations, and communities to achieve shared goals of relief, recovery, and rebuilding. In some cases, these hyperlocal organizing processes result in an "organization"—an entity with clear interpersonal and social boundaries—designed to meet unmet needs or ongoing challenges such as rebuilding, food security, temporary housing needs, and financial assistance. Like civic media, hyperlocal organizing remixes and reconfigures existing communication and organizing processes to meet the needs of people and communities for association and interaction that create space for distributed actions that replace or supplement dominant institutional framing and interests. Hyperlocal organizing and civic media both provide paths to decentralized and distributed power and responsibility.

After the disaster, organizations often face challenges in their physical, social, and interorganizational environments that diminish their ability to operate and partner in routine ways. New configurations of relationships emerge amid changes in the organizational landscape of disaster-impacted communities as the realities of the disaster and the needs of the community become clear. As people, communities, and organizations respond to disaster, new organizations may emerge to help in a highly uncertain environment undergoing disruption. Locally rooted, emergent hyperlocal organizing does not mysteriously emerge only after social disruptions leave communities feeling alone and searching for answers. Instead, I argue that hyperlocal organizing should be seen as part of a network of existing and emerging organizations loosely related to a community's plural sector.

The plural sector is a broad array of organizations existing between the private and public sectors. Often underfunded and inadequately resourced, the plural sector is often called on to solve social problems through networked community partnerships. Within this civic network of strong, weak, and latent ties, existing community organizations may take on new roles to address challenges and unmet needs emerging from crisis. For example, in coastal New Jersey, a county-wide domestic violence agency expanded its counseling and creative arts therapy programs to serve disaster-impacted residents wrestling with grief and trauma. In the same county, an affordable housing construction nonprofit expanded its geographic reach to the broader coastal New Jersey region after other nonprofits closed up shop and left before the recovery was complete. These efforts represent ways in which networked community organizations are able to assess community needs after the disaster and respond accordingly.[7]

To fully understand how long-term recovery unfolds, it is important to consider the social and organizational dynamics of impacted communities and the relational ties between organizations managing various aspects of the recovery process. Stakeholder theory and networked theories of communication provide the intellectual foundations for developing an understanding of long-term recovery as a process of connected stakeholders wrestling with the question of recovery, resilience, and community survivability. Stakeholder theory is concerned with organizational survivability and organizational agency, the sustainability of an organization's mission and purpose over the long term, and the relationships that an organization chooses to engage in, prioritize, or maintain to foster long-term survivability.

Networked stakeholders also provide the social and organizational infrastructure important for community survival. Communities consist of networks of organizations that contribute to the economic and social well-being of individual residents and the overall community. Community survivability often relies upon organizational survivability, which, in turn, rests upon the health of the overall set of social and organizational relationships in which it is embedded. Hyperlocal organizing is a critical part of community survivability and is a process through which neighborhoods, grassroots organizing, and community organizations connect and coalesce to fill in resource gaps and address institutional failures in disaster response and recovery. These hyperlocal organizing efforts may also connect with institutional response efforts, but the locus of hyperlocal organizing efforts is on the people in their neighborhoods with whom they share social ties and the bonds of place.

Organizational Networks and the Plural (Civil Society) Sector

Organizational networks mobilize resources and build social capital through cross-sector relationships that connect multiple organizations with differing capacity, mission, purpose, and roles. In a study of Sri Lankan flood response in 2016 and 2017, Karuarathne and Gress (2022) identified the importance of cross-sector networks encompassing government agencies, nongovernmental organizations, faith-based organizations, and community organizations as crucial for providing support to flood-impacted people and communities. While government agencies dominated the response and provided the catalyst for mobilization, faith-based organizations such as Buddhist Temples and Churches were crucial for shelter and the distribution of food. Similarly, Harris and Doerfel (2017) in a study of a small coastal community after Hurricane Sandy found cross-sector networks dominated by government agencies and nongovernmental organizations relied on community organizations, churches, local schools, and volunteer firehouses for sheltering and food distribution. In the political jurisdiction analyzed by Harris and Doerfel, school districts and volunteer fire departments are independent of local, county, and state elected leadership and operate quasi-independently of the municipalities of which they are a part, enabling them to act more independently.

Both the Karuarathne and Gress and the Harris and Doerfel studies identified traditional institutional responders such as the Red Cross as more peripheral to the network and local faith-based and community organizations as more central to community-level response and recovery efforts. In a study of community recovery following the Great East Japan Earthquake and Tsunami in 2011, Otsuyama and Shaw (2021) reference the strong tradition of neighborhood civic voluntary associations. In one case study, they, like Harris and Doerfel, find that local decision-making supplemented by external stakeholder networks supported both overall long-term recovery efforts and transitions from one phase of recovery to the next.[8]

Localized networked stakeholders, or civic networks (Diani 2015; Small 2009), provide the glue that holds communities together in crisis and disaster. While established community organizations play vital roles in hyperlocal organizing processes in disaster response and recovery, the studies discussed in the previous paragraph operate one level above emergent response and important interpersonal and intergroup ties. In more remote regions of Sri Lanka social networks, the interpersonal ties between people and groups were vital in the mobilization and distribution of resources to families and communities that were out of reach of existing cross-sector community response networks. In coastal New Jersey, the site of the Harris and Doerfel (2017) study of networked community stakeholders, emergent response intersected with grassroots organizations such as Burners without Borders and Occupy Sandy resulting in the establishment of field kitchens, tool libraries, and resource distribution points in impacted communities.[9]

Burners without Borders entered the Northern Bayshore of coastal New Jersey to provide on-the-ground assistance and interestingly enough began partnering with a municipality to address short- and long-term housing needs. They essentially merged grassroots and institutional response without using local emergent organizations. On the other side of New York Harbor in Staten Island, Occupy Sandy organizers connected with a plethora of hyperlocal emergent grassroots groups left to grapple with the response on their own after the island borough was cut off from the mainland after the storm. Recent studies of local responses to disaster make clear what disaster researchers have always known, that in both disaster response and more importantly, in long-term recovery after disaster, local organizing is proactive, pro-social, and that rather than being redundant, contributes to problem-solving and effective decision-making through local knowledge of geographies, cultures, identities, and histories.

Improvisational Response After Disaster: The 9/11 Boat Flotilla

Disaster often involves improvisation and distributed sensemaking among not only members of the formal institutional response but also among those immediately impacted by the disaster and by members of adjacent communities rapidly mobilizing to address the on-the-ground realities of disaster. Kendra and Wachtendorf (2016) describe the experiences of Jeff Wollman, a waterfront construction manager for Reinauer Transportation, one of the Northeast United States' oldest and most important tugboat operators. Early on 9/11, Wollman rode to Manhattan on one of the company's tugboats accompanied by his son, soon after the planes hit the World Trade Center. Kendra and Wachtendorf describe the varied and impromptu activities Wollman and his son engaged in as part of the 9/11 responses. These activities were spontaneous, yet not disconnected from the institutional response and they built on Wollman's professional experiences in construction, heavy equipment operation, and general automotive knowledge and mechanics. Wollman and his son hotwired and moved semi-trucks, delivered drinks and food by hand and by van to emerging operations and staging areas, and operated a heavily damaged police van to pick up and deliver supplies from One Police Plaza, New York City's police headquarters to various staging and rescue sites.[10]

This microcosm of activities that Wollman and his son enacted was a mirror of the larger spontaneous response being enacted by the New York/New Jersey Maritime community in response to the attacks on the twin towers. The boat lift from Manhattan Island after the collapse of the world trade centers is simultaneously little known and extensively detailed. A flotilla of boats was operated and organized by people with varying skills, expertise, occupational and personal identities, and knowledge. Together, the boats in the flotilla worked singularly, collectively, apart from, and in concert with, the New York Fire and Police Departments, the U.S. Coast Guard and countless paid and volunteer EMS squads and Fire Departments from New Jersey. NJ Fire Departments and Emergency Medical Services rapidly mobilized at New Jersey harbors as the extent of the catastrophe became clear and survivors were evacuated. The 9/11 boat flotilla is discussed as an example of a hyperlocal organizing response to a manufactured crisis or disaster in chapter 3.

Hyperlocal Organizing: Processes of Communication and Collaboration for Community Survivability After Disaster

The central thesis of this book is that recovery from crisis and disaster is organized locally at the grassroots, neighborhood, and community levels. Hyperlocal organizing is the process through which grassroots, neighborhood, and community organizations mobilize not only to engage in disaster recovery tasks but also to mitigate institutional failures, communication breakdowns, and outright isolation and abandonment of neighborhoods and communities. Through hyperlocal organizing, communities create processes of communication and organizing that allows neighborhoods and local communities to engage with state and federal government agencies and national or international disaster relief and humanitarian assistance organizations more effectively.

Institutional failures, communication breakdown, existing formal and informal work practices, and communication patterns are all present in long-term recovery. Oftentimes, local knowledge and expertise is passed over by the Federal Emergency Management Agency (FEMA) in favor of regional or national contractors and non-profits who may not understand the language, culture, rhythms, and histories of impacted families and communities. Browne (2015) terms this "The Bureaucratic Tin Ear" in her account of long-term recovery processes impacting a St. Bernard Parish family in Louisiana after Hurricane Katrina. One of her most striking accounts is of how family members, all of whom were skilled workers and laborers before the storm and who held deep knowledge of the physical infrastructure, geography, history, and culture of their parish were continually passed over by FEMA for road/home construction, transport, and debris removal business contracts despite their deep knowledge of the community and its needs. Many family members had engaged in rescue efforts during the storm and organized relocation and temporary shelter to Houston for members of their family, church, and community. After the storm, family members had even invested in new trucks and equipment to haul FEMA trailers into St. Bernard Parish, and storm debris out of the parish, in anticipation of new work associated with the recovery. Most were not able to recoup the cost of their investments once FEMA failed to award local contracts directly to local businesses and instead awarded contracts to large multinational firms. This vivid example of gaps between family, community, and larger institutional processes of recovery highlights the flaws in existing federal models of whole community recovery after disaster. Whole community models of disaster response and recovery all too often rely on outside organizations to organize the locals rather than using the locals to help the national and institutional response get organized.[11]

The organizing processes and communication practices of long-term recovery are often siloed between the public, plural, and private sectors. For the public sector, the problem is one of rebuilding public infrastructure and public assistance for impacted residents and communities. For the plural sector, the problem is one of rebuilding homes, case management for individuals and families needing services, emotional and spiritual support, financial assistance, communication flows, and information management. Private sector organizations see disaster response and recovery simply as a supply chain problem or as part of a broader corporate social responsibility strategy.

The Hurricane Sandy Rebuilding Task Force established in 2012 included only local elected leaders on the federal task force, even though plural sector organizations had boots on the ground, extensive experience in short- and long-term recovery, and were tasked with providing case management services to the most vulnerable populations in the region. A long-term recovery assessment report prepared by New Jersey

VOAD detailed the role New Jersey nonprofit organizations played in long-term recovery but focused only on relational ties with funders from the philanthropic community rather than their broader set of relational ties with public agencies and private sector providers of building materials and home goods. From the ground, it can often appear as though organizations are operating independently of one another, especially if they are operating in different organizational sectors or different regions.[12]

Addressing problems of this size, scale, scope, and complexity requires a sophisticated understanding of organizations and organizing and of the communication patterns and processes that foster the social and organizational interactions that make organizing happen. Across disciplines, scholars have sought to redefine organizations as processes and systems and move away from static conceptions of organizations as bounded containers of people and things in which messages are exchanged and tasks organized. This has entailed a move beyond the study of organizations to studies of organizing and from concerns with intra- to interorganizational communication. Organizing in this context does not mean political organizing to win elections as part of an electoral system, or social movement organizing to challenge and change institutions and institutional norms. Rather, organizing is the process through which people, communities, and yes, even organizations, interact with one another to achieve shared goals. In the Communication discipline, we see communicating as organizing, and organizing as communicating, where communication is the practices and patterns of interaction that enable coordination and the balancing of interests and needs at multiple levels and scales.

This framework of organizing has particular salience for disaster research where the fluid nature of the event, differing levels of scale and complexity, formal response protocols, spontaneous volunteers, and "pop-up" or emergent organizations vary across time, space, and place. Stepping outside traditional studies of disaster response and emergency management enables us to see disaster response not just as institutional protocols such as the Incident Command System, or social and organizational behaviors, but rather as an organizing process through which connection and coordination happen over time.

Defining Hyperlocal Organizing

Hyperlocal organizing is the process of grassroots communication and coordination to meet local needs often overlooked by institutional response efforts after disaster. These processes include both existing community and neighborhood organizations as well as "pop-up" organizations that emerge in disaster-impacted communities. An outcome of hyperlocal organizing following disaster, hyperlocal organizations are place-based organizations operating at the neighborhood or grassroots level that fill in the gaps between community needs and institutional response during times of crisis or disruption. Hyperlocal organizations may often engage in interorganizational relationships that use multi-stakeholder models of collaboration to provide resources, solve problems, and make decisions.

Hyperlocal organizing, however, provides much more than simply access to resources and assistance. Hyperlocal organizing helps provide the underlying patterns of organizational interaction that are important for local communities and governance. Ultimately, hyperlocal organizing is a form of civic engagement triggered when a shock event such as a disaster occurs. As such, hyperlocal organizing may have implications for both community resilience and democratic governance.

Following Hurricane Sandy's landfall in 2012 dozens of "hubs" and micro-organizations "popped-up" in New York City and along the New Jersey Coast. Interviews and field research across coastal New Jersey and the New York Borough of Staten Island made visible a variety of activities in which residents responded to disruption in their communities and engaged in organizing activities in the days, weeks, and years after Sandy made impact. The emergence of these organizations is consistent with past disaster research scholarship that finds spontaneous response from citizens and volunteers is a normal part of disaster response and recovery. Many of these new "pop-up" organizations and hubs connected with existing community organizations, long-term-recovery groups, and regional and national disaster relief organizations creating the cross-sector, networked stakeholder relationships through which disaster recovery unfolds. This intersection of emergent organizations with existing community organizations after disaster enacts a process of hyperlocal organizing through which community and neighborhood needs are made visible and the unmet needs of residents often met.

THE PURPOSE AND LAYOUT OF THIS BOOK

This study of hyperlocal organizing extends existing disaster research by connecting theories of communication and organizing with disaster research. It provides a more nuanced understanding of the interplay between emergent organizing and the interorganizational relationships that shape the landscape of disaster recovery. The main goal of this book is to use contemporary accounts of hyperlocal organizing to develop a robust conceptual analysis of the mechanisms and processes of organizing that contribute to disaster relief and recovery. Understanding these mechanisms and processes goes far beyond disaster relief and recovery, however. Hyperlocal organizing and the relationships of grassroots, neighborhood, and community organizations with larger, more formalized institutions have implications for resilience, governance, and civic engagement, all three of which are critical in efforts to solve complex social and political problems such as climate change and transitions to sustainability.

Chapter 1, "Communicating and Organizing after Disaster," introduces the theoretical foundation of the book and provides a snapshot of hyperlocal organizing activities after Hurricane Sandy. Using current theories of communicating and organizing, the chapter advances a framework of communicative organizing shaped by the material and organizational realities on the ground, which provides opportunities for cross-sector collaboration among grassroots, emergent, community, social movement, and institutional forms of organizing.

Chapter 2, "How Public Policy Shapes the Organizational Landscape of Recovery," discusses the organizational landscape of recovery focusing on the ways in which legislation and public policy shape organizational landscapes. The chapter focuses on federal and institutional frameworks for disaster recovery in the United States and the mix of organizations active in recovery, including coordinating entities such as the National VOAD, emergent and grassroots groups, and community organizations.

Chapter 3, "Writing Community Back into Disaster Recovery," explores the interorganizational relationships that underly hyperlocal organizing and the combination of improvisation, emergent organizing, spontaneous volunteering, and existing organizations and organizational infrastructure that shape hyperlocal organizing in crisis and disaster.

Chapter 4, "Using Stakeholder Theory to Build Theories of Hyperlocal Organizing," begins to build a theory of hyperlocal organizing using stakeholder theory as a key framework to understand the role of social and organizational infrastructure in addressing disaster recovery and broader issues of crisis and disaster. It argues that stakeholder theory can be extended to explore issues of the community as well as organizational survivability. The concept of communicative management as a key organizing framework that can be activated after disaster is also introduced in this chapter. Communicative management is a networked communication process in which organizations can identify shared interests, set joint goals, and try to balance power and leadership throughout the broader network. In hyperlocal organizing, communicative management is a process through which cooperation and coordination can emerge across the public, plural, and private sectors and between institutions and communities.

Chapter 5, "Hyperlocal Organizing after Hurricane Sandy," uses post-Sandy field research in New Jersey and New York to explore the organizing processes and networks of recovery enacted in the mid-Atlantic region of the United States after Hurricane Sandy.

Chapter 6, "Hyperlocal Organizing," explores the implications that hyperlocal organizing has for democratic governance and building resilience. I further develop the idea of associational and communal ties as cornerstones of the associational ties which underlie stakeholder theory and processes of hyperlocal organizing. Associational ties are those ties between organizations that provide a community's social infrastructure and build organizational capital, while communal ties are the social ties between family, friends, neighbors, and work colleagues that build social capital. Both types of ties are important for disaster relief and recovery as well as for building resilience and sustainability.

Chapter 6 concludes the book by asking that in light of the increasing frequency and intensity of storms, ecological and social disruption caused by climate change, and a general institutional inability to adequately address these challenges, is reliance on hyperlocal organizing the new normal in disaster response? And if so, how can we resource and build capacity for hyperlocal organizing efforts not knowing when, where, and how they might emerge?

NOTES

1. NOAA National Centers for Environmental Information (NCEI), "U.S. Billion-Dollar Weather and Climate Disasters (2021)," January 8, 2021, https://www.ncdc.noaa.gov /billions/,; "2020 U.S. Billion-Dollar Weather and Climate Disasters in Historical Context | NOAA Climate.Gov," accessed September 27, 2021, https://www.climate.gov/news-features /blogs/beyond-data/2020-us-billion-dollar-weather-and-climate-disasters-historical; Adam B. Smith, "U.S. Billion-Dollar Weather and Climate Disasters, 1980 - Present (NCEI Accession 0209268)" (NOAA National Centers for Environmental Information, 2020), https://doi.org /10.25921/STKW-7W73; CAL FIRE August 22, 2022 Stats and Events, https://www.fire. ca.gov/stats-events/ "Behind the Numbers: The Shadow of 2010's Earthquake Still Looms Large in Haiti," IDMC, accessed September 27, 2021, https://www.internal-displacement .org/expert-opinion/behind-the-numbers-the-shadow-of-2010s-earthquake-still-looms-large -in-haiti; "Haiti's Long, Terrible History of Earthquakes and Disaster," *Washington Post*, accessed September 27, 2021, https://www.washingtonpost.com/history/2021/08/14/haiti -earthquake-last-one/; Christina Maxouris, "Here's Just How Bad the Devastating Australian Fires Are -- by the Numbers," *CNN*, January 6, 2020, https://www.cnn.com/2020/01/06/us /australian-fires-by-the-numbers-trnd/index.html; "Hurricanes Irma and Maria: Impact and Aftermath," *Homeland Security Operational Analysis Center* (blog), accessed September 27, 2021, https://www.rand.org/hsrd/hsoac/projects/puerto-rico-recovery/hurricanes-irma-and -maria.html; Katie Atkins, "Nearly 1,200 Buildings in the Keys Were Destroyed by Hurricane Irma," *Miami Herald*, December 3, 2017, sec. Florida Keys, http://www.miamiherald.com/ news/local/community/florida-keys/article187816479.html; Nishant Kishore et al., "Mortality in Puerto Rico after Hurricane Maria," *New England Journal of Medicine* 379, no. 2 (July 12, 2018): 162–70, https://doi.org/10.1056/NEJMsa1803972.

2. Samantha Montano and Amanda Savitt, "Not All Disasters Are Disasters: Pandemic Categorization and Its Consequences," Social Science Research Council, *Items Insights from the Social Sciences* (blog), September 10, 2020, https://items.ssrc.org/covid-19-and-the-social -sciences/disaster-studies/not-all-disasters-are-disasters-pandemic-categorization-and-its-conse- quences/; Samantha Montano, *Disasterology: Dispatches from the Frontlines of the Climate Crisis* (Toronto: Park Row Books, 2021); Scott Gabriel Knowles and Zachary Loeb, "The Voyage of the Paragon: Disaster as Method," in *Critical Disaster Studies*, ed. Jacob A.C. Remes and Andy Horowitz (University of Pennsylvania Press, 2021), 11–31; Ryan Hagen, "Acts of God, Man, and System: Knowledge, Technology, and the Construction of Disaster," in *Critical Disaster Studies*, ed. Jacob A.C. Remes and Andy Horowitz (University of Pennsylvania Press, 2021), 32–50; Enrico L. Quarantelli and Russell R. Dynes, "Response to Social Crisis and Disaster," *Annual Review of Sociology* 3, no. 1 (1977): 23–49; Enrico L. Quarantelli, "Emergencies, Disaster And Catastrophes Are Different Phenomena," Preliminary Paper (University of Delaware Disaster Research Center, 2000); Enrico L. Quarantelli, "Catastrophes Are Different from Disasters: Some Implications for Crisis Planning and Managing Drawn from Katrina," Social Science Research Council, *Items Insights from the Social Sciences* (blog), June 11, 2006, https:// items.ssrc.org/understanding-katrina/catastrophes-are-different-from-disasters-some-implica- tions-for-crisis-planning-and-managing-drawn-from-katrina/; E. L. Quarantelli, "The Earliest Interest in Disasters and Crises, and the Early Social Science Studies of Disasters, as Seen in a Sociology of Knowledge Perspective," 2009, http://udspace.udel.edu/handle/19716/5745.

3. Andy Horowitz, *Katrina: A History, 1915-2015* (Harvard University Press, 2020); Steve Kroll-Smith, Vern Baxter, and Pam Jenkins, *Left to Chance: Hurricane Katrina and the Story of Two New Orleans Neighborhoods* (Austin, TX: University of Texas Press, 2015);

James R. Elliot and Jeremey Pais, "Race, Class, and Hurricane Katrina: Social Differences in Response to Disaster," *Social Science Research* 35, no. 2006 (2006): 295–321; Chester Hartman and Gregory D. Squires, eds., *There Is No Such Thing As A Natural Disaster: Race, Class, and Hurricane Katrina* (New York: Routledge: Taylor & Francis Group, 2006); Keith Wailoo et al., eds., *Katrina's Imprint: Race and Vulnerability in America* (New Brunswick, NJ: Rutgers University Press, 2010); Robert D. Bullard and Beverly Wright, "The Legacy of Bias: Hurricanes, Droughts, and Floods," in *The Wrong Complexion for Protection: How the Government Response to Disaster Endangers African American Communities* (New York and London: New York University Press, 2012), 47–72.

4. Claire B. Rubin, "Long Term Recovery from Disasters—the Neglected Component of Emergency Management," *Journal of Homeland Security and Emergency Management* 46, no. 6 (2009): 1; Claire B. Rubin, "Reflections on 40 Years in the Hazards and Disasters Community," *Journal of Homeland Security and Emergency Management* 12, no. 4 (January 1, 2015), https://doi.org/10.1515/jhsem-2015-0050; Claire B. Rubin and Susan L. Cutter, *U.S. Emergency Management in the 21st Century: From Disaster to Catastrophe* (New York: Routledge, 2020).

5. Jack L. Harris and Marya L. Doerfel, "Interorganizational Resilience: Networked Collaboration in Communities after Disasters," in *Social Network Analysis of Disaster Response, Recovery, and Adaptation*, ed. E.C. Jones, and A.J. Faas, 1st ed. (London: Elsevier, 2017); Katherine E. Browne, *Standing in the Need: Culture, Comfort, and Coming Home after Katrina* (Austin, TX: University of Texas Press, 2015).

6. Mario Diani, *The Cement of Civil Society: Studying Networks in Localities* (New York: Cambridge University Press, 2015); Michelle Shumate and Katherine R. Cooper, *Networks for Social Impact* (New York: Oxford University Press, 2022).

7. Henry Mintzberg, "Time for the Plural Sector," *Stanford Social Innovation Review* 13, no. 3 (2015): 28–33, https://doi.org/10.48558/0WX6-ZG74; Henry Mintzberg and Guilherme Azevedo, "Fostering 'Why Not'? Social Initiatives—beyond Business and Governments," *Development in Practice* 22, no. 7 (September 2012): 895–908, https://doi.org/10.1080/09614524.2012.696585; New Jersey Voluntary Organizations Active in Disaster (NJVOAD), "New Jersey Non-Profit Long-Term Recovery Assessment: Hurricane Sandy Recovery," October 28, 2016, http://www.njvoad.org/wp-content/uploads/2017/01/NJ-Non-Profit-Long-Term-Recovery-Assessment-print-version.pdf.

8. Ananda Y. Karunarathne and Gress, "The Role of Organizational Networks in Ameliorating Flood Disaster Impacts: A Case Study of Flood Inundated Rural and Urban Areas in Sri Lanka," *International Journal of Risk Reduction* 71, no. 2022 (2022): 1–15, https://doi.org/10.1016/j.ijdrr.2022.102819; Harris and Doerfel, "Interorganizational Resilience"; Kensuke Otsuyama and Rajib Shaw, "Exploratory Case Study for Neighborhood Participation in Recovery Process: A Case from the Great East Japan Earthquake and Tsunami in Kesennuma, Japan," *Progress in Disaster Science* 9 (January 2021), https://doi.org/10.1016/j.pdisas.2021.100141.

9. Diani, *The Cement of Civil Society*; Mario Luis Small, *Unanticipated Gains: Origins of Network Inequality on Everyday Life* (Oxford: Oxford University Press, 2009).

10. James Kendra and Tricia Wachtendorf, *American Dunkirk: The Waterborne Evacuation of Manhattan on 9/11* (Philadelphia, PA: Temple University Press, 2016).

11. Browne, *Standing in the Need*.

12. "Hurricane Sandy Rebuilding Strategy" (Hurricane Sandy Rebuilding Task Force (U.S. Department of Housing and Urban Development), August 2013); New Jersey Voluntary Organizations Active in Disaster (NJVOAD), "New Jersey Non-Profit Long-Term Recovery Assessment: Hurricane Sandy Recovery."

1

Communicating and Organizing after Disaster

Citizens, organizational leaders, and academics often conflate communication after disaster with solemn pronouncements from government officials and frantic social media posts by impacted residents and responding organizations. Communication, however, involves much more than just sending one-to-many messages through mass communication channels and online chatter. Communication itself constitutes organizing—the processes through which collectives share information, identify issues, solve problems, allocate resources, and make decisions. The public and many decision-makers in public and private organizations often view communication as crafting the right message or image to engage audiences on cable and broadcast TV, radio, Tweets, Facebook check-ins, or Instagram photos. Communication after disaster, however, involves more than designing the right messages for the best communication channels. Communication after disaster involves gathering networks of organizations and people organizing together to rebuild their communities and their lives.[1]

Communication is a relational process through which people and organizations make sense of their surrounding environment and organize to provide support, shelter, food, and healthcare to shepherd each other through the short- and long-term impacts of a disaster. These relational processes are patterns of social interaction. Stakeholders share stories and create consensus over the norms, rules, talk, codes, and contracts that shape the activities and behaviors of stakeholders over time. In turn, their organizing shapes the operating logics, mission statements, goals, and messages through which stakeholders organize their response in disaster-impacted communities.

Strategic and organizational communication serves two important roles in response and recovery: they are how we set and achieve organizational and interorganizational goals, and how we communicate with external audiences. Organizations are communicative, meaning they embody and extend institutional messages and logics through a multilevel communication process. In this process, cues extracted from our social and organizational environments are turned into plausible stories that guide actions and responses, which, in turn, create new roles, rules, norms, behaviors, and relationships designed to address issues in an organization's external environment. Communication provides the necessary link between sensemaking and organizing and enables stakeholders to achieve their stated goals. The processes through which organizations connect to their external environment and navigate external environments are crucial to understanding how people and organizations respond to and recover from crisis and disaster.[2]

PROCESSES OF ORGANIZING AND COMMUNICATION AFTER DISASTER

In coastal New Jersey in 2012, after Hurricane Sandy, Bishop John Shoal saw a need that couldn't be met through the existing network of faith-based relief organizations. Shoal was a leader in the United Methodists of Greater New Jersey, the Methodist conference that oversees congregations in the central and coastal New Jersey areas hardest hit by Hurricane Sandy. He responded by creating A Future with Hope to provide rebuilding and case management services to assist in disaster recovery. A staff of three was in place in December 2012 (within eight weeks of Sandy's landfall), 501c3 status was granted in 2013, and the first construction project was completed by the end of 2013. At the height of its operations, A Future with Hope employed 22 people, provided oversight to over 12,000 volunteers (between 2012 and 2018), and rebuilt or repaired 273 homes.[3]

By 2017, five years after Hurricane Sandy's landfall, A Future with Hope was one of four nonprofits operating as a "Nonprofit Builders Table." It was one of the few remaining organizations serving the more than 1,000 people still wrestling with rebuilding and recovery. Shoal's actions showed an organizational level response to meet gaps in recovery needs that could not be met by existing faith-based stakeholders active in community and disaster relief networks. When executive directors of the four different organizations were asked how and why they decided to work together several years into the recovery, they responded that they learned through collaboration. By working together through the early stages of long-term recovery, they were able to observe each other's working styles and communication. Open observation and communication helped them find similarities in work practices, communication, collaborative approaches, commitment to impacted residents, and enactment of their own organizational values and missions.

Community leaders and volunteers in Oceanport, a back-bay coastal New Jersey town of 5,832 people in which more than 50 percent of the homes received storm damage, created Oceanport Cares, a 501c3 nonprofit organization. Oceanport Cares collected and allocated financial donations after finding that a hybrid institutional/volunteer structure was effective at feeding and sheltering residents in town during the emergency response but was not set up to support residents' short-term housing and long-term recovery needs. Once the foundation was officially incorporated, the new organization could directly support residents struggling with complex long-term recovery needs and officially participate in county and state coalitions of organizations active in disaster (COADs and VOADs). Their activities included informal case management by volunteers, two of whom were successively employed by Catholic Charities as caseworkers and then later hired by FEMA. Oceanport Cares also assisted with grant funding and coordinating volunteers and organizations working to rebuild low-income families and senior citizens' homes. The organization and its volunteer leaders also played an important role in helping SBP, a long-term recovery-focused nonprofit founded after Hurricane Katrina out of volunteer rebuilding efforts in Louisiana's St. Bernard Parish, expand its operations out of Sea Bright, New Jersey, and into the broader coastal New Jersey region.

This new organization in Oceanport represented a move from recovery to resilience. It could directly receive funding to support residents in future crises and effectively participate in the more formal networked response and recovery networks alongside government agencies, nonprofits, and faith-based organizations. During the COVID-19 pandemic, Oceanport Cares worked with the local school board to direct food resources directly to forty-six at-risk families participating in the free and reduced-price school lunch program. They made 30-pound boxes of shelf-stable foods available to local organizations at $30 a box, the cost of which Oceanport Cares was able to cover through previously received donations and grants. By helping the local school board deliver resources directly to the school, at-risk families retained anonymity and were connected to a larger network of resources. The official nonprofit status also enabled the Sandy-created organization to work with the COAD to receive, store, and distribute 55 gallons of hand sanitizer and 2,500 cloth masks and surgical gowns directly to the county's nonprofits and faith-based organizations using their own facilities on a decommissioned Army base.

The evolution of Oceanport Cares from a hyperlocal response to Hurricane Sandy to a broader set of network activities during the COVID-19 pandemic represents a hyperlocal organizing process. Conversation among community leaders and volunteers led to emergent activities, followed by organizing relief and recovery processes, and finally resulted in formal organization. In the case of Oceanport Cares, formal organization was achieved through state incorporation and 501c3 tax status. These organizing activities didn't exist in isolation. Rather, they were embedded within localized needs as part of a set of cross-sector relationships that built social infrastructure and civic networks over time. Post-disaster organizing also operates in ad-hoc ways at the grassroots level as well.

In New York's Borough of Staten Island, a former borough resident teamed up with a childhood friend still living in the neighborhood. They showed up at their childhood parish asking what could be done to help. A parish priest directed them to Oakwood Beach, where they set up on a corner with a card table, two chairs, clipboards, and pens. They began recording residents' needs and the damage to their homes. This operation was later called Guyon Rescue and eventually operated out of a VFW Hall, before they purchased a trailer and military tent, then established a multi-year operation across the street from the VFW Hall.

Organizing processes are patterns of interaction that occur over time and are enacted at interpersonal, organizational, interorganizational levels, within and across communities of different size and complexity. Organizing depends upon the ability of people and communities to make sense of the situations they find themselves in and to foster a response by observing cues in the external environment. In disaster-impacted communities, these cues may include visible images of destruction (both in-person and mediated), reports from local neighbors or leaders, and information from official sources. Cues may also include ideas or information drawn from volunteers and relief agencies organizing in the impacted community. What matters in these cues-extracting processes is that information is deemed plausible rather than being entirely accurate. The cues and information extracted from people's surroundings enable them to shape their environment through talk, narrative, and dialogue. These patterns and processes of interaction enable people and communities to act, solve problems, and make decisions that shape their organizational and social environments.[4]

Understanding Disaster through Organization Theory

There are five families of organizational theories that help us understand the organizations, institutions, and interorganizational relationships active after disaster. At first glance, resource dependency theory (RDT) appears to be most useful in explaining post-disaster recovery networks and the shaping of the organizational landscape of disaster response and recovery. In RDT, organizations transact over time to acquire the resources needed to survive. These transactions, in turn, shape the power dynamics between organizations. For example, they might establish legitimacy, claim governance, or take leadership roles, which allow well-resourced organizations to exert authority within an interorganizational relationship.

Organizational ecology offers visibility into changes in organizational landscapes and networks. There are high rates of emergence, entrance, and exit of organizations during disaster response and recovery. In coastal New Jersey, over 300 people showed up at the first Monmouth County organizational meeting on post-Sandy recovery in December 2012. By 2018, only two of these organizations remained. A 2017 study by Harris and Doerfel in Oceanport, New Jersey, the coastal New Jersey community where the author lives, showed an increase in network centralization from 61 percent to 78 percent between the emergency response phase (October 30–November 11, 2012) and short-term recovery phases (November 11, 2012, to December 24, 2012). Network centrality scores highlight the degree of reliance among organizations in a network on any single organization in the organization for network coordination and connection to other organizations. It is through these network connections that information and resources flow. As the Oceanport network reorganized in response to network departures, the mix of hyperlocal organizations in the network declined from 87 percent of organizations in the network to 73 percent. National organizations increased from 13 percent of the network to 18 percent. The post-Sandy Oceanport organizational network illustrates how post-disaster recovery networks (a) rely on a mix of organizations to meet community needs and (b) that shifts from emergency response to short-term recovery to long-term recovery can be mapped through changes in the composition of a community's post-disaster recovery network.[5]

Organizational ecology also provides a framework for understanding differences in types of organizations in a disaster recovery network (variation); emergence and organizational change (selection); and why some organizations become core parts of post-disaster recovery networks and organizational landscapes, while others return to their usual missions or disappear completely from recovery or civic networks (retention). Community ecology, a subset of organizational ecology, provides a framework for understanding how the fluid entrance and exit of organizations in disaster recovery shapes interorganizational interactions over time. Where organizational ecology describes a community's organizational infrastructure, institutional theory highlights the connections between the social and organizational processes through which coordinated action takes place.[6]

Institutional theory provides insights into the material, symbolic, and relational constitution of organizations and how they emerge and endure. Spanning a vast body of theories and literature, institutional theory emphasizes the processes through which social formations become organizations and how in turn organizational processes institutionalize. These processes include storytelling that creates and preserves organizational memory and culture, norms that guide organizational behaviors, and external regulations that shape behaviors. Ultimately, institutional theories focus on the institutional logics that shape sensemaking, mission, and purpose, and the messages that carry these institutional framings and logics. Communication as Organizing or Communication as Constitutive of Organizing (CCO) is a framework for understanding how speech, texts, and communication practices enact organizing processes that create agendas, set goals, make decisions, and complete work. CCO theory puts communication in the center of organizing and emphasizes the role of communication practices and social interactions in organizing and organizations.[7]

Stakeholder theory emphasizes the shared interests in organizations and the universal claims that stakeholders have upon an organization. As a theory of organizing, stakeholder theory provides a framework for understanding the multilateral relationships of organizations and their importance for economic and social well-being. Ultimately, stakeholder theory is concerned with organizational survival over time. If there is no organization, there are no wages, taxes, philanthropic funds, information, or ideas to support a wider constellation of individuals, organizations, and government. The emphasis of stakeholder theory on the universal rights of stakeholders, shared interests between organizations, strategic cooperation, and workplace democracy helps us understand the interdependencies needed for long-term disaster recovery. This study uses stakeholder theory to create a framework of hyperlocal organizing to explain some of the dynamics of long-term recovery and of the interorganizational collaborations that build economic and social well-being after disaster.[8]

Gathering after Disaster

Gathering after disaster is the first stage of community response and represents a particular form of communicative organizing. Gathering after disaster enables people to make sense of the situation, understand individual and collective needs, and assess the efficacy of the institutional response. It is a first step toward organizing, as joint interests and shared goals are identified and the steps needed to collaborate and address those goals are established. As institutions respond and communities coalesce after disaster, we see parallel organizing processes and different uses of space between the impacted community and the institutions of response. Organizational identities and languages may conflict with the disaster-impacted community, even as local communities and disaster relief organizations organize to try to house and feed displaced residents and stabilize the initial disruption. Shelters and food trucks operated by the American Red Cross, Salvation Army, and FEMA are usually top of mind when government officials, disaster relief professionals, and the media think of post-disaster operations. However, post-disaster gathering usually takes place in a myriad of locations and operates very differently than envisioned by emergency managers and disaster relief professionals.

Impacted residents, community leaders, and volunteers gather in these spaces, turning them into workspaces and sites of organizing. "Organizational space" is usually defined as an office, classroom, factory floor, or even a Zoom meeting. Such bounded physical and digital environments define organizational use of space or tie organizations to particular physical sites or virtual meeting platforms. Work also takes place in "Third Spaces" such as coffee shops and libraries. During the COVID-19 crisis, what Wilhoit (2020) calls "unusual spaces"—homes, cars, community centers, and even the use of personal technologies and digital platforms—were transformed into workspaces. After disaster, converting unusual space into organizational space becomes the norm, which impacts the organizing possibilities and constraints in any given community. Gathering and organizing after disaster may take place in multiple locations and host activities and tasks in unusual spaces to facilitate post-disaster response and recovery.[9]

Physical Gathering Spaces after Disaster

Organizations active in disaster include emergent "pop-up" organizations, social movement collectives, newly created philanthropic foundations, and mutual aid efforts. Their new relief and recovery responsibilities traditionally operate outside of the disaster and humanitarian relief sector. Organizing activities take place in schools, churches, volunteer firehouses, VFW Halls, backyards, and street corners. They happen in restaurant and church parking lots, and down the streets of New York's East Village. After Hurricane Sandy, organizing efforts sprung up around field kitchens, shared tool libraries, trailers, and quickly pitched tarps. These organizing activities were grassroots efforts that connected people with locally rooted organizations. In turn, they expanded the capacity of local and regional civic networks through hyperlocal organizing. Improvisation after disaster will typically convert unusual spaces into organizational spaces. Field research after Hurricane Sandy identified multiple "unusual spaces" converted into organizing space. A list and definitions follow.

Microshelters: Small, usually impromptu shelters that "pop-up" in volunteer firehouses, schools, churches, and similar institutions. Microshelters tend to emerge from warming or cooling centers where impacted residents go to warm up or cool down according to the season, obtain water and/or other supplies, charge their electronic devices, file insurance claims, apply for government assistance, and have a meal. These spaces may be formally or informally operated by local or county offices of emergency management, community organizations, or mutual aid groups.

Volunteer Firehouses: Fire stations owned and operated by a volunteer fire department or fire district that utilizes trained volunteers for firefighting services. Volunteer fire services usually have a degree of independence from the municipal government in the jurisdictions in which they are located, by organizing as an independent fire company in a specific fire district. However, these organizations usually closely coordinate with their local governments, offices of emergency management, and other first-responder organizations.

K–12 Schools: K–12 schools may be utilized in smaller towns or regions to serve as a microshelter, and they may offer sheltering or feeding services. They are often utilized in smaller towns and regions that are more geographically remote and/or have multiple jurisdictions of governance within a single municipality. Large cities such as New York City or New Orleans typically do not utilize school building properties for response and relief. However, in Houston, schools in the hard-hit northeastern part of Harris County were utilized to launch rescues from and provide immediate relief and shelter to rescued residents.

Schools, Colleges, and Universities: Colleges and universities can also assist in emergency response and short-term recovery. Recreation and sports facilities were used to house displaced residents at Rutgers University after Hurricane Sandy. Methadone patients from Atlantic City were housed at a Rutgers-New Brunswick location where they could continue to receive treatment, after dislocation while response and recovery operations in their home communities were underway. Monmouth University (a private university) allowed its sports center to be used by the American Red Cross as a shelter. Post-Sandy, the Monmouth County Office of Emergency Management established a partnership with Brookdale Community College to offer sheltering options during future storm and weather events.

Coffee Shops: Locally owned, franchised, or corporate coffee shops where people gather to charge their phones, exchange information, and find sustenance in the early days after disaster.

Supermarkets: After Hurricane Sandy, regional supermarket chains such as Wegman's provided charging stations at their stores. In the Asbury Park, New Jersey, area, the Ocean Township Wegmans served as a point of information exchange between community members in addition to providing access to digital infrastructure. Locally owned ShopRite stores established vouchering systems so local volunteers and communities could gather food and supplies to support impacted residents before more formal systems of feeding, sheltering, and temporary housing could be established.

Churches: Churches are primary gathering spaces after most disasters. Parish halls, church basements, and even parking lots are used to provide services, food, and shelter. After Hurricane Sandy, Sea Bright used church parking lots directly across the Shrewsbury River from Sea Bright to reestablish municipal operations. These churches—Holy Cross Roman Catholic Parish, St. George's By-The-River Episcopal Church, and First Presbyterian Church of Oceanic—were all located near the Rumson-Sea Bright Bridge. They operated warming stations and provided food and supplies to impacted Sea Bright Residents. They also served as staging areas for residents looking to reenter Sea Bright to check on their homes and retrieve belongings in the evacuated town.

Parking Lots: Parking lots serve as handy and convenient open spaces in which to stage response and recovery operations, operate shelters, provide staging areas, cook meals, and exchange information. FEMA established a large sheltering, feeding, and utility company staging area in the large parking lot at Monmouth Park, a centrally located horse-racing facility in Oceanport, New Jersey. Colloquially referred to as "FEMA Tent City" by locals, the operation replaced Red Cross Sheltering operations at nearby Monmouth University and centralized FEMA operations in the area.

Parks: Parks are open or forested spaces that are used for passive and active recreation. Parks may be used as staging areas, storage areas, debris collection and removal sites, and supply depots following a disaster. In Monmouth County, New Jersey, the park system used existing buildings and their central warehouse to gather and store donated food and supplies before distributing them to individual municipalities.

Official Shelters: Official shelters are usually run by disaster relief and humanitarian assistance organizations as part of their responsibilities under U.S. or UN Disaster Response and Humanitarian Assistance Protocols. However, federal, state, county, or municipalities may operate them as well, depending on circumstances and contracts.

Reflecting on lessons learned from Hurricane Sandy, a coastal New Jersey municipal official relayed the following:

> Some of the lessons learned: to have a specific site set up for recovery for residents, where there is a generator. Not that it has to be a shelter, but a respite area, a recovery area, whether it be for Superstorm Sandy or a power outage or something like that. Don't know what Oceanport has done, but what we've done here in Little Silver is we have a women's club. And we don't really want to get into the shelter business, but a respite

area, a recovery area, just a place for the community to go. It was important for people to have a place to go that were out of their homes, where they could see their neighbors, grab a cup of coffee, charge their cellphones.

(Interview with Coastal New Jersey Municipal Official, February 2017)

This municipal official's comments reflect the importance of gathering after disaster for impacted residents. "Gathering" is not just a formal response that establishes a shelter run by an officially designated agency. It is also about making space for people to connect with one another to "see their neighbors." In these spaces, stories get told, misery shared, information circulated, and plans hatched. For hyperlocal organizing processes, physical space matters.

Reorganizing Through Gathering after Disaster

In the early days following disaster, the personal and professional lives of residents merge as impacted communities take stock of their situation and activate their personal and professional networks. This stock taking takes place individually and collectively, at home and in the disparate gathering spaces discussed previously. Through this stock taking, or sense making, residents connect with one another, seek out resources, and share information creating a second stage of disaster response and the foundation for post-disaster recovery. Personal, business, and professional lives remain disrupted for uncertain periods of time. Employees, managers, executives, and business owners all struggle to make sense of and restore some sense of normalcy to the post-disaster environment. People activated their personal and professional networks to find information, secure resources, restore business operations, and even relocated those business operations after severe disruptions caused by widespread storms such as Hurricane Katrina in 2005, Hurricane Sandy in 2012, Hurricane Maria in 2017, and Hurricane Ida in 2021.

In a 2010 study of interorganizational communication after Hurricane Sandy, Doerfel, Lai, and Chewning charted the progression from the use of interpersonal to interorganizational networks in post-disaster recovery. They found that business and personal recovery is phased, and transitions from a personal emergency phase to a professional emergency phase and finally to a transitional phase before the rebuilding phase commences. The personal emergency phase takes place in the immediate days and weeks after the physical impacts of disaster, as people use their interpersonal networks to access resources such as temporary shelter. Once people and families are secured, attention turns to people's livelihoods and they turn their attention to their jobs and businesses. This is especially true for small business owners. Business owners and leaders communicate with their employees to assess their safety, security, and ability to work. These owners and leaders also direct their employees toward available resources such as unemployment insurance. In the transitional phase, organizational leaders move from internal to external communication—engaging with key stakeholders and using legacy and social media to advise their customers and communities that they survived—to resume business. In the rebuilding phase, organizations move forward using their interorganizational networks to acquire resources, build new relationships, and communicate their survival and renewal.[10]

In a post-hurricane environment, people gather and organize across communities to share information and experiences, exchange resources, and negotiate recovery. These gatherings and exchanges of information often occur well outside the formal recovery processes and communication channels of government agencies and established disaster relief organizations. Restaurants and bars are often a site for community gathering and organizing activities, as gatherings around food have traditionally been places where family and community come together. Owners, managers, and staff may have extended personal and professional networks through which to organize, bring resources into the community, and serve as distribution and access points for community members. They can also connect with emergency responders, utility workers, and healthcare professionals struggling in the initial days and weeks after the disaster.

Local Businesses and Hyperlocal Organizing

In coastal New Jersey after Hurricane Sandy, an iconic local business quickly reopened and provided free food and a physical location for first responders and public workers to find a warm place to connect and share information. These activities served two goals. First, they supported first responders, public workers, and utility employees responding to Sandy. Second, they provided steady employment to their employees during a time of crisis and disruption. "They rely on their paycheck" BurgerBiz's (the iconic local business) co-owner stated during a 2013 interview with the author, referring to their hourly employees' need for continued employment and income and the negative impact that disruption from disaster would have on their families and livelihoods. BurgerBiz's employees were typically minimum-wage workers who relied on their weekly paychecks. By quickly getting up and running, the co-owners of BurgerBiz were able to rapidly bring their employees back to work and pay them while at the same time providing food and a warm space to rest for first responders and public workers working near round-the-clock shifts following the storm.

Many of BurgerBiz's employees themselves were directly impacted by the storm and suffered dislocation and significant housing damage. Reestablishing operations quickly provided these employees with a place to get warm and eat while earning a paycheck. These activities allowed BurgerBiz to meet multiple communities, business, and employee (stakeholder) needs while restoring their daily business operations and activities. Understanding the symbiotic post-disaster needs of the business and employees helps to develop organizational and community survivability and stability after disaster. Similarly, the owner of a local coastal New Jersey accounting firm emphasized that "our first effort was to get a handle on our people" as he relayed the steps he took after the storm to restore his business operations. BurgerBiz's co-owner used similar language in discussing their priorities stating, "our first goal was to reach out to employees."[11]

After disaster, business, personal, and professional recovery often overlap, turning workplaces, particularly small and midsized businesses, into centers of organizing and gathering as employers reach out to employees to assess their needs and their ability to recover. In these spaces, business owners can master the intricacies of both commercial and homeowners' insurance and obtain personal and business assistance from state and federal governments. Office space, or other undamaged dry space, becomes an important part of the recovery process. These spaces become places where employees can gather, do paperwork, and earn a paycheck. Restoration of businesses and workplaces help reestablish a sense of normalcy in impacted communities. In recovering communities, earning an income or a weekly paycheck becomes immensely important when temporary housing must be secured and homes eventually rebuilt.

Immediately after Hurricane Sandy, the owners of "Woody's," a prominent restaurant and bar in hard-hit Sea Bright, New Jersey, organized a gathering space in their parking lot. In this space, they cooked and built daily bonfires. Volunteers provided food, clothing, gift cards, and other resources to impacted residents. Ultimately, their humble parking lot served as a distribution point of information in a town where the power and water infrastructure had been completely destroyed. These nascent efforts later became the nucleus of the Sea Bright Resource Center and Sea Bright Rising, hyperlocal organizations whose organizational life began in a cold, dark, November parking lot.

ORGANIZING AND ORGANIZATIONS

Understanding post-disaster organizing requires planners and leaders in federal agencies and disaster relief and humanitarian assistance organizations to embrace emergent behaviors, and for organizers and leaders of emergent responses to be ready to scale into formal organizations (such as the 501c3 nonprofit described above) if needed. Disaster response and recovery, especially the long-term recovery process, requires flexibility and adaptability and the embrace of a broad organizational landscape. Organizing is dynamic and, although often centered around shared goals, it does not always result in enduring organizational forms or networks. In fact, organizing can be particularly ephemeral when self-organizing around common interests. Social interaction may result in gathering for common goals, but while social interaction may lead to organizing, organizing may not lead to the creation of a formal organization.[12]

At its simplest, organizing may be a repeated gathering of people with shared interests and goals at a specific place over time. Swimmers at Promontory Point, a man-made peninsula in Lake Michigan adjacent to Chicago's Hyde Park neighborhood, have been frequenting this cove since the early 1960s. The number of swimmers has steadily increased throughout the COVID-19 pandemic, as most gyms and pools were closed for the better part of a year. Open-water swimming has become a popular alternative over the last year, not only in Lake Michigan, but at the New

Jersey Shore, the Kettle Ponds of Cape Cod, and the lochs and beaches of Scotland. At Chicago's Promontory Point, an early morning group swims consistently throughout the year, as other individuals, couples, and groups come and go.

The entry at Promontory Point lies on the southeast side of the point. To reach the entry/exit point to the water, a swimmer must cross crumbling limestone seawalls and rocks. Sometimes, there may be an old plastic step stool to make traversing the rocks easier. Once the shore is reached, fastened to the underwater rock face is an old iron ladder and iron poles connected to an underwater wood lattice work belted across the face of the limestone. These man-made structures are not maintained by the City of Chicago due to liability issues. The area is collectively organized by the swimmers who regularly show up. At times, pink duct tape has been wrapped around the uppermost sides of the iron ladder and at the top of the adjacent pole. The brightly colored tape provides much-needed visibility when swimming back across the cove and trying to find the exit point on days when the water is choppy or the visibility is low. Swimmers have tied a thermometer (no longer working) to the closest buoy to measure water temperatures. One of the early morning swimmers has been posting water temperatures through a picture of his own thermometer on a Promontory Point Swimmers Facebook page. An ice axe for winter swimming was dropped in the water and lost in the winter of 2020–2021. Early in the summer of 2021, swimmers were joking that they should ask a nearby scuba diver who was practicing in the cove to look for the ice axe so they could have it back in time for the next winter.

The Promontory Point swimmers are not a formal organization by any stretch of the imagination (despite the presence of a Facebook page). Their activities are simply the outcome of swimmers with a shared goal of open-water swimming who must navigate the physical topography of Promontory Point to meet that goal. Conversation occurs on the rocks and on Facebook about different issues related to the physical site: what to do about boaters and jet skiers who ignore the buoys? Are there dangers of swimming on the north side versus the south side? How quickly is the lake churning and water temperatures increasing or decreasing? What should we do about the rickety ladder, or a photographer who takes images without asking permission of participants? The presence of these informal organizing activities provides a measure of safety by developing a collective sense of the physical site and the development of collective narratives about different events that occur throughout the year. Organizing activities and processes are occurring at Promontory Point within what appears at first glance to be loosely organized, ad-hoc activities in which people show up and leave according to their own schedules. So how do we understand how conversation and action foster organizing processes that meet shared goals?

Organizations have traditionally been viewed as a structured social formation in which people, conversations, technologies, symbols, rituals, and identities combine to achieve shared interests or common goals through processes of activity coordination, boundary setting, and membership negotiation. These activities and processes in turn can range from "emergent" to "institutionalized" forms. We often see emergent organizing in communities during and after crisis and disaster. Only later do they become institutionalized forms, in which organizational structure is cemented through rules and rulemaking, isomorphic processes, and institutional logics and messages. How organizing, organizations, and institutions differ are important to note as each provide different paths through which to accomplish tasks and create meanings.

Organizing processes and the social formations they foster are structured in pursuit of shared interests and common goals. We can best think of organizing and organizations as a continuum of action and presence. Organizational actions include activities and negotiations that people and leaders engage in. Through these processes, they establish rules, boundaries, and goals, then develop the processes, paths, and technologies through which their goals may be met. Presence, on the other end of the continuum, implies an organization omnipresent in the social landscape as a source of employment, resources, and volunteer labor to meet economic and social goals. Organizing can take place within organizations, between organizations, or even as a precursor to creating a new organization. Novel organizing processes and unique self-organizing activities achieve shared goals and support common interests.

Organizing, organizations, and institutions can be seen as a continuum through which coordination of roles and tasks takes place. On the "organizing" side we find highly informal organizational activities, which may become formalized organizations (connected systems of communication and coordination) within a framework of values, identities, rituals, and symbolic interactions. Between emergent and institutionalized forms of action lie organizing processes through which people communicate over shared interests and organize around activities and shared goals to support and defend them. These organizing activities further define the organization and its place within an organizational field or set of social relationships.[13]

At the far end lie institutionalized disaster response organizations such as the American Red Cross or FEMA. FEMA, for example, is embedded in the institutional processes of government agencies and the American Red Cross remains embedded within the nonprofit sector. Both are constrained by formal structures, policies, and relationships and have bureaucratic complexity that make it difficult for outsiders to collaborate or partner with them on an equal basis. Institutionalized organizations have come to dominate the organizational landscape of response and recovery. However, emergent and grassroots organizing over shared goals and values can and do operate in parallel to institutions and may sometimes be more effective than institutional organizations at achieving shared goals.

Wilhoit and Kisselburgh's (2015) exploration of bike commuters in a Midwestern City highlighted a collective of people engaged in a shared activity who held common interests in defending and supporting those interests. These bike commuters were not formally organized to engage in grassroots organizing or direct political engagement. While some bike commuters did organize and engage politically to support their transit activities, most of the commuters in the study did not identify as a collective in any formal way. Neither regular communication nor membership bounded or defined bike commuters as a group. Rather, they were engaged in a shared activity in the same space. Their aggregate actions through space—the geographic boundaries of the city, the road networks, and bike lanes—over time demonstrated the presence of bike commuting as a viable transit activity in two Midwestern cities.[14]

Like the loosely organized swimmers at Chicago's Promontory Point, the bike commuters engaged in communicative and technical actions to maintain the viability of their shared interests. Most importantly, neither the bikers nor swimmers view their engagement and activities as an organization, or even as a set of coordinated organizing activities. Both grassroots groups organized around specific physical features important to achieving shared goals and personal objectives—a cove and man-made peninsula in Lake Michigan near Chicago's Hyde Park neighborhood, and roads and bike lanes in a Midwestern city. In some cases, the bike commuters in Wilhoit and Kisselburgh's study even sought to distance themselves from other bike commuters (i.e., undergraduate and casual cyclists) much as the swimmers started to develop a shared identity through the purposeful action of open-water swimming.

Swim caps and goggles distinguished members of the Promontory Point tribe from the more casual swimmers who came out to paddle and splash around in the summer, or tourists that popped in for a quick swim while visiting Chicago. Floating orange personal buoys further distinguished the tribe and kept them visible to boaters and each other while providing a dry bag to keep personal items safe. For the bike commuters, the bikes, roads, and the commute itself provided the technology and process through which they traversed the city space between work and home. Both the Promontory Point swimmers and the bike commuters embody the physical, material, seen and unseen aspects of self-organizing to accomplish shared goals that exist in specific spaces and times. Seasonal and annual time defined the swimmers' actions at Promontory Point, while the exigencies and dangers of daily and weekly commutes shaped the bike commuters' daily rhythms. Seasons and events shaped the collective actions they engaged in to make biking and swimming a safer and more welcoming activity in their respective cities.

After disaster, a range of organizing activities influenced by the physical and material realities of the impacted communities and regions shape the organizational landscape and interorganizational relationships of response and recovery. The type, size, scope, and complexity of a disaster influence how the organizational landscape and interorganizational relationships emerge after disaster. During response and recovery communicating, organizing and sensemaking will range from spontaneous or self-organized activities to institutionalized ones that enact a script establishing particular disaster response and recovery protocols. Both informal organizing and institutionalized organizing will vary in suitability for organizing the recovery and rebuilding processes of the impacted communities or region.

NOTES

1. Francois Cooren et al., "Communication, Organizing and Organization: An Overview and Introduction to the Special Issue," *Organization Studies* 32, no. 9 (September 1, 2011):

1149–70, https://doi.org/10.1177/0170840611410836; Barbara Czarniawska, "Organizations as Obstacles to Organizing," in *Organizations and Organizing: Materiality, Agency, and Discourse*, ed. Daniel Robichaud and Francois Cooren (New York: Routledge, 2013), 4–22; Linda L. Putnam and Robert D. McPhee, "Theory Building: Comparisons of CCO Orientations," in *Building Theories of Organization: The Constitutive Role of Communication* (New York: Routledge, 2009), 187–205.

2. Peter R. Monge and Noshir S. Contractor, *Theories of Communication Networks* (New York: Oxford University Press, 2003); Klaus Weber and Mary Ann Glynn, "Making Sense with Institutions: Context, Thought and Action in Karl Weick's Theory," *Organization Studies* 27, no. 11 (November 2006): 1639–60, https://doi.org/10.1177/0170840606068343; William H Starbuck, "Karl E. Weick and the Dawning Awareness of Organized Cognition," *Management Decision* 53, no. 6 (July 13, 2015): 1287–99, https://doi.org/10.1108/MD-04-2014-0183.

3. Interviews with Coastal New Jersey Nonprofit Executives, July 2016; August, December 2017.

4. Karl E. Weick, *Sensemaking in Organizations* (Thousand Oaks, CA: SAGE Publications, Inc, 1995); Karl E. Weick, Kathleen M. Sutcliffe, and David Obstfeld, "Organizing and the Process of Sensemaking," *Organization Science* 16, no. 4 (August 2005): 409–21, https://doi.org/10.1287/orsc.1050.0133; K. Weick, "The Collapse of Sensemaking in Organizations: The Mann Gulch Disaster.," *Administrative Science Quarterly* 38 (1993): 628–52.

5. Jack L. Harris and Marya L. Doerfel, "Interorganizational Resilience: Networked Collaboration in Communities after Disasters," in *Social Network Analysis of Disaster Response, Recovery, and Adaptation*, ed. E.C. Jones, and A.J. Faas, 1st ed. (London: Elsevier, 2017); Stanley Wasserman and Katherine Faust, *Social Network Analysis Methods and Applications* (Cambridge: Cambridge University Press, 1994); S.P. Borgatti, Martin G. Everett, and Jeffrey C. Johnson, *Analyzing Social Networks* (SAGE, 2013); S.P. Borgatti, "Centrality and Network Flow," *Social Networks* 27, no. 1 (January 2005): 55–71, https://doi.org/10.1016/j.socnet.2004.11.008; S.P. Borgatti and Daniel S. Halgin, "On Network Theory," *Organization Science* 22, no. 5 (2011): 1168–81, https://doi.org/10.1287/orsc.1110.064; S.P. Borgatti and L.C. Freeman, *Ucinet for Windows: Software for Social Network Analysis* (Harvard, MA: Analytic Technologies, 2002).

6. Jeffrey Pfeffer and Gerald R. Salancik, *The External Control of Organizations* (New York: Harper & Row, 1978); John H. Freeman and Pino G. Audia, "Community Ecology and the Sociology of Organizations," *Annual Review of Sociology* 32, no. 1 (August 2006): 145–69, https://doi.org/10.1146/annurev.soc.32.061604.123135; Chih-Hui Lai, Chen-Chao Tao, and Yu-Chung Cheng, "Modeling Resource Network Relationships between Response Organizations and Affected Neighborhoods after a Technological Disaster," *VOLUNTAS: International Journal of Voluntary and Nonprofit Organizations* (June 6, 2017), https://doi.org/10.1007/s11266-017-9887-4.

7. Philip Selznick, "Institutionalism 'Old' and 'New'," *Administrative Science Quarterly* 41, no. 2 (June 1996): 270, https://doi.org/10.2307/2393719; Paul J. DiMaggio and Walter W. Powell, "Introduction," in *The New Institutionalism in Organizational Analysis* (Chicago: University of Chicago Press, 1991), 1–38; Joep P. Cornelissen et al., "Putting Communication Front and Center in Institutional Theory and Analysis," *Academy of Management Review* 40, no. 1 (January 1, 2015): 10–27, https://doi.org/10.5465/amr.2014.0381; J.R. Taylor, "Organization as an (Imbricated) Configuring of Transactions," *Organization Studies* 32, no. 9 (September 1, 2011): 1273–94, https://doi.org/10.1177/0170840611411396; Timothy R. Kuhn, "A Communicative Theory of the Firm: Developing an Alternative Perspective on

Intra-Organizational Power and Stakeholder Relationships," *Organization Studies* 29, no. 8–9 (August 1, 2008): 1227–54, https://doi.org/10.1177/0170840608094778.

8. R. Edward Freeman, *Strategic Management: A Stakeholder Approach* (Marshfield, MA: Pitman Publishing, 1984); Robert Phillips, R. Edward Freeman, and Andrew C. Wicks, "What Stakeholder Theory Is Not," *Business Ethics Quarterly* 13, no. 4 (October 2003): 479–502, https://doi.org/10.5840/beq200313434; R. Edward Freeman, Robert Phillips, and Rajendra Sisodia, "Tensions in Stakeholder Theory," *Business & Society* 59, no. 2 (February 2020): 213–31, https://doi.org/10.1177/0007650318773750; R. Edward Freeman and Sergiy Dmytriyev, "Corporate Social Responsibility and Stakeholder Theory: Learning From Each Other," *Symphonya. Emerging Issues in Management*, no. 1 (December 21, 2017): 7–15, https://doi.org/10.4468/2017.1.02freeman.dmytriyev.

9. Elizabeth Wilhoit Larson, "Where Is an Organization? How Workspaces Are Appropriated to Become (Partial and Temporary) Organizational Spaces," *Management Communication Quarterly* 34, no. 3 (August 2020): 299–327, https://doi.org/10.1177/0893318920933590; Elizabeth D Wilhoit, "Space, Place, and the Communicative Constitution of Organizations: A Constitutive Model of Organizational Space," *Communication Theory* 28, no. 3 (August 1, 2018): 311–31, https://doi.org/10.1093/ct/qty007; Leah Sprain and David Boromisza-Habashi, "Meetings: A Cultural Perspective," *Journal of Multicultural Discourses* 7, no. 2 (July 2012): 179–89, https://doi.org/10.1080/17447143.2012.685743; E. Goffman, *Behavior in Public Places: Notes on the Social Organization of Gathering* (New York: Free Press, 1963).

10. Marya L Doerfel, Chih-Hui Lai, and Lisa V Chewning, "The Evolutionary Role of Interorganizational Communication: Modeling Social Capital in Disaster Contexts," *Human Communication Research* 36, no. 2 (2010): 125–62, https://doi.org/10.1111/j.1468-2958.2010.01371.x; Marya L Doerfel, Lisa V Chewning, and Chih-Hui Lai, "The Evolution of Networks and the Resilience of Interorganizational Relationships after Disaster," *Communication Monographs* 80, no. 4 (2013): 533–59, https://doi.org/10.1080/03637751.2013.828157.

11. Interview with local business owners, January, October 2014.

12. Dennis Schoeneborn, Timothy R. Kuhn, and Dan Kärreman, "The Communicative Constitution of Organization, Organizing, and Organizationality," *Organization Studies* 40, no. 4 (April 2019): 475–96, https://doi.org/10.1177/0170840618782284; Shiv Ganesh and Cynthia Stohl, "Community Organizing, Social Movements, and Collective Action," in *The SAGE Handbook of Organizational Communication*, 3rd ed. (Thousand Oaks, CA: Sage, 2014), 743–66; Marya L. Doerfel and Maureen Taylor, "The Story of Collective Action: The Emergence of Ideological Leaders, Collective Action Network Leaders, and Cross-Sector Network Partners in Civil Society," *Journal of Communication* 67, no. 1 (2017): 920–43, https://doi.org/10.1111/jcom.12340; J. A. A. Sillince, "Can CCO Theory Tell Us How Organizing Is Distinct from Markets, Networking, Belonging to a Community, or Supporting a Social Movement?," *Management Communication Quarterly* 24, no. 1 (February 1, 2010): 132–38, https://doi.org/10.1177/0893318909352022.

13. Schoeneborn, Kuhn, and Kärreman, "The Communicative Constitution of Organization, Organizing, and Organizationality"; Weber and Glynn, "Making Sense with Institutions."

14. Elizabeth D. Wilhoit and Lorraine G. Kisselburgh, "Collective Action Without Organization: The Material Constitution of Bike Commuters as Collective," *Organization Studies* 36, no. 5 (May 2015): 573–92, https://doi.org/10.1177/0170840614556916.

2

How Public Policy Shapes the Organizational Landscape of Recovery

Policy shapes organizational landscapes, the possibilities of organizing, and the configuration of institutions. Policymaking is a communicative process of organizing and discourse, which shapes the institutional messages through which governments execute policy and frame action. Issues and policies may move back and forth between experts in tightly bounded subgroups (such as disaster recovery planners and emergency managers) to institutions such as FEMA and the American Red Cross, elected officials, and broader publics, as shared meanings are developed and executable plans take shape in disaster response. Policymaking not only crafts policy language and sets operational realities, it also reflects broader institutional messages established over time. Both policymaking and institutional messages rest upon a foundation of cognitive and semantic structures that continuously shape how publics and decision-makers create, respond, and react to the discursive and organizing activities that comprise policy development. Policymaking's communicative processes, in turn, are embedded within histories, identities, and cultures that constrain and enable organizing. Scotland's support of renewable energy and community enterprises are particularly good examples of how policymaking shapes organizational landscapes.[1]

SHAPING ORGANIZATIONAL LANDSCAPES THROUGH PUBLIC POLICY: EMPOWERING COMMUNITY IN SCOTLAND

Scotland helps us understand how public policies shape organizing and organizational landscapes. There are 5,600 social enterprises in Scotland employing 80,000 people. These social enterprises earn £3.8 billion per year collectively and contribute

£2 billion annually to Scotland's economy. Social enterprises are particularly important in Scotland's rural communities, where 34 percent of Scotland's social enterprises operate in a region that holds only 18 percent of Scotland's population.
In line with a Scottish culture that supports the independence and leadership of
women, 64 percent of Scotland's social enterprises are led by women. Community
Energy Scotland, a registered charity with a mission to support the development
of community-owned energy projects across Scotland, reports 428 members and
754 supported community projects in 2022. The 2021 UK Community Energy
sector survey reports that seventy-two separate community organizations were
responsible for generating 110MW of renewable energy, with sixteen organizations
engaged in direct land acquisition to support community energy projects. The Scottish community energy sector is the most well-resourced and developed of any of
the United Kingdom's community energy sectors (England, Scotland. Wales, and
Northern Island) due to specific Scottish laws and commitments to the development
of community-owned renewable energy projects.[2]

Scottish law is designed to foster community empowerment. Following the devolution of political powers from the United Kingdom of Great Britain and Ireland
to Scotland in 1998 and the re-establishment of the Scottish Parliament in 1999,
Scotland's Parliament enacted multiple laws making community ownership and
social ventures key elements of Scottish policy. The Land Reform Act of 2003, the
Community Empowerment act of 2015, and The Islands (Scotland) Act of 2018.
Each of these laws provides partial answers to the centuries-old Scottish question:
who owns the land and has use of it? The initial Land Reform Act of 2003 not only
expanded public access and rights of way through private and public properties, it
established a community "right to buy" through registered companies or charitable
institutions. These organizations are established by communities that register an
interest in purchasing land, water, or limited fishing and mineral rights to foster
sustainable development. The Community Empowerment Act of 2015 extended the
community right to buy certain public (government) lands and buildings or to lease
or manage them for community benefit. The act promotes community planning
and participatory budgeting activities to boost community participation in public
decision-making at local and regional levels.[3]

The establishment of community businesses on the Island of Jura through the
Jura Development Trust (JDT) illustrates how national policy decisions and cross-
sector collaborations at national and transnational levels may shape the social and
organizational infrastructure of a community. Jura is a remote island community
off of Islay, a large Scottish island in the Inner Hebrides known for its smoky
whisky. George Orwell, who wrote much of *1984* there, once described the island
as "un-gettable to." Established in 1997, five years before the Land Reform Act of
2003, the trust operates as a community company with charitable (nonprofit) status
allowing it to own and operate businesses (social enterprise). It is eligible to receive
funding through government agencies, charitable institutions, and nongovernmental
organizations. Scottish law and policy support organizational forms that support
the community and impact the public good. Through funding from cross-sector

partners—including The Scottish Government, the European Agricultural Fund for Rural Development, the Scottish Rural Development Programme, Highlands and Island Enterprise, and Argyll and the Islands LEADER 2014–2020 Program—the JDT has repaired the island's community infrastructure. It purchased and rebuilt the only community store and its only petrol pump, established a community internet access and business hub, and purchased and maintained the island's stone pier for fishing and boating purposes. The stone pier supports commercial and recreational boating, both critically important for the island's economy. The JDT has been able to continually maintain "The Antlers" through leasing and operator changes over the course of the JDT's twenty-five-year history. "The Antlers" is a bistro and shop that showcases Jura history and sells local crafts opposite the community store just down the road from the island's only Hotel and Pub, and nearly adjacent to the distillery founded in 1808. These community enterprises are designed to make a profit but may not be viable or sustainable for a sole proprietor.

Given the small year-round population of the island, it would be difficult to maintain this basic level of businesses and services. The ability to maintain a basic level of social and organizational infrastructure in a remote location is an outcome of national Scottish law and policy. It prioritizes the maintenance of communities and the businesses they support. Jura is a particularly interesting case since most of the land on the island continues to be owned by a very small number of wealthy land-owners who are not year-round residents. This owned land continues to be organized as estates and plantations for timber and wild game. Island employment is currently concentrated around the Jura Distillery, small women-owned businesses like Lussa Gin, Tourism & Hospitality, Fishing, Boating, Household Agriculture, and employment on the estates and plantations. National and transnational support for local organizations in remote regions in Scotland creates an independent social and organizational infrastructure that lessens resident dependence on wealthy landowners and singular businesses such as the distillery. Challenges remain, such as consistent access to healthcare and the still unfolding impact of Brexit, but Jura residents have access to community enterprises and an organizational infrastructure that supports work and life on the island. Together, it forms a foundation for collaborations with the government and the larger Scottish Civil and Voluntary Sector, or CVS.

UNDERSTANDING THE ORGANIZATIONAL LANDSCAPE OF DISASTER RECOVERY

Like robust island communities working to maintain year-round viability, recovery after disaster requires multiple organizations to collaborate in a vast array of activities. Just as single organizations differentiate tasks and coordinate activities inside their organization to achieve their goals, organizations engaged in long-term recovery after disaster differentiate tasks and coordinate activities across organizations and sectors. Organizations active after disaster may include for-profit private sector firms, public agencies (e.g., Federal Emergency Management Agency), offices of emergency management (at state, city, or county levels of government), The Department of Housing and Urban Development, and nonprofit organizations like the American Red Cross and Salvation Army. Existing community organizations are often overlooked by emergency management professionals and elected leaders but play an important role in response and recovery. They organize the efforts of spontaneous volunteers and emergent organizational responses to meet resident and community needs after disaster. This mix of existing and emergent community organizations comprises the social and organizational infrastructure of disaster recovery.

Almost a century of social and organizational research has established an understanding of the emergent and institutional responses that occur after disaster. However, with few exceptions, disaster researchers across sociology, public administration, and communication have failed to account for the dynamic complexity of the post-disaster organizational landscape of recovery and the interorganizational relationships that underpin recovery. In turn, legal and policy frameworks in the United States have empowered a small number of institutional players while ignoring the grassroots efforts that are key parts of disaster response and recovery efforts. Consequently, we lack a robust organizational theory for understanding disaster response and recovery that emphasizes the role of networked organizing and stakeholders in creating the conditions for recovery. Network and interorganizational research on disasters often focuses on formal emergency management networks of response, rather than broader post-disaster recovery networks that traverse the public, plural, and private sectors. Cross-sector networks include nonprofits and faith-based organizations as well as public agencies, private sector partners with construction, logistics, and supply chain expertise, and new organizations that emerge in response to local conditions on the ground. These networks build connections between community organizing efforts and the institutionalized activities of disaster response and recovery.[4]

Typologies of Disaster Response

Organizational Roles after Disaster

A classic approach for understanding the organizational landscapes of recovery is to develop typologies that categorize organizational response by organizational sector or field. These typologies classify organizations according to their primary social roles and activities in responding to disaster. In a classic framework, Bosworth and Kreps (1986, 1993, 2007) frame organizational responses after disaster as Type 1, Type 2, Type 3, and Type 4 responses.[5] The Bosworth and Kreps frameworks have stood the test of time and provide a very useful way to envision the organizational landscape of recovery. Their framework makes space for the continuum of organizing in response to disaster, revealing the salience of both institutional responsibility and the importance of emergent organizing.

Type 1 responses are the traditional first responder activities provided by police, fire, paramedics, community first aid squads, and offices of emergency management.

These responses also include the continued operation (or restoration) of community infrastructures such as hospitals and utilities. Type 1 responses are the backbone upon which disaster response and short-term recovery succeed or fail. Type 2 responses are conducted by traditional disaster relief agencies such as the American Red Cross or Salvation Army. Organizations engaged in humanitarian assistance and disaster relief as part of their core mission or purpose generally conduct Type 2 responses. Organizations designated within the Stafford Act, Emergency Support Functions, or Recovery Support Functions through legislation and policies enacted by Congress, FEMA, and the Department of Homeland Security as part of national disaster response and recovery frameworks fall into this type as well. Type 2 organizations, along with most of the Type 3 and Type 4 organizations (described below) fall into the "plural sector"—a broad range of organizations that are neither public agencies nor for-profit firms.

Type 3 disaster responses are a series of emergency response and post-disaster recovery activities in which existing community organizations extend their roles to meet the needs of their disaster-impacted community or region. Unlike emergent organizations (Type 4, discussed below), community organizations are typically rooted within their communities and may be either a local nonprofit or business. After Hurricane Sandy, a locally owned pizzeria filled in the gaps of disorganized food response from the American Red Cross in Oceanport, New Jersey, and nearby communities. Meanwhile, a regional supermarket, ShopRite, implemented a voucher system where local organizations could access fruits, vegetables, cleaning supplies, paper plates, paper towels, and other household goods to support local warming centers, microshelters, and first responders. In the same region, a domestic violence agency expanded its creative arts therapy and counseling programs to support the mental health needs of impacted residents and extended shelter operations to administer and distribute grants for housing assistance. These expanded mental health and administrative operations were supported through grants provided by foundations and state and federal agencies. Finally, Type 4 disaster responses are "emergent," conducted by neighbors helping neighbors, friends, helping friends, and strangers helping strangers. These activities usually occur during the emergency response phase of disaster response and recovery and fade as the complexity, bureaucracy, and funding needs of the recovery require increasing amounts of time and understanding of arcane processes and procedures. Increasingly, social entrepreneurial enterprises and mutual aid organizations have actively conducted Type 3 and Type 4 activities.

Bosworth and Kreps' structural model of disaster response provides an institutional lens on disaster response and recovery and helps shed light on the prevalence of particular types of disaster response and recovery activities and relationships. Type 3 and Type 4 responses are important, but often overlooked components of disaster response and recovery. While implied in the language of "whole community" response, the narrow range of partners identified in federal planning documents obscures the important role that local organizations, hyperlocal organizing, and emergent response play in disaster response and recovery. An institutional lens helps us to begin to understand why public agencies over-rely on select disaster relief organizations, even as the number and intensity of disasters requiring coordinated state and federal response grows. Understanding the institutional perspective on disaster response and recovery enables a better understanding of the role and importance of hyperlocal organizing in disaster response and recovery.

Blueprints for Organizational Action

Federal Disaster Policy and Organizing Outcomes

The planning, policy, and legislative texts described below represent the sum of interactions of a broad array of stakeholders at moments when individual lives and whole communities are disrupted. These texts are not simply words on a page or a federal policymaking and rulemaking process. Rather, these texts represent both words and action, or conversation and activities over time that provide a blueprint for federal disaster planning and response. Through this blueprint, institutional partners are selected as primary stakeholders while local partners and hyperlocal organizing are subordinated to standard processes of institutional response and recovery. Authoritative texts shape the organizing processes through which meaning and legitimacy are created in and across organizations. What is represented in an organizational text often reflects the institutional processes through which work gets done and lines of communication and authority are legitimated. Organizations are inherently communicative, meaning work practices, collaboration, public policies, organizational strategies, and meaning making are accomplished through communication. This communication includes speech, activities, and texts that contribute to the communication and organizing that shapes the organizational and interorganizational processes through which work gets done and goals are met.[6]

In the United States, the National Frameworks for Response and Disaster Recovery and their associated Recovery Support Functions (RSFs) are static, textual representations of a late-twentieth-century model of emergency management, adapted to the institutional failures of Hurricane Katrina. Along with the Stafford Act and its amendments, they constitute the official policy framework through which disaster response and recovery are conducted in the United States. Organizations operating within these frameworks share similar operating models and institutional logics that generally reflect (a) the culture and material realities of impacted communities and regions, (b) the dynamic changing processes of networked response and recovery in impacted communities after disaster, and (c) the rapidly changing nature of the global and national-level disaster landscape.

Enacted in 1988, the Stafford Act is the legislation that established the Federal Emergency Management Agency (FEMA) and authorized the establishment of national response and recovery frameworks. Within these documents, certain organizations are designated as federal partners. Title III of the Stafford Act (Major Disaster and Emergency Assistance Administration) specifically names only the American Red Cross, the Salvation Army, and Mennonite Disaster Relief, qualifying the language to read "and other relief or disaster organizations which agree to operate

under this advice or direction." In practice, "other relief or disaster assistance organizations" generally refer to the National Voluntary Organizations Active in Disaster (NVOAD or the National VOAD) in federal disaster planning. The National
VOAD comprises fifty-seven state and territory VOADs, each of which serves as
an umbrella organization or roundtable for nonprofit and faith-based organizations
active in disaster relief in their own states or territories. It is generally understood
that faith-based organizations from the major religious denominations in the United
States will engage in disaster relief efforts after major disasters.[7]

The National VOAD is not designated in the Stafford Act nor named as a
critical partner in the post-Katrina emergency management reform efforts organized between 2006 and 2009 but appears in post-Sandy federal disaster planning
documents. The National VOAD's increasing presence in federal and state disaster
planning may reflect the evolving and changing landscape of disaster response. It
also may signal an increasing reliance by impacted communities and states on a
much broader array of organizations to meet their disaster recovery needs. FEMA
designates the National VOAD along with the American Red Cross as a supporting
organization under Annex E (Health and Social Services) of the 2016 Recovery Federal Interagency Operational Plan. The National VOAD is tasked with plural sector
communication and coordination efforts among, and guidance on, best practices for
the seventy-three nonprofit, and faith-based organizations and fifty-seven state and
territory VOADs. Under Annex E, the American Red Cross is designated as the supporting partner for case management, mental health, and public health assistance.
In practice, a much wider range of organizations will engage in these functions in
disaster-impacted communities.[8]

The American Red Cross and National VOAD are also designated support
organizations for housing recovery, designated as Annex F (Housing) in the
2016 Interagency Operational Plan. The American Red Cross is designated as a
primary partner for mass care operations (feeding and sheltering) as well as a support organization for case management, post-disaster housing assessment, and the
establishment of Long-Term Recovery Groups (LTRGs). Like their Health and
Human Services functions, the National VOAD's support primarily involves communication, coordination, and best practices. While a broader range of organizations
are listed as part of the Housing Recovery Support Function, these organizations
are designated as "Private Sector and Nonprofit Partners, Resources and Expertise"
rather than as supporting organizations.

Within the Housing Recovery Support Function of the National Disaster
Recovery Framework, last updated in 2016, these other organizations are not listed
out as "Supporting Organizations." This also holds true for the Health and Social
Services Recovery Support Function, in which only the American Red Cross and
the National VOAD are named as specific organizations supporting the mission
of housing recovery. FEMA does clarify the operational plan and recovery support
functions with standard language in the RSF PDFs that emphasizes the need for new
partners (Type 3 Organizations in the Bosworth and Kreps framework) in newly
disaster-impacted communities or regions. These RSF PDFs are located on FEMA's

Recovery Support Functions page and are working documents intended to familiarize government, community, nonprofit, and business leaders with the federal process for allocating resources and supporting state and local efforts in response and recovery. The National Disaster Recovery Framework introduced six RSFs in 2011 that are led by designated federal coordinating agencies at the national level. RSFs involve partners in the local, state, and tribal governments and private and nonprofit sectors not typically involved in emergency support functions but critically needed in disaster recovery. These new partners may include public and private organizations that have experience with permanent housing financing, economic development, advocacy for underserved populations, and long-term community planning.[9]

According to FEMA's interagency operational plan, however, only the American Red Cross and National VOAD are officially designated plural sector support organizations. These RSFs and Interagency Operational Plans rely overwhelmingly on federal government agencies as primary and supporting organizations. Only these two clearly identified plural sector supporting organizations are designated as nongovernment operating partners. When FEMA and other federal agencies do turn to the plural sector in disaster planning and preparation, it is primarily to the American Red Cross—the only congressionally chartered nonprofit in the United States.[10]

Following the well-documented failures in response and recovery following Hurricane Katrina in 2005, the Post-Katrina Emergency Reform Act of 2006 was passed to address this national catastrophe. One provision of the act established a National Disaster Recovery Strategy to assess the current state of emergency management and disaster relief efforts in the United States. Between 2009 and 2011, 600 stakeholders provided comments on drafts of a proposed National Disaster Recovery Strategy. In 2011, the National Disaster Recovery Strategy was finally published as the National Disaster Recovery Framework, five years after the initial congressional enabling legislation, and a revised version of the framework was published in 2016. The goals of the recovery framework are implementing eight core principles to guide recovery. These principles clarify the roles and responsibilities of the (federal agencies and supporting plural and private sector) organizations responsible for vital recovery tasks, an interorganizational coordinating structure, and recovery processes that incorporate resilience as well as recovery. The RSFs provide the federal framework through which to coordinate recovery across six areas: (a) economic, (b) Health & Social Services, (c) Housing, (d) Community Planning & Capacity Building, (e) Infrastructure Systems, and (f) Natural and Cultural Resources. RSFs were enacted through the establishment of the National Disaster Recovery Framework in 2011.[11]

While there was extensive stakeholder outreach throughout these processes, most stakeholders were only brought in to review the plan and provide feedback after the drafting stage was complete. Nongovernmental stakeholders were not included as key partners in the interorganizational collaboration or drafting processes that shaped these texts. This approach also informed the establishment of the Hurricane Sandy Rebuilding Task Force on December 7, 2012. While widely regarded as an outstanding "whole of government" approach and an example of interorganizational collaboration across federal agencies and intergovernmental cooperation, the task force did not include one nongovernmental stakeholder from either the plural or private sector. Nongovernmental stakeholders were relegated to roles of subject matter experts and cheerleaders rather than collaborators and decision-makers. The introduction to the Sandy rebuilding task force reads: "The Task Force was in near constant contact with a wide range of stakeholders from residents, non-profits, think tanks, academia, and the private sector. These groups offered not only their opinions and expertise, but their support."[12] The Hurricane Sandy rebuilding task force represents core issues with federal thinking about disaster response, and more importantly long-term recovery after disaster. While the language of federal policy documents and their supporting strategic communications emphasizes collaboration and connections with stakeholders, primary drafting and decision-making responsibility for policymaking in disaster response and recovery rest with federal agencies.

FEMA'S 2022–2026 STRATEGIC PLAN: RETHINKING INSTITUTIONAL FRAMEWORKS

In late 2021, FEMA released a new five-year strategic plan. While the strategic plan does not replace prior national response plans and recovery frameworks, it does attempt to better address the legacy of institutional failures that have impacted communities of color and socioeconomically disadvantaged communities disrupted by disaster. The 2022–2026 FEMA strategic plan explicitly recognizes that disasters, response, and recovery occur in specific community, cultural, economic, and historical contexts. It presents equity as the first of the three goals that connect climate resilience, disaster preparedness, and vulnerable communities as part of a whole community approach to disaster response and recovery. Key changes in FEMA's five-year strategic plan are discussed below.[13]

The strategic plan leads with *Goal 1: Instill Equity as a Foundation of Emergency Management* (p. 9):

> Disasters impact people and communities differently. Every disaster occurs within a unique context based on a community's geographic, demographic, political, historical, and cultural characteristics. These unique contexts require tailored solutions that are designed to meet their unique needs.

Immediately followed by specific references to inequalities in traditional disaster response and recovery (p. 9):

> Underserved communities, as well as specific identity groups, often suffer disproportionately from disasters. As a result, disasters worsen inequities already present in society. This cycle compounds the challenges faced by these communities and increases their risk to future disasters.

By linking equity, resilience, and disaster preparedness, FEMA has taken initial steps to ensure a more comprehensive understanding of the intersection of emergency management with the human dimensions of complex environmental change. FEMA uses executive authority pursuant to Presidential Executive Order 13985 to establish new operating principles to enact new organizational and interorganizational frameworks and strategies for disaster planning, response, and recovery. Organizational dimensions of FEMA's 2021 strategic plan emphasize workplace diversification through partnerships with Historically Black Colleges and Universities (HBCUs). Such diversification seeks to foster a new generation of emergency management professionals, support employee-based resource groups that foster inclusion and equity practices within FEMA, and develop action plans to improve FEMA employees' awareness of multicultural issues impacting disaster, planning, response, and recovery, and FEMA's relationship with disaster-impacted communities and individuals. Improvements to FEMA's client-facing dimensions include expanding the types of documentation required to prove homeownership, prioritizing agency casework that emphasizes outreach to homeowners deemed eligible based on occupancy or ownership criteria, and changing calculations for eligibility of direct housing assistance. Together, these updates to organizational guidelines should address key institutional failures in federal disaster response.

Black families in disaster-impacted communities have been disproportionately impacted by federal assistance rules that require a property title for homeowner assistance. In many black southern neighborhoods and communities, property often passes from generation to generation without clear title, as families navigated slavery, freedom, and Jim Crow and sought to build homes and homesteads as stable places for family, community, and gathering. Often when parents or grandparents died, land and property were simply passed onto children and grandchildren without title transfers ever being executed with a county or municipal recorder of deeds. As a result, homes and land ended up held solely by a descendant who lacked a clear title to the land because of either a failure to record deeds and titles at times of property transfer, or held legal titles that were never clearly drawn. More common and much more contentious is the issue of "heirs' property," in which untitled claims are held by multiple descendants.

Heirs' property is quite common in the coastal Carolinas and the coastal parishes of Louisiana. Where the centuries-old legacies of slavery and plantation economies intersects with centuries of hurricanes, the problem of heir's property has contributed to significant losses of land and property wealth in black families and communities throughout the twentieth century and well into the twenty-first century. When land is considered heirs' property, individual owners who live on or work the property are ineligible for federal loans and disaster relief because the land is assumed to be held in common regardless of informal understandings of ownership, residency, and use of the land for livelihoods among heirs and descendants. Post-Katrina estimates of recovery assistance applications suggest that at least 250,000 properties were restricted from accessing rebuilding grants and loans due to heirs' property status, and upward of $165 million of recovery funds were unclaimed because of unclear or contentious titles.[14]

By centering equity and developing a set of client-facing principles designed to mitigate inequities in rebuilding and recovery assistance, FEMA has taken the first steps in moving toward more equitable outcomes in federal disaster assistance activities. The development of partnerships with HBCUs and efforts to build a more diverse and inclusive federal disaster workforce may help to rectify problems with FEMA's "bureaucratic tin ear" and historic inabilities to adapt organizational processes and federal policy to differing cultural and historic contexts. Diverse and inclusive teams should be able to identify problems of inequity rooted in history and culture, identify workarounds, and shape policies that address the wide-ranging problems of disaster response and recovery rooted in culture, history, language, and institutional expectations. Such efforts should build more effective "whole of community" responses able to grapple with increasing complexity and a broader set of stakeholders.[15]

Goal two of the 2022–2026 strategic plan (pp. 14–18) is a holistic community approach to climate resilience as part of FEMA's overall disaster preparedness activities. Under this strategic plan, FEMA will engage with multiple stakeholders to address the impacts of climate change on emergency management and the development of resilience strategies to address the increasing intensity and frequency of storms and natural hazards events. For the most part, this goal is aspirational and leverages existing tools and training processes to increase awareness of climate risks and vulnerable populations. It fails to take concrete actions such as the allocation of resources for resilience-building activities, support for emergent organizing activities, development of grassroots- or neighborhood-level capacity, and capability for addressing resilience-building efforts and emergency response. However, this goal represents a devolution of sorts in which risks, risk identification, and the development of resilience strategies are moved to the community level and become the responsibilities of localities rather than federal agencies and policymakers. No clear funding sources or resource allocation processes are established to deal with increasingly hazardous environmental conditions and a growing number of communities at risk from sea level rise, wildfires, and catastrophic weather events. Lack of funding and unclear intergovernmental lines of authority and interest make the interorganizational dimensions of resilience more important for communities wrestling with climate change.

Goal three of the most recent FEMA strategic plan addresses interorganizational processes through Objective 3.3 (p. 25):

> Disaster mitigation, preparedness, response, and recovery are not the responsibility of just one agency. Rather, these functions are a shared responsibility requiring coordination of federal agencies, private and social sectors, state, local, tribal, and territorial governments, and other partners. FEMA is uniquely postured to lead the federal government in integrating delivery of federal resources through leveraging both nationwide

initiatives through the Emergency Support, Recovery Support, and Mitigation Support Functional Leadership groups.

This objective is similar to previous iterations of the National Response Plan and National Disaster Recovery Framework. It recognizes shared responsibilities and the importance of coordination of interagency and interorganizational processes. However, only a very narrow set of agencies and organizations are tasked with disaster preparation, response, and recovery in planning documents and enabling legislation. Even with the explicit acknowledgment of nonfederal partners and the foregrounding of ongoing operational processes to better support community resilience and interorganizational coordination at multiple levels of disaster preparedness, very little space is given to nonfederal partners as equal partners in disaster planning and readiness. Measures are established to track each of the three goals and their objectives, yet what is missing is an understanding of the organizing processes through which community preparedness and resilience are built.

THE INSTITUTIONAL MESSAGES OF FEDERAL DISASTER RESPONSE

Public policy provides the architecture through which the institutions and organizing processes of disaster recovery are created. Federal frameworks detailing policy, strategy, and operations create the institutional messages through which disaster response and recovery is enacted in the United States. These messages in turn shape the organizational landscape of disaster response and recovery and its overreliance upon government agencies and a limited number of nongovernmental partners as supporting organizations coordinating with other nongovernmental organizations. Institutional messages represent the interactions through which assemblages of thoughts, patterns, belief, and rules are conveyed over time. They may represent the values or identities of organizations, convey meaning, establish rules or guidelines, inform publics, and promote organizations or ideas. They are broad frames of understanding through which people and organizations understand their roles and constraints. They also delineate boundaries of accepted thought and action within and across the institutional environments they are operating in. Institutional messages are not simply a signal to act, they embody meaning and patterns of behavior enacted through speech and texts over time. Institutional messages may encumber stakeholders to operate within the guidelines or frameworks conveyed through institutional messages, become established over time based on the frequency of their use and repetition, vary in the size and impact of the stakeholder communities they reach, and take on a life of their own beyond the stated speech or text embodied in the institutional message.[16]

Table 2.1:   Primary Textual Documents Shaping U.S. Disaster Response and Recovery: 1950–2021

Pre-Stafford Act—Sets the foundation for modern disaster relief in the United States

1950: The Federal Disaster Relief Act of 1950. (P.L. 81-875).
1966: The Federal Disaster Relief Act of 1966. (P.L. 89-796)
1968: National Flood Insurance Act of 1968. (NFIA P.L. 89-796).
1972: The Federal Disaster Relief Act of 1974 (P.L. 93-288).
1978: National Governor's Association Emergency Preparedness Project Final Report (Washington D.C.: NGA, 1978).
1978: President's Reorganization Project, Federal Emergency Preparedness and Response Historical Survey (Washington D.C.: US Office of Management and Budget, 1978).
1979: Executive Order 12127, 44 Federal Register (March 31, 1979).
1979: Executive Order 12148, 44 Federal Register (July 20, 1979).

Stafford Act and Post-Stafford Act—Establishes the Organizational Landscape, Interagency, and Interorganizational Relationships of U.S. Disaster Response and Recovery

1988: Robert T. Stafford Disaster Relief and Emergency Assistance Act (P.L. 100-707).
2000: Disaster Mitigation Act of 2004 (P.L. (106-390).
2002: The Homeland Security Act of 2002 (P.L. 107-296).
2006: Post-Katrina Emergency Reform Act of 2006 (P.L. 109-25).
2007: The American National Red Cross Governance Modernization Act of 2007 (P.L. 110-26, May 11, 2007).
2008: US Government Accountability Office, Actions Taken to Implement the Post-Katrina Emergency Management Reform Act of 2006 (GAO-09-59R).
2008: National Response Framework
2011: Presidential Policy Directive 8: National Preparedness (March 30, 2011).
2011: National Disaster Recovery Framework: Strengthening Disaster Recovery for the Nation (September 2011).
2013: National Response Framework (2nd edition)
2013: Hurricane Sandy Rebuilding Task Force. Hurricane Sandy rebuilding strategy. Washington D.C. Hurricane Sandy Rebuilding Task Force; 2013.
2013: Sandy Recovery Improvement Act of 2013 (P.L. 113-2, January 24, 2014).
2014: Recovery Federal Interagency Operational Plan
2016: Recovery Federal Interagency Operational Plan (2nd Edition).
2016: US Governmental Accountability Office: Report to Congressional Requestors: DISASTER RECOVERY: FEMA Needs to Assess its Effectiveness in Implementing the National Disaster Recovery Framework (May 2016).
2016: National Disaster Recovery Framework (2nd Edition, June 2016).
2018: Disaster Recovery Reform Act of 2018 (DRRA, Division D of P.L. 115-254, October 5, 2018).
2019: Disaster Recovery Reform Act (DRRA) Annual Report (October 2019).
2019: Reforming Disaster Recovery Act of 2019 reintroduced in the U.S. Senate
2021: H.R. 2809 Natural Disaster Recovery Program Act of 2021 introduced in the U.S. House of Representatives.

Created by Author.

IMPLICATIONS OF CURRENT FEDERAL DISASTER POLICY FOR ORGANIZING

Federal Disaster Policy has transmitted a series of institutional messages that constrain the imagination of emergency management professionals and elected leaders wrestling with the dual challenges of disaster response and climate change. The language of the National Response and National Disaster Recovery frameworks emphasizes a "whole community approach" to disaster response and recovery, and federal policy designates local or state government as the lead on disaster response in their respective cities and states. As a result, the organizational landscapes shaped through U.S. disaster policy are tightly constrained. The institutional messages of federal disaster policy fail to account for the dynamic, relational aspects of disaster recovery, emergent organizing, and the crucial role of plural sector organizations in long-term recovery. While federal funding plays a critical role for individuals and communities recovering from disaster, federal funding often falls short, requiring foundations and philanthropic organizations to close the gap. Plural sector organizations are then called to navigate the interorganizational labyrinths of state and federal recovery processes, meaning each disaster recovery process unfolds differently after every disaster.

THE PLURAL SECTOR AND THE ORGANIZATIONAL LANDSCAPE OF DISASTER

The plural sector is the broad array of organizations that are neither public (government and quasi-governmental agencies and authorities primarily funded through tax revenues and debt) nor private (for-profit firms funded primarily through customer revenues, shares, debt, and licensing fees) sector organizations. The plural sector represents a long tradition of voluntary associations in the United States, through cooperatives, nonprofits, nongovernmental organizations, and social enterprises and many also engage in global activities. During and after disaster, plural sector organizations assist relief and recovery efforts alongside local first responders, city and community leaders, and a broad array of state and federal agencies, each tasked with separate facets of relief and recovery efforts. Plural sector organizations operate shelters, provide food, reunite families, operate Multi-Agency Resource Centers, provide short-term financial assistance through cash and gift cards, and run the case management processes that will connect disaster-impacted residents with the resources needed for long-term recovery.[17]

Collaborative efforts in disaster response and recovery, such as coordination and communication, often fall to plural sector organizations. The National VOAD's role as a supporting organization in FEMA's Health and Human Services and Housing RSFs is defined as collaboration. The organization's purpose statement and website states the National VOAD "facilitates communication, cooperation, coordination, and collaboration between NVOAD partners and throughout communities to better prepare for and respond to disaster and and other emergency incidents." Its additional roles include informing the government or National VOAD members about member capabilities and capacities, information sharing, and guidance on best practices, rules, and norms across a range of recovery functions. These functions include survivor mass care, emotional and spiritual support, housing, rebuilding and repair, long-term recovery, volunteer management, and donation management.

The National VOAD was founded in 1970 by seven organizations representing primarily faith-based organizations active in crisis response and disaster relief. The National VOAD consists of fifty state organizations, the District of Columbia, and seven VOADs located in U.S. territories as well as foundation, corporate, nonprofit, government, and academic partners. Their mission and values of "communication, coordination, collaboration, and cooperation" ("the 4Cs") are reflected in the Annexes of FEMA's Recovery Federal Interagency Operational Recovery. The "4Cs" are used to shape consensus, decision-making, and operating frameworks for the National VOAD as well as their state and territory partners.[18]

The National VOAD reflects a model of cross-sector collaboration connecting plural, public, and private sector organizations to build multi-stakeholder initiatives for disaster response and recovery. VOADs may also be named Community Organizations Active in Disaster (COADS), and the names are somewhat interchangeable. The difference is that VOADS are voluntary organizations and employ an organizational model of professionally staffed and led organizations that recruit and deploy volunteers from among their membership or the membership of corporate and similar partners. COADs often consist of organizations already located in a community with missions and portfolios much broader than simple disaster response and recovery. Within the Kreps and Bosworth framework, the slight differences in name and operations reflect differences between Type 2 and 3 organizations.

VOADS and COADs are multilevel organizations with collaborations active at the city, county, regional and state, and national level. They are nested networks of recovery that connect organizations of different size, scope, and roles and provide a trusted partner for state and federal government through which to connect with a multiplicity of organizations. Like the LTRGs discussed below, VOADs and COADs have both organizational and network elements. However, participation by hyperlocal organizations and community-focused organizations such as mutual aid groups in state and local VOADs is largely missing. Making space for, or even being aware of, the critical role of emergent and hyperlocal organizing in response and recovery continues to be a challenge for VOADs.

Another model of coordination and collaboration recognized by the federal disaster recovery framework are LTRGs. LTRGs are established in disaster-impacted areas to coordinate the flow of resources necessary for rebuilding and the recovery process. Like VOADS and COADs, LTRGs are comprised of organizations with different missions, roles, sizes, and capacities. LTRGs can be established simply as a coordinating entity, a fiscal agent, or a combination of both. They may be organized and run through community voluntary organizations or set up independently and staffed with a director, case managers, construction officials, and volunteer coordinators. LTRGs are formed through a convening process several weeks to several months after disaster, when organizations active in the disaster-impacted community are united by a plural sector organization with experience and capacity to provide scope and scale to a bootstrap operation. Previously, United Ways often served as fiscal agents for the impacted communities of which they are a part. However, as United Way has consolidated catchment areas and moved away from disaster relief funding, they appear to be less likely to convene LTRGs. In states with a strong state-level VOAD, that state's VOAD may help convene the organizations needed for long-term recovery and help launch the LTRG itself. In two of the hardest-hit coastal counties in the mid-Atlantic after Hurricane Sandy, each county LTRG was convened through meetings of the recovery network in November and December 2012 with over 200 organizations active in response and recovery present at each meeting. By the end of 2017, only three recovery organizations and one LTRG were still active and by the summer of 2020 only two organizations and no LTRGs were still active.

LTRGs often serve as a backbone organization within a broader recovery network. As a backbone organization, LTRGs provide fiscal, organizational, logistics, and case management support for rebuilding and recovery efforts in an impacted community or region. LTRGs have both organizational and network elements. They are composed of multiple organizations active in the recovery network of an impacted region and may also add staff to provide specific disaster-recovery functions such as case management, volunteer coordination, and support for rebuilding housing.

The plural sector is a vital part of disaster response and recovery. However, the full range of organizations necessary for effective response and recovery is not recognized by policymakers and planners who design disaster response and recovery frameworks. Plural sector organizations are asked to review but rarely asked to participate in plans and policies. This leads to an overreliance on the same institutional partners to execute federal response and recovery strategies. Institutions often lack adaptability and flexibility and fail to engage with Type 3 (existing) and Type 4 (emergent) community organizations as equal partners. As disaster becomes more complex and more frequent in response to changing climate conditions, community and emergence need to be written into federal policy and institutions reorganized to become more flexible and adaptable in their ability and willingness to partner with communities, emergent organizations, and spontaneous volunteers.

NOTES

1. Kathleen Carley and Michael Palmquist, "Extracting, Representing, and Analyzing Mental Models," *Social Forces* 70, no. 3 (March 1992): 601, https://doi.org/10.2307/2579746; Kathleen Carley, "Extracting Culture through Textual Analysis," *Poetics* 22, no. 4 (June 1994): 291–312; Kathleen M. Carley and David S. Kaufer, "Semantic Connectivity:

An Approach for Analyzing Symbols in Semantic Networks," *Communication Theory* 3, no. August (1993): 183–213.

2. "Social Enterprise in Scotland: Census 2017" (Community Enterprise in Scotland, 2017), https://socialenterprise.scot/files/4de870c3a3.pdf; "Community Energy: State of the Sector Report 2021" (Community Energy England, Wales, and Scotland, 2021).

3. "The Land Reform (Scotland) Act 2003" (2003), https://www.legislation.gov.uk/asp /2003/2/contents; "Community Empowerment (Scotland) Act 2015" (2015), https://www .legislation.gov.uk/asp/2015/6/contents/enacted; "Islands (Scotland) Act 2018" (2018), https://www.legislation.gov.uk/asp/2018/12/contents; Islands (Scotland) Act 2018; Matthew Hoffman, "Why Community Ownership? Understanding Land Reform in Scotland," *Land Use Policy* 31, no. March (2013): 289–97; Frank Rennie, *The Changing Outer Hebrides: Galson and the Meaning of Place* (Stornoway, Isle of Lewis: Acair Books, 2020).

4. Daniel P. Aldrich, *Black Wave: How Networks and Governance Shaped Japan's 3/11 Disasters* (Chicago and London: University of Chicago Press, 2019); Christopher A. Airriess et al., "Church-Based Social Capital, Networks and Geographical Scale: Katrina Evacuation, Relocation, and Recovery in a New Orleans Vietnamese American Community," *Geoforum* 39, no. 3 (May 2008): 1333–46, https://doi.org/10.1016/j.geoforum.2007.11.003; Elizabeth J. Carlson et al., "A Study of Organizational Reponses to Dilemmas in Interorganizational Emergency Management," *Communication Research* (January 6, 2016), 0093650215621775, https://doi.org/10.1177/0093650215621775; Marya L Doerfel, Lisa V Chewning, and Chih-Hui Lai, "The Evolution of Networks and the Resilience of Interorganizational Relationships after Disaster," *Communication Monographs* 80, no. 4 (2013): 533–59, https://doi.org/10 .1080/03637751.2013.828157; Jack L. Harris and Marya L. Doerfel, "Interorganizational Resilience: Networked Collaboration in Communities after Disasters," in *Social Network Analysis of Disaster Response, Recovery, and Adaptation*, ed. E.C. Jones, and A.J. Faas, 1st ed. (London: Elsevier, 2017); Naim Kapucu, Tolga Arslan, and Matthew Lloyd Collins, "Examining Intergovernmental and Interorganizational Response to Catastrophic Disasters: Toward a Network Centered Approach," *Administration & Society* 42, no. 2 (April 2010): 222–47, https://doi.org/10.1177/0095399710362517; Naim Kapucu and Qian Hu, "Understanding Multiplexity of Collaborative Emergency Management Networks," *The American Review of Public Administration* 46, no. 4 (October 23, 2014): 399–417, https://doi.org/10.1177 /0275074014555645; Chih-Hui Lai and Ying-Chia Hsu, "Understanding Activated Network Resilience: A Comparative Analysis of Co-Located and Co-Cluster Disaster Response Networks," *Journal of Contingencies and Crisis Management* 27, no. 1 (January 2019): 14–27, https://doi.org/10.1111/1468-5973.12224.

5. Susan Lovegren Bosworth and Gary A. Kreps, "Structure as Process: Organization and Role," *American Sociological Review* 51, no. 5 (October 1986): 699, https://doi.org/10 .2307/2095494; Gary A. Kreps, "Disaster, Organizing, and Role Enactment: A Structural Approach," *American Journal of Sociology* 99, no. 2 (September 1993): 428–63; Gary A. Kreps and Susan Lovegren Bosworth, "Organizational Adaptation to Disaster," in *Handbook of Disaster Research* (New York: Springer-Verlag, 2007), 297–315.

6. Timothy R. Kuhn, "A Communicative Theory of the Firm: Developing an Alternative Perspective on Intra-Organizational Power and Stakeholder Relationships," *Organization Studies* 29, no. 8–9 (August 1, 2008): 1227–54, https://doi.org/10.1177/0170840608094778.

7. "Robert T. Stafford Disaster Relief and Emergency Assistance Act," Pub. L. No. 93–288, as amended, 42 42 U.S.C. 5121 et. seq., and Related Authorities (1988); Federal Emergency Management Agency (FEMA), "National Response Framework" (Washington, DC: Department of Homeland Security, January 2008); Federal Emergency Management

Agency (FEMA), "National Response Framework (2nd Edition)" (Washington, DC: Department of Homeland Security, May 2013), http://www.fema.gov/media-library-data/20130726-1914-25045-1246/final_national_response_framework_20130501.pdf; Federal Emergency Management Agency (FEMA), "National Disaster Recovery Framework" (Washington, DC: Department of Homeland Security, September 2011); Federal Emergency Management Agency (FEMA), "National Disaster Recovery Framework (Second Edition)" (Department of Homeland Security, June 2016).

8. Federal Emergency Management Agency (FEMA), "Recovery Federal Interagency Operational Plan," August 2016; "Disaster Recovery: FEMA Needs to Assess Its Effectiveness in Implementing the National Disaster Recovery Framework" (U.S. Government Accountability Report, May 2016); "THE RESILIENT SOCIAL NETWORK: @OccupySandy #SuperstormSandy," RP12-01.04.11-01 (Falls Church, VA: Department of Homeland Security, Science and Technology Directorate, Homeland Security Studies and Analysis Institute, September 30, 2013), http://homelandsecurity.org/docs/the%20resilient%20social%20network.pdf; Federal Emergency Management Agency (FEMA), "Lessons from Community Recovery: Seven Years of Emergency Support Function #14, Long-Term Recovery from 2004 to 2011" (Washington, DC: Department of Homeland Security, April 2012); Divya Chandrasekhar, Yang Zhang, and Yu Xiao, "Nontraditional Participation in Disaster Recovery Planning: Cases from China, India, and the United States," *Journal of the American Planning Association* 80, no. 4 (October 2, 2014): 373–84, https://doi.org/10.1080/01944363.2014.989399; Claire B. Rubin, "The Community Recovery Process in the United States after a Major Natural Disaster," *International Journal of Emergencies and Mass Disaster* 3, no. 2 (1985): 9–28.

9. "Recovery Support Functions | FEMA.Gov," accessed September 23, 2021, https://www.fema.gov/emergency-managers/national-preparedness/frameworks/national-disaster-recovery/support-functions; Federal Emergency Management Agency (FEMA), "National Disaster Recovery Framework" (Washington, DC: Department of Homeland Security, September 2011); Federal Emergency Management Agency (FEMA), "National Disaster Recovery Framework (Second Edition)" (Department of Homeland Security, June 2016).

10. Kevin R. Kosar, "The Congressional Charter of the American National Red Cross: Overview, History, and Analysis" (Congressional Research Service, The Library of Congress, March 15, 2006), http://oai.dtic.mil/oai/oai?verb=getRecord&metadataPrefix=html&identifier=ADA462052; "American Red Cross Governance for the 21st Century: A Report to the Board of Governors" (Washington D.C.: The American Red Cross, October 2006); Alan Feuer, "Where FEMA Fell Short, Occupy Sandy Was There," *The New York Times*, November 9, 2012, http://www.nytimes.com/2012/11/11/nyregion/where-fema-fell-short-occupy-sandy-was-there.html; Justin Elliot and Justin Eisinger, "PR Over People: The Red Cross' Secret Disaster," *Pro Publica*, October 29, 2014, https://www.propublica.org/article/the-red-cross-secret-disaster; Justin Elliott and Jesse Eisinger, "How Fear of Occupy Wall Street Undermined the Red Cross' Sandy Relief Effort," *ProPublica*, December 11, 2014, https://www.propublica.org/article/how-fear-of-occupy-wall-street-undermined-the-red-cross-sandy-relief-effort; Justin Elliott, Jessica Huseman, and Decca Muldowney, "Texas Official After Harvey: The 'Red Cross Was Not There,'" *ProPublica*, October 2017, https://www.propublica.org/article/texas-official-after-harvey-the-red-cross-was-not-there; Derek Kravitz, "Red Cross 'Failed for 12 Days' After Historic Louisiana Floods," *ProPublica*, October 3, 2016, https://www.propublica.org/article/red-cross-failed-for-12-days-after-historic-louisiana-floods; Ruth McCambridge, "As Storm Season Looms, Miami Drops Reliance on the

Red Cross.," *Nonprofit Quarterly*, June 6, 2018, https://nonprofitquarterly.org/2018/06/06/as-storm-season-looms-miami-drops-reliance-on-red-cross/; Kyle Dickman, "The Future of Disaster Relief Isn't the Red Cross," August 25, 2016, https://www.outsideonline.com/2106556/team-rubicon-takes-red-cross.

11. Douglas Brinkley, *The Great Deluge Hurricane Katrina, New Orleans, and The Mississippi Gulf Coast* (New York: Harper Perennial, 2006); Chester Hartman and Gregory D. Squires, eds., *There Is No Such Thing As A Natural Disaster: Race, Class, and Hurricane Katrina* (New York: Routledge: Taylor & Francis Group, 2006); James R. Elliot and Jeremey Pais, "Race, Class, and Hurricane Katrina: Social Differences in Response to Disaster," *Social Science Research* 35, no. 2006 (2006): 295–321; David L. Brunsma, David Overfelt, and J. Steven Picou, eds., *The Sociology of Katrina: Perspectives on a Modern Catastrophe* (New York: Rowan & Littlefield Publishers Inc., 2007); Keith Wailoo et al., eds., *Katrina's Imprint: Race and Vulnerability in America* (New Brunswick, NJ: Rutgers University Press, 2010).

12. "Hurricane Sandy Rebuilding Strategy" (Hurricane Sandy Rebuilding Task Force (U.S. Department of Housing and Urban Development), August 2013).

13. "2022–2026 FEMA Strategic Plan Building the FEMA Our Nation Needs and Deserves" (Washington D.C.: Federal Emergency Management Agency, 2021), 2022–2026 FEMA Strategic Plan Building the FEMA our Nation Needs and Deserves.

14. Kenneth A. Weiss, "Clearing Title in Katrina's Wake," *Probate and Property*, October 2006; "No Title? No Easy Access to Post-Katrina Aid," *All Things Considered* (NPR, April 28, 2008), https://www.npr.org/templates/story/story.php?storyId=90005954; Richard Kluckow, "The Impact of Heir Property On Post-Katrina Housing Recovery In New Orleans" (Thesis, Fort Collins Co, Colorado State University, 2014); Laura Bliss, "After Florence, the Gullah Could Face New Threats," *Bloomberg CityLab* (blog), September 15, 2018, https://www.bloomberg.com/news/articles/2018-09-15/hurricane-florence-threatens-the-gullahs-of-south-carolina; Lizzie Presser, "Their Family Bought Land One Generation After Slavery: The Reels Brothers Spent Eight Years in Jail for Refusing to Leave It.," *ProPublica*, July 15, 2019, https://features.propublica.org/black-land-loss/heirs-property-rights-why-black-families-lose-land-south/.

15. Katherine E. Browne, *Standing in the Need: Culture, Comfort, and Coming Home after Katrina* (Austin, TX: University of Texas Press, 2015); Robert D. Bullard and Beverly Wright, "The Legacy of Bias: Hurricanes, Droughts, and Floods," in *The Wrong Complexion for Protection: How the Government Response to Disaster Endangers African American Communities* (New York and London: New York University Press, 2012), 47–72; Wailoo et al., *Katrina's Imprint*.

16. John C. Lammers, "How Institutions Communicate: Institutional Messages, Institutional Logics, and Organizational Communication," *Management Communication Quarterly* 25, no. 1 (February 1, 2011): 154–82, https://doi.org/10.1177/0893318910389280; John C. Lammers and Joshua B. Barbour, "An Institutional Theory of Organizational Communication," *Communication Theory* 16, no. 3 (2006): 356–77, https://doi.org/10.1111/j.1468-2885.2006.00274.x; William Ocasio, Jeffrey Loewenstein, and Amit Nigam, "How Streams of Communication Reproduce and Change Institutional Logics: The Role of Categories," *Academy of Management Review* 40, no. 1 (January 1, 2015): 28–48, https://doi.org/10.5465/amr.2013.0274.

17. Henry Mintzberg et al., "The Invisible World of Association," *Leader to Leader* 2005, no. 36 (2005): 37–45, https://doi.org/10.1002/ltl.126; Henry Mintzberg, "Time for the Plural Sector," *Stanford Social Innovation Review* 13, no. 3 (2015): 28–33, https://doi.org/10.48558/0WX6-ZG74; Katharina Kaltenbrunner and Birgit Renzl, "Social Capital in

Emerging Collaboration Between NPOs and Volunteers: Performance Effects and Sustainability Prospects in Disaster Relief," *VOLUNTAS: International Journal of Voluntary and Nonprofit Organizations* 30, no. 5 (October 2019): 976–90, https://doi.org/10.1007/s11266 -019-00123-6; Micheal L. Shier and Femida Handy, "From Advocacy to Social Innovation: A Typology of Social Change Efforts by Nonprofits," *VOLUNTAS: International Journal of Voluntary and Nonprofit Organizations* 26, no. 6 (December 2015): 2581–603, https://doi .org/10.1007/s11266-014-9535-1; Sara Bondesson, "Vulnerability and Power: Social Justice Organizing in Rockaway, New York City after Hurricane Sandy" (Dissertation, Uppsala, Sweden, Uppsala University, 2017), http://uu.diva-portal.org/smash/record.jsf?pid=diva2 %3A1084218&dswid=8530; Minkyung Kim et al., "Serving the Vulnerable While Being Vulnerable: Organizing Resilience in a Social Welfare Sector," *Nonprofit and Voluntary Sector Quarterly* Online First (2021), https://doi.org/0.1177/0899764021103912.

18. "About Us," Organizational, *National Voluntary Organizations Active in Disaster* (blog), November 13, 2018, https://www.nvoad.org/about-us/.

3

Writing Community Back into Disaster Recovery

Hyperlocal Organizing and Interorganizational Relationships

HYPERLOCAL ORGANIZING

Connecting Community and Institutions

Hyperlocal organizing relies upon robust interorganizational relationships that connect people and organizations to knowledge and material resources. It derives its power from integrating emergent organizing and spontaneous volunteering with community organizations that are expanding their roles in local disaster response and recovery. This integration of individual action, collective activities, and organizational processes creates relationships that solve problems in real time, both in the immediate hours and days after disaster and during the months and years of long-term recovery.

Ultimately, hyperlocal organizing is about place and the social and interorganizational relationships that form the fabric of the community. Disaster response and recovery activities are location specific; people and communities respond to an event that takes place in a geography they inhabit and that disrupts their lives. Impacted people and communities, in turn, engage with each other, local community organizations, and national and transnational disaster relief and humanitarian assistance organizations to ensure a full range of organizing across Type 1, Type 2, Type 3, and Type 4 responses. Collectively, individual, institutional, and organizational activities are critical parts of neighborhood and community response to disaster. Research on network inequalities, social impact networks, social capital, and community resilience all agree that *organizational* relationships connect people to the resources and knowledge needed to increase individual and community well-being, rather than personal ties and connections. In other words, organizational relationships build the social capital of people and communities.[1]

Social capital is primarily thought of as connections between people. These individual network ties create social capital, which, in turn, improves individual and community resilience. Social capital is created through social interactions and provides the bonds or glue that connect people and provide access to information and resources that might otherwise be inaccessible. Social interactions can enable or constrain the development of personal relationships, given people's opportunities or chances to connect through organizations or informal gathering places. For example, Small (2009) argues that social interaction is shaped by organizing. In a study of network inequalities, he finds that organizational context or connections are what matter most for childhood development and well-being. These organizational relationships connect mothers to services, material goods, and information via organizational networks. These networks in turn provide the relationships through which organizational credibility is established, mothers and children locate appropriate resources, and organizations forge collaborations to address individual and community needs.[2]

The ability of organizations and organizational leaders to broker connections among individuals and organizations creates the social and organizational capital necessary for individual and community well-being. Simply put, social ties exist within the organizations and interorganizational relationships that shape the possibilities or constraints of interaction. In other words, they are embedded within overlapping organizational and civic networks—complex webs of social and organizational relationships. Similarly, Shumate and Cooper's (2022) exhaustive, multiyear study of civic networks found that social impact networks are "sensitive" to their organizational and social environments (pp. 20–21, 187–188). They learn from and adapt over time to changing social and organizational conditions. Social impact networks are "configurable" (p. 24) because they make use of current organizational culture(s), partnerships, and resources, funding availability, leadership capabilities, capacities, public/plural/private (cross-sector) relationships, local knowledge, and community insights to configure interorganizational relationships to meet a particular community's needs.[3]

During disaster, ad-hoc or emergent activities often emerge in informal "third spaces." Parking lots, sidewalks, street corners, restaurants, and supermarkets can be configured for meetings, distributing resources, staging operations, collecting information, and providing access to information and applications for financial and housing assistance. Civic infrastructure is composed of existing and emergent organizations rooted in a particular place and the networks that they form to impact economic and social well-being. These interorganizational relationships shape the possibilities and limitations of social and organizational interactions that give rise to emergency response, disaster relief, and post-disaster hyperlocal organizing efforts. Some of these relationships may be built through years of interpersonal and interorganizational relationships, while others may spontaneously emerge as people and communities grapple with disaster and try and make sense of unfolding events. Hyperlocal organizing is the process through which ad-hoc individual and collective activities merge with existing civic networks and institutional partners to address unfolding disasters and their attendant recovery processes.[4]

HYPERLOCAL ORGANIZING AFTER 9/11:
INSTITUTIONAL AND IMPROVISATIONAL RESPONSE

One of the most successful examples of hyperlocal organizing in recent decades was the rapid and spontaneous organizing of a boat flotilla to rescue people stranded in lower Manhattan on 9/11. Over 500,000 people were ferried from lower Manhattan by 150 commercial vessels to landing zones throughout New York Harbor. New York City is a seaborne city where 25 percent (2.6 million residents) of the New York City metro region commuted into Manhattan pre-pandemic. Synonymous with New York City, Manhattan is an island borough accessible only by bridge or tunnel and is the financial and media capital of the world. Of the four other New York City boroughs, only the Bronx sits on the mainland of the United States. Staten Island is an island connected only by ferry to Manhattan, and just four bridges connect Staten Island to mainland New Jersey and Brooklyn (three to New Jersey and one to Brooklyn, leaving tenuous connections of one ferry and one bridge to the city and state political jurisdictions that Staten Island is a part of). Brooklyn and Queens sit at the extreme western end of Long Island and are accessible only by bridge or tunnel from the other three boroughs of New York City and the U.S. mainland.[5]

The Port of New York and New Jersey is the largest container port on the East Coast of the United States. It has terminals located throughout New York City and northeastern New Jersey and moves an average of 82,215 metric tons of freight per year. On a clear day, from the northern-most New Jersey beaches, cargo ships can be seen lined up steaming toward New York Harbor or rounding Sandy Hook to head toward Newark Bay. Twenty-one ferry routes serviced New York City, moving a pre-pandemic average of 18,000 commuters a day, most from New Jersey. The Staten Island Ferry moved an average of 25,000 commuters per day pre-pandemic. New York's proximity to bays, sounds, tidal rivers, and tidal estuaries puts residents at great risk to storms and terror attacks. On 9/11, the maritime industry that serves this area self-organized by connecting with larger institutional players. It rapidly emerged as a major player in evacuation, emergency response, and in the supply chain servicing response and recovery efforts at the site of the collapsed towers.[6]

Soon after the two planes hit the World Trade Center, boat captains converged on lower Manhattan and began rescuing the people who flowed south toward Battery Park and the adjacent waterfront to escape the fires and smoke at the trade center. One of the first boats to reach lower Manhattan was the *Amberjack V* out of Sheepshead Bay, captained by Vincent Ardolino. Ardolino simply told his wife, "I've got to go." Party boats, fishing boats, and ferries quickly began ferrying people out of Manhattan, docking wherever they could and in many cases simply pulling alongside the lower Manhattan bulkheading, which people climbed over or were lifted onto the waiting boats. Crewmen used acetylene torches to cut through railings to access the shore and open abandoned and disused piers. After picking up survivors, the boats sped off across the harbor and unloaded them on the New Jersey side before heading back across the bay to rescue more people. The boat flotilla lasted nine hours on 9/11 and rescued more people in those nine hours than had been evacuated from Dunkirk over three days during the early days of World War II.[7]

It was not an officially organized and sanctioned operation, despite loose and spontaneous connections with the formalized emergency response. Even the institutionalized, formal response represented by police, fire, Emergency Management Services (EMS), local and state Offices of Emergency Management (OEM), and the U.S. Coast Guard was simply responding to events as they unfolded. Radio communication broke down and plans went out the window. Ad-hoc configurations of responders banded and disbanded throughout the day on and off the water as tasks unfolded, were completed, and new events on the ground demanded new tasks that needed to be completed. Off-duty firefighters and police officers grabbed their gear and ran to the scene. Supervisory and superior officers who were disconnected from the chain of command in the chaos following the tower's collapse made spontaneous on-the-ground decisions to draft decommissioned fireboats into fire suppression operations. They enlisted knowledgeable and skilled workers, such as Steven Wollman, the waterfront construction manager for a marine transportation company who we met in the first chapter. Participants, observers, reports, and academic studies all characterized the operations of spontaneous volunteers and loosely connected emergency responders active in the boat flotilla as orderly, yet not organized in any meaningful sense. The organizing happened as people made sense of the situation, assessed their immediate environment, and used their skills, capabilities, personal networks, and the tools at hand to intervene, evacuate people, and construct preliminary systems of cross-sector response. These emergent, adaptive responses on 9/11 are reflective of a century's worth of findings on social behavior during and after disaster. People are proactive and willing to help and engage in activities that support their neighbors and communities in the aftermath of crisis and disaster.[8]

Interactions between the U.S. Coast Guard and New York Harbor pilots are particularly instructive of how spontaneous and emergent response and systems emerge through convergence. Specifically, they illustrate how institutional adaptability and flexibility can leverage hyperlocal organizing efforts to create larger systems of response that exceed the existing skills and capacity of a particular community, organization, or interorganizational relationship. Kendra and Wachtendorf (2016) describe how leaders of the New York maritime community near Staten Island responded when the twin towers were hit and began to crumble; By chance, several leaders in the New York maritime community had scheduled meetings at the Coast Guard station that day or were passing through on their way to work at one of their maritime facilities. At the Coast Guard Station on Staten Island, they began to make sense of the situation as the towers fell, responding individually and collectively, moment by moment, in what Kendra and Wachtendorf describe as a blur of sensemaking and decision-making.[9]

The decision at the New York Coast Guard station that saved the day was made by a U.S. Coast Guard Officer, Lieutenant Jack Day. He spontaneously transformed the harbor pilot boat *New York* into a Coast Guard Command Center by hoisting the Coast Guard flag and sailing with a mix of Coast Guard personnel and New York Harbor pilots into the harbor. Harbor pilot boats control traffic into and out of busy harbors like New York and serve as a base of operations for harbor pilots with local knowledge to deploy to maritime vessels unfamiliar with the area. Positioning the harbor pilot boat *New York* in a visible harbor location clearly identified as a vessel under the command of the U.S. Coast Guard paid dividends when electronic communications collapsed or became overwhelmed with traffic on 9/11.

The *New York* became a mobile command post for maritime operations. Coast Guard personnel and New York Harbor pilots were able to visually see the 9/11 operations area. Responding boats could pull alongside the pilot boat for information or instructions. The Coast Guard officer in charge (Lieutenant Day) could direct boats to specific Manhattan landing points and then onto harbor routes back to New Jersey and Staten Island. The mix of Coast Guard expertise in maritime operations and response, law enforcement, national defense, and search and rescue combined with the harbor pilots' mastery of the geography of New York Harbor. They leveraged the expert knowledge and the capacity and capabilities of individual boats and maritime shipping and transportation companies, enabling them to quickly connect with and coordinate the emerging boat flotilla. Recollections of the exact sequence of events on the morning of 9/11 are muddled, as is to be expected in the moments and hours after disaster or a terrorist attack. Individuals interviewed over the ensuing decade who were active in the boat flotilla have given differing accounts in academic interviews, news stories, documentaries, and films about exactly when the Coast Guard's request for "all available boats report to Governors Island" was made. They also weren't certain whether the call was made in response to boats already crowding together in the waters off Manhattan and picking up survivors, or was a spontaneous Coast Guard decision made by Lieutenant Day to dispatch boats both afloat and docked for maritime rescues off of lower Manhattan. What is known is that ferries had already headed back to Manhattan to rescue their passengers as soon as the second plane hit the tower. People made their boats, workplaces, and other spaces along the harbor available to engage in the biggest maritime evacuation since World War II.

Adaptable Institutions: The U.S. Coast Guard and Disaster Response

The 9/11 Boatlift highlights the unique role of the U.S. Coast Guard in crisis and disaster and its "hi-flex" operating philosophy. Hi-flex operations is the capacity of institutions to remain flexible and adaptable during fluid complex events, and is exceedingly rare. Similar to high-reliability organizations (HROs), hi-flex organizations are able to consistently adapt to fluid and changing circumstances. Where HROs are typically organized around safety, hi-flex organizations routinely decentralize decision-making to those with the relevant expertise or knowledge, or those closest to the event. Hi-flex operations allow for the reconfiguration of people, organizations, and systems as events are interpreted and made sense of. HROs and hi-flex operating philosophies are not mutually exclusive, as the Coast Guard has demonstrated elements of being both a HRO and a hi-flex one. HROs emphasize training, procedures, and backup systems (redundancy) to build processes and cultures of safety. Organizations with hi-flex cultures and operations emphasize adaptability and autonomy in response to uncertainty (Weick 1987; Weick & Sutcliffe

2006; Roberts 1990; Klein, Bigley, & Roberts 1995; Ginter, Duncan, McCormick, Rucks, Wingate, & Abdolrauslina 2001).

Unlike many government institutions, the Coast Guard is stakeholder oriented, nimble, and able to connect with a wide array of partners regardless of the events or conditions on the ground. It also operates in both adversarial and cooperative postures with its stakeholders, given its overlapping law enforcement, intelligence, regulatory, and rescue missions. Over the past two decades, the U.S. Coast Guard has been the go-to partner for early rescue and response activities during catastrophic weather events. During Katrina, the Coast Guard rescued 33,500 people including medical patients that needed immediate evacuation. Seven helicopters launched while tropical storm force winds were still blowing and began rescuing people from their homes, hospitals, and school rooftops. During 2017's Hurricane Harvey, a four-person aircrew out of Mobile, Alabama, made the first air rescue of Hurricane Harvey. Over ten hours, they flew a dozen missions that rescued fifty-four people, continuously improvising and often violating standard operating procedures to extract families from flooded homes and getting them to safety. The Coast Guard eventually rescued 11,022 people and 1,384 pets over a four-day period during and after Hurricane Harvey.[10]

The U.S. Coast Guard's history, operating philosophy, and culture are rooted in an ethos of decentralized expertise and decision-making that allow for rapid adaptation and organizational transformations. Founded in 1790 as the Revenue Cutter Service of the U.S. Department of Treasury, the Coast Guard is the United States' oldest seagoing service. The Coast Guard today is the outcome of more than a century of mergers and consolidations. Organizations with seagoing and navigation missions were combined and integrated to create a maritime agency with robust search and rescue capabilities. Organizations with missions as diverse as the Steamboat Inspection Service, the U.S. Lifesaving Service, the U.S. Lighthouse Service, and the Bureau of Navigation were all combined with the Revenue Cutter Service between 1790 and 1946. Each of these organizations has become a distinct mission area that the Coast Guard is responsible for. The Coast Guard has also been housed in multiple executive homes throughout its 230-year history, and during wartime was absorbed into the Department of Defense. The U.S. Coast Guard also has been part of both the U.S. Department of Treasury and the U.S. Department of Transportation at different times in its history and several of its mission areas have historically been part of the U.S. Department of Commerce. Finally, in 2003, the Coast Guard became part of the newly created Department of Homeland Security created in the aftermath of 9/11 but continued its key maritime safety and search and rescue roles even as port security, law enforcement, and intelligence operations took precedence in their new organization. The Coast Guard's changing organizational history demonstrates the importance of understanding the context in which communicating and organizing occurs. History, culture, and (individual and collective) identities put communication into context and shape how organizing processes and collaborative possibilities unfold. For the Coast Guard, history, culture, and identity means adaptability at the level of individuals and small groups to complete a mission successfully or to change its scope and scale given pressing realities.[11]

Building Institutional Adaptability through Stakeholder Relationships

As a mission-driven, stakeholder-oriented organization, the Coast Guard interacts with a wide range of maritime stakeholders that comprise the Coast Guard's twenty-four distinct mission areas. After 9/11 these mission areas were organized into five main mission categories, each comprising a subset of related, individual missions. These mission categories include marine safety, maritime mobility, maritime security, national defense, and protection of natural resources. The breadth of the Coast Guard's mission connects them with a wide range of stakeholders and numerous, shifting operational realities during routine sea, port, and air operations. These shifting operational realities foster a culture of institutional adaptability that connects the Coast Guard to the communities they serve as a networked stakeholder capable of both emergent and institutional action.[12]

The 9/11 mariners who rescued 500,000 people from the shores of Manhattan are stakeholders of the U.S. Coast Guard as well as members of their own community of boat captains, harbor pilots, and crew. In turn, the 9/11 mariners are part of a broader New York Harbor community of people and communities who make their living working the water. Membership in the New York Harbor Community is vast and varied and includes dockworkers, welders, and mechanics, restaurant owners and workers who own and work harborside and dockside facilities, gate attendants, and the front-office administrative, clerical, and logistics staffs that keep it all running smoothly. The Coast Guard interacts with all members of this community through the routine execution of its missions. The 9/11 maritime rescue efforts highlight how overlapping organizing efforts are a web of (a) individual, spontaneous actions in response to a situation, (b) hyperlocal organizing activities among members of a specific physical, social, or occupational community, and (c) institutions with specific expertise or authority.

As a stakeholder-focused organization with a culture of adaptability, the Coast Guard can rapidly connect with its stakeholders even amidst the chaos and uncertainty of a terrorist attack. Instances of equal participation between hyperlocal organizing efforts and institutions during crisis and disaster are rare and need to be explored further, and ultimately integrated into disaster response and recovery planning and scenarios. A key challenge for policymakers is to understand and make space for emergence in response and recovery, while accepting that the actual parameters of emergent organizing and relationships will remain largely unknown until after a specific crisis or disaster occurs.

EMERGENT ORGANIZING AND LONG-TERM RECOVERY AFTER DISASTER

Recent research has uncovered the prevalence of emergent organizing several years into a long-term recovery process, even as resource needs changed and community networks evolved. Localization of disaster recovery in impacted communities and neighborhoods may mean that some local emergent responses become institutionalized. The years-long duration of disaster response and recovery requires transitions and handoffs from one organizational sector to another. Emergency response evolves into short-term recovery, and short-term recovery morphs into long-term recovery. Some of the most interesting innovations in disaster response and recovery have occurred since Hurricane Katrina, with the emergence of SBP out of Louisiana's St. Bernard Parish and Compass 82 out of coastal New Jersey's Ocean County.

SBP emerged to work on the rebuilding process and typically does not enter an impacted community until after a year and the long-term recovery process has begun. Compass 82 applied lessons learned in disaster case management to projects in Florida after Hurricane Maria. They also served as a key component of the disaster planning and resilience infrastructure in Ocean County, New Jersey. Both these organizations emerged out of complex and fraught recovery processes and rose to be active players in long-term recovery processes. Long-term recovery after disaster is an often overlooked and ignored component of disaster response and recovery efforts and does not have the immediate measurable results that emergency response and short-term relief efforts offer to volunteers, funders, and responding organizations. Organizations with the maturity and patience to slog through years of recovery efforts and gain knowledge of the complex long-term recovery process are significantly underrepresented in the organizational landscape of disaster response and recovery.

Emergent organizing is a common phenomenon after disaster, yet existing research often focuses on how pre- and post-disaster social structures foster emergence. It neglects the dynamic organizing processes that emerge in the moment to fill in the gap between official, formal response, and recovery processes and the on-the-ground realities in impacted communities. Disaster response and long-term recovery are carefully orchestrated patterns of organizing and communicating processes that unite different types of organizations to provide specific types of services and complete tasks. Disasters are localized, and thus specific to a locality's social, economic, and historical context, as well as reflective of larger social and organizational processes that generate civic networks and social capital.[13]

Like emergent organizing, volunteers converging to the scene of crisis or disaster has long been observed by researchers and professionals alike. Spontaneous volunteers have always been present in disaster response, and the role of unaffiliated volunteers has a long history in disaster scholarship. Unorganized, individualized volunteers converging on a scene and spontaneously volunteering are often an important concern of emergency managers and humanitarian assistance professionals. Some of the institutionalized disaster relief and humanitarian assistance organizations seek to funnel spontaneous volunteers into their own organized volunteer efforts and membership base. They hope to better coordinate communication and avoid duplication of effort and services without understanding the context of convergence and citizen response.

Emergent citizen response is not only a naturally occurring response to crisis and disaster; it often appears in response to actual or perceived gaps and failures in institutional response efforts. These responses, in turn, may motivate "pop-up" organizations at the local or grassroots level to address gaps and failures in institutional response efforts. NJVOAD, New Jersey's National Voluntary Organizations Active in Disaster (VOAD) affiliate, took on the responsibility of brokering volunteers during the COVID-19 crisis. Working with the New Jersey Governor's Office of Volunteerism, they utilized an online platform through which individuals could volunteer, and nonprofit organizations could sign up and list their volunteer needs. Volunteers could then be assigned to specific organizations with specific needs, such as meal delivery or meal packaging and shopping for senior citizens and immune-compromised residents. One of the challenges of volunteering during a pandemic was ensuring safety, making spontaneous volunteering riskier than usual forms.[14]

Mutual Aid is increasingly becoming a significant part of the landscape of emergent organizing and spontaneous volunteering. Mutual Aid involves grassroots collectivities of people working toward common goals of care and solidarity. It differs from traditional notions of charity, philanthropy, and volunteerism because their service is less driven by values or generosity and more by the notion that, at the grassroots, "I am my brother's keeper." Mutual Aid may be either political or apolitical. Many Mutual Aid organizations operate from a premise of anti-capitalism or anarchist organizing, even if they generally eschew politics and policy advocacy. While Mutual Aid—and more broadly self-help—have long been present as grassroots organizing phenomena, Hurricane Maria, the COVID-19 pandemic, and 2021's Winter Storm Uri in Texas have led to an explosion of Mutual Aid organizing. Twin hurricanes, a 6.4 magnitude earthquake, and decades of austerity and privatization severely weakened Puerto Rico's social and organizational infrastructure. Neighbors and communities worked together to find clean water, procure food and supplies, jury rig power sources, and find healthcare resources, all while providing each other emotional and spiritual support.

Similar patterns have emerged in New Orleans, where consecutive years of intense hurricanes and flooding have left many neighborhoods and communities devastated and state and federal capabilities frayed. Following Hurricane Ida, Mutual Aid groups reactivated, and new Mutual Aid groups emerged to feed, house, and support people throughout New Orleans and along the bayous and rivers of South Louisiana. Winter Storm Uri in Texas left almost 5 million residents without power in freezing temperatures. Indifference by the state government and federal elected officials to quickly solving the problem and activating state and federal assistance led to a proliferation of Mutual Aid efforts across the state. Many of these Mutual Aid groups organized in response to the COVID-19 crisis and simply expanded their operations during Winter Storm Uri. We can expect Mutual Aid to play an increasingly larger role in grassroots response to crisis and disaster. Much as experiences with the anti-Wall Street Occupy movement led participants to create a new organizing process called Occupy Sandy for post-disaster recovery after Hurricane Sandy, experiences with COVID-19 and failed public sector responses will lead to new and expanded roles in emergent and grassroots organizing, and within the broader organizational landscape of disaster recovery.[15]

HYPERLOCAL ORGANIZING AND THE CHANGING LANDSCAPE OF DISASTER RECOVERY

Hyperlocal organizing involves the emergent and established aspects of disaster response and recovery. In hyperlocal organizing, established community organizations will typically coalesce through a VOAD or Long-Term Recovery Group (LTRG) and then connect with national and regional disaster relief organizations. Often left out of initial convening efforts are the ad-hoc efforts in neighborhoods and communities to map damage, secure resources, and exchange information. Over time, these emergent neighborhood and community efforts may become structured and more formally organized, as a way to shift hyperlocal efforts from response to relief and ultimately, recovery. As this process of emergence and organizing unfolds, these ad-hoc and "pop-up" organizations may begin to engage with and participate in local VOADs and LTRGs. New federal response and recovery frameworks were enacted after Hurricane Katrina in 2005 and revised after Hurricane Sandy in 2012 to better clarify organizational roles and responsibilities. Additionally, communication technologies have enabled a broader array of spontaneous volunteering and emergent organizing. New frameworks and technologies have expanded the organizational landscape of disaster recovery far beyond the face-to-face activities of traditional hyperlocal emergent organizing efforts. Federal disaster response and recovery frameworks still struggle to account for the known social and organizational processes and behaviors of disaster response and the widely varied and diverse organizational landscape through which response, relief, and recovery are enacted.

After Hurricane Harvey in 2017, the Cajun Navy launched boat rescues using information from crowdsourced phone calls and emails, as residents used social media to request a rescue from rapidly flooding neighborhoods and homes. A phone number was even designated by crowdsourced volunteers, enabling stranded residents to call in if they couldn't reach 9-11. Cloud software such as Google Maps and GIS mapping software were then used to identify residents' precise locations and the boats nearest to them. While these efforts were going on, local schools, community organizations, and businesses mobilized to find dislocated residents' temporary shelter and move them from "lily pads" to more safe and secure locations.[16] From there, grassroots rescuers and local organizations connected rescued residents with family or friends or found them local shelter in schools and community organizations. They filled in when established national disaster relief organizations failed to adequately establish and staff mass care operations and shelters in the days and weeks after Harvey's landfall.

In the immediate aftermath of Hurricane Harvey, three parallel processes assisted impacted residents in the Houston metro area: (1) the traditional first responder network of police, fire, EMS, and OEM, (2) a local community effort organized through local schools, businesses, and nonprofits, and (3) a digital crowdsourced effort utilizing the experiences and expertise of a loosely organized organization colloquially known as the Cajun Navy. The Cajun Navy consisted primarily of volunteers from Louisiana who fish, hunt, and boat. Typically well equipped with personally owned outdoor gear, these volunteers will self-deploy and connect with local and hyperlocal response and relief efforts when local authorities and the national response are overwhelmed. The effort was launched as an ad-hoc response for failed city, state, and federal relief efforts after Katrina and has continued for almost two decades. Less organized and structured than other emergent efforts that emerged after Katrina (SBP) and the 2010 earthquake in Haiti (Team Rubicon) and that later became go-to disaster relief players, the Cajun Navy is representative of a broad array of organizing efforts that support hyperlocal response with outside resources and expertise.

The organizational landscape of recovery is driven by overlapping networks of interorganizational relationships that are already present in a community when disaster strikes. Hyperlocal organizing is primarily, though not always, a process of emergent networked organizing in a disrupted region. That is, both new and existing organizations connect in new patterns of interaction and relationships to address the problem at hand. Grassroots and neighborhood organizing efforts usually give rise to new forms of organizing and organization in disaster-impacted communities. Existing community organizations also engaged in disaster relief and recovery will often connect with these emergent organizations and spontaneous volunteers, as well as with the more formally organized and organizationally stable disaster and humanitarian relief organizations. These connections and interorganizational relationships dynamically reshape the organizational landscape of disaster by connecting the hyperlocal organizing efforts of both emergent and established community organizations within the broader institutional landscape of response and recovery.

HOW DOES HYPERLOCAL ORGANIZING WORK?

Hyperlocal organizing activates a blended local stakeholder network that remixes face-to-face and digital organizing processes to respond to institutional failures in crisis and disaster. It is neither a fully emergent nor a fully established community stakeholder network. Instead, hyperlocal organizing integrates emergent organizing and established grassroots, neighborhood, and community organizations into disaster response and recovery networks. These networks then facilitate grassroots collaboration to meet local needs that are often overlooked by institutional response efforts after disaster. Like hyperlocal media, hyperlocal organizing has a community orientation, varying geographic reach, and the potential to drive civic engagement.

Unlike hyperlocal media, which also fills in the response gaps left by institutions, hyperlocal organizing does not *require* web and digital technologies. The same parallels hold true between hyperlocal organizing and connective logics. Both connect individuals (such as spontaneous volunteers) with broader frames of action and a wider network of organizations. However, connective logics rely much more on digital mobilization to connect widely scattered, decentralized individuals with like-minded others engaged in political and social activities. Hyperlocal organizing may indeed utilize digital infrastructures to connect local communities with digitally networked grassroots organizations, such as Burners without Borders and Occupy Sandy. But even these efforts are ultimately place-based—geographically bound to where communication and organizing activities related to disaster response and recovery are taking place.

Understanding Hyperlocal Organizing through Theories of Civic Media

Both hyperlocal organizing and civic media share underlying communication and organizing principles that emphasize connection and the creation, recreation, configuration, and reconfiguration of organizing processes in response to changes in social, economic, and environmental conditions. As a participatory phenomenon, civic media involves the creation of new communication channels and tools that increase the possibility of public engagement in civic life. To achieve these goals, civic media engages people and communities in the co-production of locally oriented media through processes of information creation and sharing. Hyperlocal organizing uses similar information and communication processes to build needed interorganizational relationships that engage people and communities in shared problem-solving after disaster. Most simply, civic media can be defined as communication that strengthens community social bonds or increases civic engagement among citizens. It is both emotional and aspirational, as it seeks to increase the connections and emotional bonds between citizens, their neighbors, communities, and organizational associations.

Civic media is not just simply a technical fix or technological solution to participation. Instead, civic media is a framework through which associational activities are made possible. Similar to "convergence" or "remix" cultures, civic media is a process of creation and recreation in which content flows across different media platforms and through different media sectors. It relies on partnerships to cross-fertilize ideas, stories, and strategies. These varied partnerships are networked stakeholder relationships in which each partner has a claim to, or stake in, the creation of open-source technologies that facilitate the flow of civic information. In civic media, fluid and changing audiences shape and reshape content and culture, using tools of participatory culture and interactive communication technologies to create "mashups" of new and existing information and media.[17],[18]

These participatory cultures, tools, and technologies have given rise to a system of connective logics that provides a new digital and networked basis for political participation, social action, and civic engagement. Connective logics bring atomized publics together with broader networks of political and social action. In this way, they connect individualized actors with larger movements of social and political action through dense patterns of interpersonal and interorganizational communication. Connective logics emphasize the connection of individuals to larger civic action networks by enabling individuals to act on or activate their belief systems and personal values by connecting with a broader network of individuals who share similar values and commitments. In her account of the digitally enabled protest, Tufecki (2017) remarks that loose connections of activists, across multiple protests and geographic spaces, were facilitated by sharing in-person experiences and digital technologies. While protests such as those marking the Arab Spring or Turkish protests in Gezi Park were local, individually shared experiences of protest and social advocacy also rapidly mobilized individuals worldwide who were advocating for democracy and civic space. New organizations emerged out of shared advocacy experiences, similar to earlier anti-WTO mobilizations, which were then able to build on these experiences to connect protestors on the ground with digital-only engaged protestors. Technology-enabled connections and digitally mediated associations build not only networks of action—they also create new patterns of associational activity and change the organizational logics of existing organizations and the sectors they operate in.[19]

Connective logics are both online and offline processes of communicating and organizing. Rather than serving as a standard channel of political communication in which information is exchanged and received and in which communication channels serve as paths for the communication of reputation, identity, and financial resources among stakeholders, connective logics pattern the interactions of those engaged in political and social action. As an organizational logic, connective logics link individuals to larger patterns of political activity and discourse, which increase civic engagement. Civic engagement ranges from "slacktivism" to the creation of new tools that enable citizens to access, mine, and understand complex or hidden public data, or actively participate in public meetings, actions, and protests.

Foundational theories of civic media were created before the emergence of harmful misinformation and network propaganda that spread during Brexit, the Trump presidency, and the COVID-19 pandemic. With very few exceptions, civic media was largely seen as a pro-social technological advancement that enabled voluntary associations and bolstered civic life. The Cambridge Analytica scandal, political efforts to cast doubt on the legitimacy of the 2020 U.S. presidential election, and anti-vaccine mobilizations have all challenged our understanding of civic media and digitally networked communication as positive developments for civic engagement. They have rendered plainly visible the dark shadows of populist demagoguery and disinformation in an era of distributed communication and institutional failures. Accessibility, configurability, and connectivity can be used to foster community or to tear it down.

Civic media are configurable and customizable technologies and tools that improve political communication and policymaking processes. It has the potential to unite citizens, civic leaders, elected officials, and experts. It is not simply another term for citizen journalism or hyperlocal media organizations that report on grassroots and neighborhood concerns. Rather, citizen journalism and hyperlocal media can be thought of as strands of civic media. Civic media also is a process of communicating and organizing. It operates at the individual, organizational, interorganizational, community, national, and international levels and can be configured to represent local values and needs. Initially, civic media was seen as a way to increase civic engagement and boost local democratic practices through distributed deliberation in politics and governance using digital tools and information. However, civic media also enables collective social movements and participation in contentious politics. It serves as a "disruptive" technology and platform that erodes traditional notions of credibility, expertise, legitimacy, and authority. Within civic media environments, expertise is widely distributed, and credentials often suspect. Like all technologies, civic media can be harnessed for good or evil.

Civic media has traditionally relied on a foundation of convergence (or "remix") culture. By crossing cultural, social, and organizational boundaries, civic media has enabled new participants to engage in activities that traditionally required capital, expertise, or time. Remix culture hinges on the ability of audiences and producers to combine existing texts, sounds, images, and artifacts into new configurations that appeal to existing and new audiences. It uses digital technologies to create distributed peer-peer communication, moving away from traditional political and media models of one-to-many and top-down communication. By moving beyond the mass communication models of institutionalized twentieth-century communication, twenty-first remix culture democratized participation and engagement in politics and popular culture. Remix culture rests upon foundations of code and open-source architectures that move media production, information gathering, and audiences beyond the traditional centralized, capital-intensive infrastructures that have traditionally dominated mass and political communication. These dispersed and digital challenges to traditional sources of news, information, and culture have significantly eroded the agenda-setting and gate-keeper functions of mass media and elite institutions. They have also amplified peer-to-peer communication about social and political crises and issues through a digital technology environment that encourages the direct creation of content and extended interactions with experts and media organizations.

Ultimately, civic media is the expression of remix culture in more institutionalized and associational forms. It is a stream of organizing processes and communication flows that build connections between citizens, communities, and institutions. Similarly, hyperlocal organizing relies upon remixed communication and organizing processes to create a digital coordinating framework through which disaster-impacted residents and communities can intervene in the top-down decision-making processes typical of short- and long-term recovery after disaster. Hyperlocal organizing is essentially an organizational remix, in which emergent and existing organizations restyle civic networks to best meet the needs of impacted residents and communities.

Hyperlocal Organizing: Remixing Organizing and Communicating on Staten Island

Occupy Sandy's connection with hyperlocal organizing in the New York City Borough of Staten Island after 2012's Hurricane Sandy illustrates the physical and digital remixing of organizing processes and social interactions. An organizer active in the Occupy Wall Street movement lived on the Lower East Side of the Borough of Manhattan in New York City. Since he owned a motorcycle and could easily maneuver around the closed-off, storm-impacted streets and bridges, he was asked by other Occupy Sandy organizers to go to Staten Island to check on the damage and resident's needs. Once there, the organizer was able to connect with spontaneous volunteers and emergent organizing efforts, assess their efforts, and bring that information back over the bridges to Occupy Sandy coordinators located in Manhattan and the NYC Borough of Brooklyn. This early reconnaissance effort occurred while the region's communications infrastructure was severely damaged, prompting a reliance on physical, face-to-face communication, even among digital technology-savvy organizations such as the Occupy Movement.

Once Occupy Sandy coordinators in Brooklyn received information from Staten Island and other similarly impacted communities, they were able to use existing digital infrastructure. They set up an Amazon wedding registry to connect donors to community needs and deliver critical supplies like gas, diapers, battery-operated radios, and bottled water directly to communities. The Occupy Sandy coordinator who made the initial motorcycle run stayed connected with hyperlocal organizing efforts in Staten Island. They later became extensively involved in interorganizational organizing efforts with emergent and faith-based recovery on Staten Island. Occupy Sandy provided not just boots on the ground and digital infrastructure but also collaborative leadership with grassroots and faith-based organizations that resulted in the formation of the Staten Island Long-Term Recovery Organization (SILTRO).

Community Information Ecosystems as Civic Media

Community information ecosystems provide the organizational and institutional infrastructure that connects civic media to place-based processes of hyperlocal organizing and civic engagement. The concept of a community information ecosystem represents multiple ways of thinking about the use and role of information within a community. At a broad level, information ecosystems can be defined as complex systems of exchange in which ideas and technologies are developed and diffused over time among different populations. Internews' Center for Innovation and Learning describes information ecosystems as how "local communities exist and evolve within particular information and communication systems," noting that "the term broadly refers to a loose, dynamic configuration of different sources, flows, producers, consumers, and sharers of information interacting within a defined community or space."

These information ecosystems are not fixed in time or by the constraints of physical or digital infrastructures, rather they are continually evolving. Following disaster, information ecosystems may rapidly evolve and make use of functional communication technologies at hand. Findings from a post-Sandy study of information ecosystems in New York City commissioned by Internews found that electronic and digital communication was severely constrained by power outages and disrupted electricity flows. Residents and organizational leaders turned to corded landline phones and ham radios. They increasingly relied on face-to-face communication to gather and distribute information. In short, information ecosystems can remix old and new technologies to rapidly reconfigure organizing processes to work around disrupted communication and organizing processes. Community information ecosystems provide a framework from which to understand civic media as a process of citizen engagement based on the availability, use, and application of information and data through different communication channels.[20]

Civic institutions such as community libraries and hubs—as physical spaces through which people can connect physically and virtually—give physical shape and presence to local information ecosystems. Historically, the United States Post Office, free public libraries, and free public schools were established to foster an information-rich republic in which participation in community life was valued. Civic institutions and civic engagement are core hyperlocal organizing processes and represent an associational politics rooted in the panorama of civic and political life painted by Tocqueville in his travels across the United States in the early days of the republic. For Tocqueville, voluntary associations and township governance were foundational units of American democracy. Local associations (and later local chapters of national voluntary associations) and township governance provided the organizational and spatial places from which to engage in democracy through civic institutions. A broader "society of organizations" was thought to mitigate socio-economic and ecological externalities generated by organizations in the public and private sectors. What we now call civic engagement is the communicative interplay between individuals and civic organizations, which may exist either virtually or physically. Digital tools differentiate current modes of civic engagement from past modes of civic engagement, which required face-to-face conversations in shared physical and organizational spaces. Digital tools allow for digital citizens to access streams of civic information, analyze publicly available data sets, and share and distribute this civic information and public data sets in ways that challenge official logics, frames, positions, and narratives.[21]

PLACE, COMMUNICATION, AND ORGANIZING

Communication always occurs in context. Material circumstances, identities, cultures, the socioeconomic and political landscape, and even physical place all impact the quality and efficacy of communication activities. Organizing always requires two-way communication in which interactions and meaning are co-constructed among participants. We can map, measure, and analyze the formal structures and networks of organizational and interorganizational communication. Still, context matters, and local identities and cultures will often shape who talks to and connects with whom, thus impacting the membership and configuration of these networks.

In coastal New Jersey, interviews about the interorganizational relationships of organizational leaders engaged in long-term recovery invariably coalesced into three distinct patterns. Mayors and other elected officials pointed to other mayors and government agencies as their primary relationships, while Municipal Business Administrators referred to other Municipal Business Administrators, and nonprofit leaders connected mainly with other nonprofit leaders. In Staten Island, the situation was even more clear cut. Existing community organizations and nonprofits coalesced around the pre-existing Staten Island Community Organizations Active in Disasters (SICOAD) while emergent and faith-based organizations coalesced primarily into the newly organized SILTRO. Identities, cultures, and homophily shape interorganizational relationships even in disaster-impacted communities experiencing social and technological disruptions.

Geographic, organizational, or physical place shapes the organizational interactions and networked relationships that ultimately underlie communication and organizing processes. The density of community organizations in a specific community or neighborhood may be a better predictor of civic engagement and social well-being than either the personal social ties or memberships in traditional organizations that we usually define as social capital and use as a predictor of resilience. Network density may vary across communities and neighborhoods, though the actual measured network density of a community or neighborhood may not truly capture the overall density of community organizations in those places. It is the presence and interaction of organizations in communities and neighborhoods that open possibilities for increased civic engagement, associational politics, and increased organizational capital, all of which are important factors in recovery from disaster or crisis.[22]

NOTES

1. Michelle Shumate and Katherine R. Cooper, *Networks for Social Impact* (New York: Oxford University Press, 2022).

2. Mario Luis Small, *Unanticipated Gains: Origins of Network Inequality on Everyday Life* (Oxford: Oxford University Press, 2009).

3. Shumate and Cooper, *Networks for Social Impact*.

4. Joonmo Son and Nan Lin, "Social Capital and Civic Action: A Network-Based Approach," *Social Science Research* 37, no. 1 (March 2008): 330–49, https://doi.org/10.1016 /j.ssresearch.2006.12.004; Mario Diani, *The Cement of Civil Society: Studying Networks in Localities* (New York: Cambridge University Press, 2015); Shumate and Cooper, *Networks for Social Impact*.

5. "4 Bridges Connect Staten Island to the Rest of The World," *Staten Island Advance*, March 4, 2019, https://www.silive.com/guide/2012/04/4_bridges_connect_staten_island_to _the_rest_of_the_world.html.

6. "2019 Trade Statistics" (New York: Port Authority of New York and New Jersey, 2020); "The Ins and Outs of NYC Commuting: An Examination of Recent Trends and Characteristics of Commuter Exchanges between NYC and the Surrounding Metro Region" (New York City Department of Planning, September 2019).

7. James Kendra and Tricia Wachtendorf, *American Dunkirk: The Waterborne Evacuation of Manhattan on 9/11* (Philadelphia, PA: Temple University Press, 2016); Eddie Rosenstein, *BOATLIFT: An Untold Tale of 9/11 Resilience* (Brooklyn, NY: Eyepop Productions, 2011),

https://www.youtube.com/watch?v=18lsxFcDrjo; *The 9/11 Boat Rescue That Saved Half a Million People | I Was There* (Vice Productions, 2021), https://youtu.be/XyS-tYoOj6g; *Rescue at Water's Edge: The U.S. Merchant Marine Response to 9/11* (New York: U.S. Department of Transportation, 2011), 11, https://youtu.be/yc66PsnXPoA.

   8. Kendra and Wachtendorf, *American Dunkirk: The Waterborne Evacuation of Manhattan on 9/11*; Gregory J Sanial, "The Response to Hurricane Katrina: A Study of the Coast Guard's Culture, Organizational Design & Leadership in Crisis" (Masters of Management, Cambridge MA, Massachusetts Institute of Technology, 2007); Karl E. Weick, "Enacted Sensemaking in Crisis Situations [1]," *Journal of Management Studies* 25, no. 4 (1988): 305–17; K. Weick, "The Collapse of Sensemaking in Organizations: The Mann Gulch Disaster," *Administrative Science Quarterly* 38 (1993): 628–52; Karl E. Weick and Kathleen M. Sutcliffe, *Managing the Unexpected: Assuring High Performance in an Age of Complexity* (San Francisco: Jossey-Bass, 2001); Enrico L. Quarantelli and Russell R. Dynes, "Response to Social Crisis and Disaster," *Annual Review of Sociology*, 1977, 23–49; Enrico L. Quarantelli, "Conventional Beliefs and Counterintuitive Realities," *Social Research* (2008): 873–904; E. L. Quarantelli, "The Earliest Interest in Disasters and Crises, and the Early Social Science Studies of Disasters, as Seen in a Sociology of Knowledge Perspective," 2009, http://udspace.udel.edu/handle/19716/5745; Kathleen J. Tierney, "From the Margins to the Mainstream: Disaster Research at the Crossroads," *Annual Review of Sociology* 33 (2007): 503–25.

   9. Kendra and Wachtendorf, *American Dunkirk: The Waterborne Evacuation of Manhattan on 9/11*.

   10. Douglas Brinkley, *The Great Deluge Hurricane Katrina, New Orleans, and The Mississippi Gulf Coast* (New York: Harper Perennial, 2006); Evan Cadet Twarog, "Hurricane Ready: Coast Guard Adapts to the Social Media Storm," *Proceedings of the U.S. Naval Institute* 144, no. 10 (October 2018), https://www.usni.org/magazines/proceedings/2018/october/hurricane-ready-coast-guard-adapts-social-media-storm; Julian Smith, "The Untold Story of Hurricane Harvey's First Urban Air Rescue Mission," *Esquire*, September 1, 2020, https://www.esquire.com/news-politics/a33611137/hurricane-harvey-coast-guard-rescue/.

   11. Sanial, "The Response to Hurricane Katrina: A Study of the Coast Guard's Culture, Organizational Design & Leadership in Crisis"; Thomas H. Collins, "Change and Continuity—The U.S. Coast Guard Today," *Naval War College Review* 57, no. 2 (Spring 2004): 2–19.

   12. P.J. Chief Petty Officer Capelotti, *Rouge Wave: The U.S. Coast Guard on and after 9/11* (Washington, DC: U.S.US Coast Guard Historians Office, 2003); Garret M. Graff, "Escape from New York the Great Maritime Rescue of Lower Manhattan on 9/11," *New York Magazine*, September 11, 2021, https://nymag.com/intelligencer/2021/09/the-great-maritime-rescue-of-lower-manhattan-on-9-11.html.

   13. Sarah Lee Saunders and Gary A. Kreps, "The Life History of Emergent Organization in Times of Disaster," *The Journal of Applied Behavioral Science* 23, no. 4 (1987): 443–62; Thomas E. Drabek and David A. McEntire, "Emergent Phenomena and the Sociology of Disaster: Lessons, Trends, and Opportunities from the Research Literature," *Disaster Prevention and Management* 12, no. 2 (2003): 97–112, https://doi.org/10.1108/09653560310474214; Thomas E. Drabek, "Community Processes: Coordination," in *Handbook of Disaster Research*, 2007, 217–33; Veronica Strandh and Niklas Eklund, "Emergent Groups in Disaster Research: Varieties of Scientific Observation over Time and across Studies of Nine Natural Disasters," *Journal of Contingencies and Crisis Management* 26, no. 3 (2017): 1–9; A. Majchrzak, S. L. Jarvenpaa, and A. B. Hollingshead, "Coordinating Expertise among Emergent Groups Responding to Disasters," *Organization Science* 18, no. 1 (2007):

147–61; A. J. Porter, "Emergent Organization and Responsive Technologies in Crisis: Creating Connections or Enabling Divides?," *Management Communication Quarterly* 27, no. 1 (February 1, 2013): 6–33, https://doi.org/10.1177/0893318912459042.

14. Robert A. Stallings and E. L. Quarantelli, "Emergent Citizen Groups and Emergency Management," *Public Administration Review* 45 (January 1985): 93, https://doi.org/10.2307 /3135003; Margaret Harris et al., "The Involvement/Exclusion Paradox of Spontaneous Volunteering: New Lessons and Theory From Winter Flood Episodes in England," *Nonprofit and Voluntary Sector Quarterly* 46, no. 2 (April 2017): 352–71, https://doi.org/10.1177 /0899764016654222; John Twigg and Irina Mosel, "Emergent Groups and Spontaneous Volunteers in Urban Disaster Response," *Environment and Urbanization* 29, no. 2 (October 2017): 443–58, https://doi.org/10.1177/0956247817721413; Ruth Simsa et al., "Spontaneous Volunteering in Social Crises: Self-Organization and Coordination," *Nonprofit and Voluntary Sector Quarterly* 48, no. 2_suppl (April 2019): 103S–122S, https://doi.org/10.1177 /0899764018785472.

15. Isa Rodríguez Soto, "Mutual Aid and Survival as Resistance in Puerto Rico: Faced with an Onslaught of Disasters, Government Mismanagement of Life-Threatening Crises, and the Injustices of Colonialism, Puerto Rican Communities Have Bet on Their Own Survival. Their Mutual Aid Efforts Testify to Both the Power of Grassroots Organizing and the Scale of State Neglect," *NACLA Report on the Americas* 52, no. 3 (July 2, 2020): 303–8, https://doi.org /10.1080/10714839.2020.1809099; Simon Springer, "Caring Geographies: The COVID-19 Interregnum and a Return to Mutual Aid," *Dialogues in Human Geography* 10, no. 2 (July 2020): 112–15, https://doi.org/10.1177/2043820620931277; Daniela G. Domínguez et al., "Leveraging the Power of Mutual Aid, Coalitions, Leadership, and Advocacy during COVID-19," *American Psychologist* 75, no. 7 (October 2020): 909–18, https://doi.org/10 .1037/amp0000693; Amy McCarthy, "When Government Could Not, Mutual Aid Kept Texans' Needs Met Through Winter Storm Uri," February 22, 2021, https://houston.eater .com/22293485/mutual-aid-groups-disaster-relief-texas-winter-storm-uri; Alexandria Herr, "'Solidarity, Not Charity': Mutual Aid Groups Are Filling Gaps in Texas' Crisis Response," *Grist*, February 26, 2021, https://grist.org/justice/solidarity-not-charity-mutual-aid-groups -are-filling-gaps-in-texas-crisis-response/; "Texas Organizers Discuss Mutual Aid Responses to Storm," *It's Going Down* (Pacifica Radio Network: 94.1 KPFA, March 12, 2021), https:// kpfa.org/episode/its-going-down-march-12-2021/.

16. "Lily pads" was the term used by local residents and community leaders to describe a school or business with an above-water parking lot from which boat rescues could be launched and residents brought to safety.

17. W. Lance Bennett and Alexandra Segerberg, *The Logic of Connective Action: Digital Media and the Personalization of Contentious Politics* (Cambridge University Press, 2013); Bruce Bimber, Andrew J. Flanagin, and Cynthia Stohl, *Collective Action in Organizations: Interaction and Engagement in an Era of Technological Change* (New York: Cambridge University Press, 2012); Chris Wells, *The Civic Organization and the Digital Citizen: Communicating Engagement in a Networked Age* (Oxford University Press, 2015); Zeynep Tufekci, *Twitter and Tear Gas: The Power and Fragility of Networked Protest* (New Haven and London: Yale University Press, 2017); Sheetal D. Agarwal et al., "A Model of Crowd Enabled Organization: Theory and Methods for Understanding the Role of Twitter in the Occupy Protests," *International Journal of Communication* 8 (February 14, 2014): 27.

18. Bennett and Segerberg, *The Logic of Connective Action*; Bimber, Flanagin, and Stohl, *Collective Action in Organizations: Interaction and Engagement in an Era of Technological*

Change; Wells, *The Civic Organization and the Digital Citizen*; Agarwal et al., "A Model of Crowd Enabled Organization."

19. Tufekci, *Twitter and Tear Gas.*

20. Nancy Kranich and Jorge Reina Schement, "Information Commons," *Annual Review of Information Science and Technology* 42, no. 1 (2008): 546–91; Internews, "Information Ecosystems in Action: New York" (Internews, November 2014), http://www.internews.org/sites/default/files/resources/Internews_Information_Ecosystems_in_Action-NewYork.pdf.

21. Nancy Kranich, "Civic Partnerships: The Role of Libraries in Promoting Civic Engagement," *Resource Sharing & Information Networks* 18, no. 1–2 (August 10, 2005): 89–103, https://doi.org/10.1300/J121v18n01_08; Lynette Kvasny, Nancy Kranich, and Jorge Reina Schement, "Communities, Learning, and Democracy in the Digital Age," in *Learning in Communities* (Springer, 2009), 41–44, http://link.springer.com/chapter/10.1007/978-1-84800-332-3_9; Alexis de Tocqueville, *Democracy in America*, ed. Harvey C. Mansfield and Winthrop (Chicago, IL: University of Chicago Press, 2000).

22. Robert J. Sampson, *Great American City: Chicago and the Enduring Neighborhood Effect* (University of Chicago Press, 2012); Steve Kroll-Smith, Vern Baxter, and Pam Jenkins, *Left to Chance: Hurricane Katrina and the Story of Two New Orleans Neighborhoods* (Austin, TX: University of Texas Press, 2015); Vikki S. Katz and Keith N. Hampton, "Communication in City and Community: From the Chicago School to Digital Technology," *American Behavioral Scientist* 60, no. 1 (2016): 3–7; B. Palser, "The Hazards of Hyperlocal: Why Neighborhood News Online Is a Dicey Proposition," *American Journalism Review* 32 (2010): 68–69.

4

Using Stakeholder Theory to Build Theories of Hyperlocal Organizing

> How do you not have a stake in the situation, in the recovery, if you're part of the community?
>
> (Author Interview with Grassroots Organizer,
> Coastal New Jersey, March 2017)

FROM ORGANIZATIONAL SURVIVABILITY TO COMMUNITY SURVIVABILITY

The survivability of communities in the face of increasing climate change, more intense storms, and growing inequalities in disaster-impacted communities is the grand challenge of the twenty-first century. Meeting this challenge requires organizing to generate solutions. Understanding the broader landscape of stakeholder relationships and community collaboration in post-disaster recovery shows how to respond: by extending stakeholder theory to community survivability. Stakeholder theory provides a theoretical framework through which to create new government disaster policies that better account for the diverse interorganizational relationships that make disaster response and recovery happen.

At its heart, stakeholder theory is a theory of organizing and interconnection. It has traditionally been concerned with issues of organizational survivability and the claims that stakeholders—organizations, communities, and people—make upon one another. Stakeholders are mutually dependent and able to affect the achievement of organizational goals in both stable and turbulent environments. Stakeholders may provide financial, material, or communicative resources. They can also trade power, status, and prestige, which offer a way to navigate interorganizational complexities and negotiate uncertainty. Stakeholder relationships are processes of interaction among organizations with shared goals and joint problem-solving interests. These interactions enable the social and organizational ties that allow organizations to achieve shared goals by making collaborative decisions to solve problems. In so doing, interorganizational interactions shape and reshape the social and organizational landscape of communities. It is from these organizational landscapes that complex public problems, such as long-term recovery from disaster or social resilience, may finally be solved. Stakeholder theory is a dynamic, empirical framework through which common organizational and interorganizational interests and goals are refined and developed, expanding the framework of moral considerations and social expectations. While stakeholder theory is not a broad theory of political economy, it can be applied to broader social, economic, and ecological problems that impact community and social well-being—problems like disaster response and recovery.

Within Nordic countries,[1] stakeholder interests have been expanded to include issues of child labor, human rights, long-term investments in communities, and sustainability. Nordic organizational theorizing has long considered the role of communities in stakeholder relationships and how the political, economic, and social stakes of stakeholders are entwined. A Nordic notion of citizenship includes broad participation in the political process, an emphasis on social benefits and human development, and equal consideration of both worker and management rights in governance. Nordic civic and political concepts broadly reflect the required processes of long-term recovery after disaster, in which networked stakeholders collaboratively identify problems and needs; develop solutions; divide up tasks and roles; choose leadership of the coordinating LTRG or VOAD; and coordinate resources.[2]

Successful long-term recovery requires active stakeholder participation, balanced governance, and an emphasis on social benefits and community well-being. To achieve these goals, long-term recovery requires networked collaborations that connect stakeholders across the public, private, and plural sectors. Equal weight should be given to the interests, skills, and expertise of each participating organization as the parameters of the disaster, and individual and community needs become clear. As the parameters of the disaster emerge, tasks and roles can be collaboratively assigned to organizations with the appropriate expertise and resources, regardless of their position in the hierarchies and landscapes of recovery. Community collaboration, citizen or spontaneous volunteering, "pop-up" organizations, and hyperlocal organizing are all organizational phenomena that enable a community to react, respond, and recover from disaster. Long-term recovery and post-disaster recovery (more broadly) provide opportunities to extend stakeholder theory from a concern with organizational survivability to a broader focus on *community* survivability through collaborations that leverage existing social and organizational infrastructure.

Hyperlocal Organizing and Networked Stakeholders: Organizational Theorizing for the Twenty-First Century

Stakeholder theory accounts for interactions that define contemporary economic and social life. These interactions occur between institutional and noninstitutional actors, as well as across the public, plural, and private organizational sectors. As a relational theory of organizing, stakeholder theory describes how interorganizational interactions generate shared meanings of events and activities, and shape subsequent organizational actions. Stakeholder theory also provides an ethical basis for understanding social and organizational relationships as voluntary associations between organizations sharing mutual concerns.[3]

"By their groups ye shall know them." In his aphorism, the twentieth-century Unitarian-Universalist theologian and social ethicist James Luther Adams expressed a profound belief in the power of voluntary associations to mediate relationships between individuals and the state. Adams argued that religious faith and organizational ethics can only be truly understood through action. In other words, what actions does an individual's faith or ethics prompt them to take in response to specific economic, social, or political concerns? What associational activities do they engage in that may express their faith or ethics in concrete, meaningful ways? We find echoes of Adams' concern with voluntary association in the political philosophy of Wilson Carey McWilliams. A twentieth-century political philosopher, McWilliams, like the theologian and social ethicist Adams, emphasized the associational bases of political and social life. Where Adams saw voluntary association as a mediating force between individual agency and state power, McWilliams was concerned with the ties that bind people to the community. These ties formed the moral bases of politics, much as Adam Smith framed commercial society as resting upon a series of rules-based and internalized moral attributes guiding individual and social relations.[4]

In the atomized landscape of late industrial democracy, McWilliams argued ties became frayed. It was only through localized connections and friendships that people were able to find community. However, localized ties and the community they build remained elusive. They were also often subject to larger economic and political forces that isolated people and dissolved local associations. Trust and faith were increasingly institutionalized as institutions replaced associational and communal ties. Worse, they could be radically narrowed to connect only homogenous people and organizations that shared common ideas and backgrounds, regardless of their veracity or impact on democratic governance, with the value of difference in building strong democratic communities belittled or ignored. Crisis and disaster often temporarily reversed these forces, if only for a moment. Crises and disasters disrupt the social fabric, at which point voluntary associations among people, communities, and organizations become critical to survival and recovery.[5]

The health of voluntary association is critical for community survivability and solving grand challenges. Adams' and McWilliams' concerns broadly reflect the organizational theorist Henry Mintzberg's concern with "balance" across the public, plural, and private sectors, and how associations mitigate "worldly" problems such as climate change. Mintzberg has forcefully argued that the mid-twentieth-century business success and social progress in advanced Western industrial democracies was possible because of shared responsibilities and obligations across all three sectors. However, current Western approaches to economy and society ignore or significantly downplay the plural sector's expertise in associational politics and governance, according to Mintzberg. Neglecting the plural sector limits our capacity for solving complex ecological and social problems at the grassroots and institutional levels. Stakeholder theory adds organizational and interorganizational boundaries to these associational processes, creating a framework for understanding the mutual obligations of people and organizations to each other and their communities. As a relational theory of organizing about the attributes of organizational actors and the relationships between them, stakeholder theory is particularly well suited to addressing the complex interplay between social and ecological challenges and the interorganizational relationships needed to mitigate or solve these challenges.[6]

Mutual dependencies and tensions between the state and society give rise to organizing processes that shape the organizational landscape of a given community, region, and nation. In Perrow's 1991 accounting of "a society of organizations," complex organizations serve both social and economic purposes. When income and employment become the responsibility of large, complex for-profit organizations through wage dependency, rules and norms shape formal and informal communication and processes of work, management, and governance (bureaucracy). The social and ecological costs of organizations are externalized or outsourced, as profit-centered complex organizations give rise to other complex organizations in the public and plural sectors. To Perrow, these dependencies and tensions ultimately give rise to a constellation or "society" of organizations that addresses gaps and inequities in communities, regions, and nations. Multi-stakeholder collaboration among public, private, and plural sector organizations may mitigate these inequities and provide a process for solving complex social, economic, ecological problems caused by profit-first complex organizations.[7]

Who Has a Stake?

Stakeholder theory argues that all stakeholders with moral or legal rights or obligations have a stake in an organization. While not all stakeholders may claim their stake, they remain present as a networked stakeholder connected by an absent or latent tie. These absent or latent ties hold the potential for activation as social, economic, or organizational circumstances change. Stakeholder theory emphasizes shared interests held by organizations with different missions, operating models, capacities, and experiences. All stakeholders have equal claims to an organization's purpose and resources crucial to an organization's survival. Early attempts at more precisely defining stakeholder theory often segmented organizations and constituent groups with "stakes" in the organization as primary and secondary stakeholders (or internal and external stakeholders). Each type was dependent upon the other to achieve mutual goals, even though they often were economically interdependent. This division of stakeholder responsibilities between corporate and social environments is most clearly viewed when stakeholder theory is framed as a local theory of strategic management, to organize the relationships between an organization and its external environments to achieve narrow corporate goals. These distinctions have less utility when considering the social and political interdependencies between organizations and society that shape economic action.[8]

Traditionally, Anglo-American versions of stakeholder theory have emphasized for-profit firms and their interdependencies with other organizations and directly affiliated organizational constituents (such as customers and employees). This stakeholder framework situated a profit-based organization as a central organizing entity within an organizational field. It erected boundaries between the organization and its external environment, rather than regarding the organization as part of an interdependent web of social and organizational relationships embedded within a community, state or province, region, or country. There remains a clearly stated moral and ethical dimension found within stakeholder theory that emphasizes organizational responsibility to the community. However, traditional Anglo-American emphasis on the profit motive and individual agency in economic relationships has obscured the moral and ethical dimensions at the heart of classic stakeholder theory, which are also found in social and political theories of voluntary association. Problems with Anglo-American models of stakeholder theory become particularly acute in the face of cascading institutional failures and rapidly growing ecological challenges. By bringing the associational and communal ties of the community into stakeholder theory, we can reorient institutions and community organizations toward collaboration.[9]

COMMUNICATIVE MANAGEMENT AND THE ROLE OF COMMUNITY IN STAKEHOLDER THEORY

Community is a core stakeholder in Nordic versions of stakeholder theory. Specifically, the importance of community has been expressed through the idea of communicative management, a theory and process that emphasizes strategic cooperation to achieve shared goals. Rather than a for-profit firm residing at the center of a series of relationships with stakeholders, in communicative management, organizations are networked within a larger community and set of social relationships. Communities may represent shared physical locations (place), shared practices (common identities, beliefs, relationships, and associations), or professions (shared skills, knowledge, and experiences). Communities are physical or virtual spaces for individual and organizational interactions, and they bound participants through shared geographies and identities. For example, in Staten Island after Hurricane Sandy, residents in specific neighborhoods (place) interacted through physical, face-to-face communication by driving and walking around their neighborhoods and asking questions of their neighbors, postal employees, first responders, and at local bakeries and pizzerias. They also connected with family and friends via social media (practices) and leveraged professional connections through churches and unions (associations). As the recovery unfolded, residents and businesses were invited into a series of planning and architectural workshops to envision what a post-Sandy Staten Island might look like. In this case, residents and businesses are each considered a stakeholder with a shared concern with reimagining place and association in a community severely impacted by a major coastal storm.[10]

Stakeholder processes employed in natural resources management, planning, and international development have conceptualized stakeholder management as a way of identifying people sidelined or ignored in planning and environmental decision-making and bringing them into decision-making and governance. Natural resources management and planning take a much broader view of who constitutes a "stakeholder" and what is a "stake." This emphasis on stakeholder relationships as people rather than organizations aligns natural resources models of stakeholder engagement with contemporary models of Nordic stakeholder engagement, in which democratic participation, collaborative communication, and stakeholder relationships are embedded within communities and social relationships. One organizational leader in coastal New Jersey described stakeholders in broad terms as individuals, communities, and organizations. To this leader, stakeholders had both a fiduciary responsibility and a social obligation:

> Well, I think that clearly the homeowners are stakeholders. Communities and townships are stakeholders. And this is getting somewhat broad and philosophical, but then because all of us live in these communities, we're all stakeholders. And so I think that's more at an individual/corporate/social obligation to each other. And then I guess if you think about nonprofits who stakeholders are, by merit of . . . grantors who raise large amounts of money under the pretense of "it's going to Sandy survivors," they're a stakeholder now because they've raised that money. And then we as a grantee who have received that money, we become stakeholders because we've taken on the fiduciary responsibility to get that money to individual homeowners.
>
> (Author Interview with Faith-Based Organization [FBO]
> Executive Director, Coastal New Jersey, March 2017)

Although the focus on participation and inclusion is paramount for stakeholder engagement within the natural resources' community, problems of power and manipulation may still arise and adversely impact the inclusion and attention paid to marginalized communities. Problems of environmental quality and hazardous waste siting decisions often generate conflict among different groups of stakeholders in a community, and tests community and elected officials' commitments to participatory decision-making. Often, participatory practices end up simply reinforcing traditional community power structures. Low land values, ineffective approaches to managing toxic waste disposal, and lack of organized community stakeholder opposition usually result in replicating existing decision-making practices and land use policies that disproportionately harm communities of color, vulnerable populations, and low-income residents.[11]

Stakeholder engagement in natural resources management is not solely about "giving voice to the voiceless" by including the dispossessed in land and natural resources governance. Stakeholder engagement can also be used as a tool for decision-makers and power brokers to gain support for policies, overcome local opposition, and exclude adversarial stakeholders. The mayor of a beach town in coastal New Jersey described stakeholders as, "year-round residents, summer residents, business owners. Those who pay taxes." The OEM director of a nearby Bayside town defined stakeholders as "definitely the town, only because these people have paid taxes in town. They expect to get some type of services. Unfortunately to me, it's beyond the capabilities of most towns to deal with." In these narrow definitions, the stakeholder is a taxpayer rather than a "resident" or "voter" or even "citizen." There is an implicit bias toward defining stakeholders as less than a more expansive view of citizens or community members.[12]

Instrumental approaches tend to privilege technical problem-solving, organizational leadership, and elite agenda setting over bottom-up approaches to information gathering, problem definition, stakeholder identification, and stakeholder inclusion. These problems in natural resources management and planning mirror the issues of power and authority within the processes of decision-making in advanced industrial democracies raised by Rhenman (1968) and issues of representation and control identified by Deetz (1992, 1995, 2017) as obstacles to consensus building for complex governance issues that cross public/private boundaries. When stakeholder engagement is conducted instrumentally through top-down decision-making and expertise, community members may feel excluded or that they lack the knowledge and connection needed to participate in and contribute to solving the complex problems facing their communities. When that happens, the legitimacy of the public problem-solving process may be called into question.[13]

Forging Consensus through Communicative Management

Communicative management is a management process that emphasizes the role of communication in forging consensus over joint interests and shared goals by mitigating overt conflict over power and resources. It was conceptualized in the middle part of the twentieth century as Nordic countries industrialized and navigated a middle way between dominant frames of Anglo-American free market capitalism and a highly centralized Soviet economy. Communicative management emerged as a practice in which competing interests among industrialists, landowners, farmers, workers, and professionals could be organizationally and politically balanced. Communicative management emerged first to manage political conflict and tensions, and second as a communication and organizing process underlying Nordic industrial democracy and management theory in the second half of the twentieth century.

Cross-sector collaborations, mutual dependencies, and organizational tensions all regularly emerge in areas disrupted by disaster, since they are part of the processes of response and recovery. While government agencies and large, complex disaster relief organizations are tasked with response and recovery, their agenda, goals, and understanding of the culture and community may differ from that of local residents and organizations. In long-term recovery, there are often competing agendas between the impacted community; grassroots and emergent organizations; the local community's established nonprofit and faith-based social infrastructures; government agencies;

and large national and international nonprofit organizations. How joint interests and common goals are recognized, important and achievable goals decided upon, financial and material resources secured, and individuals supported over time as the disaster timeline moves from response to recovery are all fundamental problems that communities and organizations grapple with in crisis and disaster.

Communicative management emphasizes communication, collaboration, and coordination among stakeholders with very different values, missions, and operating capacity. Networked stakeholder relationships are needed in long-term recovery to provide assistance, rebuild homes, and reconstruct communities. They are also essential to ensuring that adequate emotional, spiritual, and social support are available to residents and responders. Communicative management is necessary for effective long-term recovery processes and requires an understanding of the larger social and organizational relationships and market forces operating within a particular community.

Hyperlocal Organizing as Communicative Management

Disaster response, particularly long-term recovery, is shaped by the communication practices of the organizations collaborating in an impacted community or region. Communication practices are speech-oriented communication processes that use gatherings, meetings, digital tools, and structured forms of talk to organize language and interaction within an interorganizational collaboration. These communication practices enable collaborating organizations and impacted communities to connect the ideas, activities, goals, and desired outcomes of the long-term recovery process. In organizing, communication practices are typically constructed through the comprehensive application of organizational communication processes and personal and social communication technologies. These technologies may include personal productivity software, email, statistical tools, relational databases, and mapping software. Communication practices may include routine face-to-face interactions to set and review shared goals, organizational and public meetings, agenda setting, rulemaking, strategy development, and implementation. Through communication practices, agencies and emergent organizers active after the disaster connect the thoughts, activities, goals, and desired outcomes needed to make sense of the current situation and identify possible future states in the disaster-impacted area. These communicative practices, in turn, constitute the organizing processes of long-term recovery after disaster. Communication practices are what translate thoughts into action by developing shared meanings through social and interorganizational interactions.

Communicative management uses these communication practices to enable collaborative communication among networked stakeholders in disaster response and recovery. Social media and mobile communication are critical in the early hours of a disaster to provide real-time information to impacted communities and serve as a platform for a crowdsourced response. As response morphs into recovery, organizations quickly find themselves shifting to face-to-face communication. The executive directors of several different LTRGs emphasized the importance of face-to-face meetings for building trust and credibility among participants tackling difficult problems. During long-term recovery, the complexity of people's rebuilding cases increases even as the recovery network and resources available shrink. As organizations left the recovery network or dumped their most difficult rebuilding cases onto the LTRGs, an LTRG executive director asked clients to bring in hard copies of their "paperwork," which they photocopied and placed in file boxes. These filed copies were kept on-site at the LTRG's offices. On-site storage ensured that client paperwork was not lost or displaced as clients were moved from one nonprofit to another. Federal and state program requirements shifted over time, often requiring new filings and new types of documentation from impacted residents. Bobbi, the leader of a faith-based organization, often chose to communicate over the phone rather than through email. Making a phone call was simply a quicker way to find out specific information or build consensus on a particular case or interorganizational goal. Many organizations engaged in the painstaking work of long-term recovery chose to regularly meet face-to-face to build an interorganizational recovery network. They used common communication practices to set shared goals and forge consensus in a fast-moving, high-stress, and disrupted environment.

Putting Communicative Management into Practice in Disaster Recovery

Communicative management is about communication in practice and a core practice of hyperlocal organizing. Organizations are not always one-size-fits-all, and there are multiple ways to achieve community and interorganizational goals. In fact, organizing activities and communication practices are not always part of formal or even informal organizations; cooperation and a desire to achieve shared goals may be expressed through common activities without formal organizations or organizing processes in place. Like the swimmers at Promontory Point and the Midwestern bike commuters discussed in the first chapter, people can achieve shared goals simply through repeated interactions in pursuit of shared goals and desired outcomes. Communicative management enables the remixing of communication and organizing in disrupted environments and is the process through which interorganizational collaboration and stakeholder engagement are built. To be effective, communicative management of disaster recovery should ask five key questions of participants:

1. What's the situation?
    a. The short-term situation?
    b. The medium-term situation?
    c. The long-term situation?
2. Who's at the table?
    a. Who's not at the table?
    b. Who should be at the table?
3. What expertise do we have?
    a. What local/community-based expertise do we have?

    b. What domain expertise & subject matter experts do we have, or have
       access to?
    c. What expertise is needed?
4. What resources are in place, and what resources are needed?
5. What relationships among organizations are already in place that can facilitate
   recovery?
    a. Board or Leadership level
    b. Employees/Volunteers
    c. Formal Agreements
    d. Informal working relationships

Stakeholders engaged in long-term recovery after disaster must also clarify the
problem-solving processes that organizations need to engage in as they develop
strategies for recovery and identify resources and needs. There are five key questions
that stakeholders need to ask each other as they come together to make sense of the
situation and clarify their roles:

1. What needs are we trying to meet?
2. What information and resources do we have at our disposal?
3. What problems need to be solved in order to meet the needs of impacted
   residents and communities?
4. What are our decision-making criteria as a recovery network? What measures
   define success?
5. What neighborhood and grassroots organizations have mobilized to address
   facets of the recovery problem?
6. How are we connected to these neighborhood and grassroots recovery
   organizations?
7. How frequently and in what ways should we communicate and meet?

Communicative management is how stakeholders govern and collaborate in
areas impacted by disaster. It opens a path to build consensus, solve problems, and
achieve shared goals. Post-disaster recovery is a messy and complicated process that
affects people's lives in disrupte communities in which their homes are destroyed.
To achieve balance and normalcy, impacted residents, grassroots groups, local community organizations, new or emergent groups, and spontaneous volunteers need
to unite. Remixing organizations and organizing processes creates a parallel process
of hyperlocal disaster recovery with its own purpose, knowledge, and resources.
This parallel process of hyperlocal organizing does not oppose federal frameworks
of recovery, or the state and federal disaster recovery efforts that mobilize state and
federal resources. Rather, hyperlocal organizing processes are the core of "whole
community" approaches to disaster recovery that link grassroots and institutional
stakeholders through a process of communicative management that emphasizes
shared goals and purpose. Hyperlocal organizing may compensate for institutional
failures in the short term. More long term, it has the potential to foster proactive

strategic cooperation by bringing together local knowledge with national resources in a process of collaborative communication that values and respects differences in organizational perspectives and individual experiences.

Post-disaster recovery ultimately helps communities survive and thrive. To achieve this goal, hyperlocal organizing should be institutionally valued and resourced, defined as a fundamental part of the federal response. Only then might recovery frameworks and clear communication practices foster strategic coopera-tion and balance interests among communities and organizations. In other words, hyperlocal organizing is the next frontier in disaster research and policymaking. The need for hyperlocal organizing will only increase in importance, given the increasing frequency and severity of storms and wildland fires, and growing threats from coastal inundation and wetlands loss. Balancing shared goals and purpose through commu-nicative management processes that emphasize connection and cooperation provides a way to bridge community needs, institutional responses, and long-term recovery.

NOTES

1. The Nordic countries include Denmark, Norway, Sweden, Iceland, and Finland. The term "Scandinavia" or "Scandinavian" refers to a subregion of Denmark, Norway, and Sweden. The autonomous territories of Greenland and the Faroe Islands are often included within broader definitions of the region. Scotland has historic ties to the Nordic region with the exploration of Scottish/Nordic trade and political ties expanding as part of the twin trends of Brexit, the United Kingdom's exit from the European Union, and the push for Scottish independence from the United Kingdom. Both Scotland and the Nordic countries see social and economic well-being as intrinsically interconnected and of the economy as embedded in a web of social relations, rather than as independent of community and society. This has significant implications for governance in the workplace, community, and politics.

2. Robert Strand and R. Edward Freeman, "Scandinavian Cooperative Advantage: The Theory and Practice of Stakeholder Engagement in Scandinavia," *Journal of Business Eth-ics* 127, no. 1 (March 2015): 65–85, https://doi.org/10.1007/s10551-013-1792-1; Robert Strand, "Scandinavian Stakeholder Thinking: Seminal Offerings from the Late Juha Näsi," *Journal of Business Ethics* 127, no. 1 (March 2015): 89–105, https://doi.org/10.1007/s10551 -013-1793-0; Øystein Pedersen Dahlen and Helge Skirbekk, "How Trust Was Maintained in Scandinavia through the First Crisis of Modernity," *Corporate Communications: An Inter-national Journal* 26, no. 1 (January 1, 2021): 23–39, https://doi.org/10.1108/CCIJ-01-2020 -0036; Haldor Byrkjeflot, "The Nordic Model of Democracy and Management," in *The Democratic Challenge to Capitalism: Management and Democracy in the Nordic Countries*, ed. Haldor Byrkjeflot et al. (Bergen: Fagbokforlager Vigmostad & Bjorke AS, 2001); Haldor Byrkjeflot, "Nordic Management: From Functional Socialism to Shareholder Value?," in *The Northern Lights: Organization Theory in Scandinavia* (Herndon, VA: Copenhagen Business School Press, 2003), 471.

3. André O. Laplume, Karan Sonpar, and Reginald A. Litz, "Stakeholder Theory: Review-ing a Theory That Moves Us," *Journal of Management* 34, no. 6 (December 2008): 1152–89, https://doi.org/10.1177/0149206308324322; R. Edward Freeman, Robert Phillips, and Rajendra Sisodia, "Tensions in Stakeholder Theory," *Business & Society* 59, no. 2 (February

2020): 213–31, https://doi.org/10.1177/0007650318773750; Samantha Miles, "Stakeholder: Essentially Contested or Just Confused?," *Journal of Business Ethics* 108, no. 3 (July 2012): 285–98, https://doi.org/10.1007/s10551-011-1090-8; Samantha Miles, "Stakeholder Theory Classification: A Theoretical and Empirical Evaluation of Definitions," *Journal of Business Ethics* 142 (2017): 437–59, https://doi.org/10.1007/s10551-015-2741-y; Strand and Freeman, "Scandinavian Cooperative Advantage"; Adriane MacDonald, Amelia Clarke, and Lei Huang, "Multi-Stakeholder Partnerships for Sustainability: Designing Decision-Making Processes for Partnership Capacity," *Journal of Business Ethics* (2018): 1–18.

4. James Luther Adams, *Voluntary Associations* (Chicago: Exploration Press: Chicago Theological Association, 1986); Stephen C Rowe, "Toward a Postliberal Liberalism: James Luther Adams and the Need for a Theory of Relational Meaning," *American Journal of Theology & Philosophy* 17, no. 1 (January 1996): 51–70; Wilson Carey McWilliams, *The Idea of Fraternity in America* (Berkeley, CA: University of California Press, 1973); Jesse Norman, *Adam Smith: What He Thought and Why It Matters* (Milton Keyens, UK: Allen Lane, 2018).

5. Wilson Carey McWilliams, "In Good Faith: On the Foundations of American Politics," in *Redeeming Democracy in America*, ed. Patrick J. Deneen and Susan J. McWilliams (Lawrence, KS: University Press of Kansas, 2011), 107–26; Wilson Carey McWilliams, "Democracy and the Citizen: Community, Dignity, and the Crisis of Contemporary Politics in America," in *Redeeming Democracy in America*, ed. Patrick J. Deneen and Susan J. McWilliams (Lawrence, KS: University Press of Kansas, 2011), 9–28; Wilson Carey McWilliams, "The Search for a Public Philosophy," in *The Democratic Soul: A Wilson Carey McWilliams Reader* (Lexington: The University Press of Kentucky, 2011), 336–52; Wilson Carey McWilliams, "Toward Genuine Self-Government," in *The Democratic Soul: A Wilson Carey McWilliams Reader*, ed. Patrick J. Deneen and Susan J McWilliams (Lexington: The University Press of Kentucky, 2011), 353–60.

6. Henry Mintzberg, Dror Etzion, and Saku Mantere, "Worldly Strategy for the Global Climate," *Stanford Social Innovation Review* 16, no. 4 (2018): 42–47; José Carlos Marques and Henry Mintzberg, "Why Corporate Social Responsibility Isn't a Piece of Cake," *MIT Sloan Management Review* 56, no. 4 (2015): 7–11; Henry Mintzberg et al., "The Invisible World of Association," *Leader to Leader* 2005, no. 36 (2005): 37–45, https://doi.org/10.1002/ltl.126; Henry Mintzberg, *Rebalancing Society: Radical Renewal beyond Left, Right, and Center* (Oakland, CA: Berrett-Koehler Publishers, 2015); Bobby Banerjee and Diane-Laure Arjaliès, "Celebrating the End of Enlightenment: Organization Theory in the Age of the Anthropocene and Gaia (and Why Neither Is the Solution to Our Ecological Crisis)," *Organization Theory*, Forthcoming 2021; Nneka Logan, "A Theory of Corporate Responsibility to Race (CRR): Communication and Racial Justice in Public Relations," *Journal of Public Relations Research* (February 16, 2021): 1–17, https://doi.org/10.1080/1062726X.2021.1881898.

7. Charles Perrow, "A Society of Organizations," *Theory and Society* 20, no. 6 (December 1991): 725–62, https://doi.org/10.1007/BF00678095; Barbara Czarniawska, "Complex Organizations Still Complex," *International Public Management Journal*, no. 10 (2007): 137–51.

8. R. Edward Freeman, *Strategic Management: A Stakeholder Approach* (Marshfield, MA: Pitman Publishing, 1984); R. Edward Freeman et al., *Stakeholder Theory: The State of the Art* (Cambridge, UK: Cambridge University Press, 2010); Max B. E. Clarkson, "A Stakeholder Framework for Analyzing and Evaluating Corporate Social Performance," *The Academy of Management Review* 20, no. 1 (January 1995): 92, https://doi.org/10.2307/258888; Stanley A. Deetz, *Democracy in an Age of Corporate Colonization: Developments in Communication and*

the Politics of Everyday Life (Albany, NY: State University of New York Press, 1992); Miles, "Stakeholder"; Miles, "Stakeholder Theory Classification."

9. Herve Mesure, "A Liberal Critique of the Corporation as Stakeholders," in *Stakeholder Theory: A European Perspective*, ed. Maria Bonnafous-Boucher and Yvon Pesqux (New York: Palgrave MacMillan, 2005), 185; Michael E. Porter and Mark Kramer, "Creating Shared Value," *Harvard Business Review*, no. January-February (2011): 4–17; Mark Aakhus and Michael Bzdak, "Stakeholder Engagement as Communication Design Practice: Stakeholder Engagement," *Journal of Public Affairs* 15, no. 2 (May 2015): 188–200, https://doi.org/10.1002/pa.1569; Colin Crouch, "Models of Capitalism," *New Political Economy* 10, no. 4 (2005): 439–56; Jamie Peck and Nik Theodore, "Variegated Capitalism," *Progress in Human Geography* 31, no. 6 (December 2007): 731–72, https://doi.org/10.1177/0309132507083505; Gregory Jackson and Richard Deeg, "From Comparing Capitalisms to the Politics of Institutional Change," *Review of International Political Economy* 15, no. 4 (October 27, 2008): 680–709, https://doi.org/10.1080/09692290802260704.

10. Laura Dunham, R. Edward Freeman, and Jeanne Liedtka, "Enhancing Stakeholder Practice: A Particularized Exploration of Community," *Business Ethics Quarterly* 16, no. 1 (2006): 23–42; Lewis A. Friedland, "Networks in Place," *American Behavioral Scientist* 60, no. 1 (2016): 24–42, https://doi.org/10.1177/0002764215601710; Emily Chamlee-Wright and Virgil Henry Storr, "'There's No Place Like New Orleans': Sense of Place and Community Recovery in the Ninth Ward After Hurricane Katrina," *Journal of Urban Affairs* 31, no. 5 (December 2009): 615–34, https://doi.org/10.1111/j.1467-9906.2009.00479.x; Tom Piazza, *Why New Orleans Matters* (New York: HarpersCollins Publishers, 2005); bell hooks, *Belonging: A Culture of Place* (New York: Routledge, 2009).

11. Dianne Scott and Catherine Oelofse, "Social and Environmental Justice in South African Cities: Including 'Invisible Stakeholders' in Environmental Assessment Procedures," *Journal of Environmental Planning and Management* 48, no. 3 (May 2005): 445–67, https://doi.org/10.1080/09640560500067582; Robert D. Bullard and Beverly Wright, "The Legacy of Bias: Hurricanes, Droughts, and Floods," in *The Wrong Complexion for Protection: How the Government Response to Disaster Endangers African American Communities* (New York and London: New York University Press, 2012), 47–72; Gustavo A. García-López, "The Multiple Layers of Environmental Injustice in Contexts of (Un)Natural Disasters: The Case of Puerto Rico Post-Hurricane Maria," *Environmental Justice* 11, no. 3 (June 2018): 101–8, https://doi.org/10.1089/env.2017.0045; Zachary A. Morris, R. Anna Hayward, and Yamirelis Otero, "The Political Determinants of Disaster Risk: Assessing the Unfolding Aftermath of Hurricane Maria for People with Disabilities in Puerto Rico," *Environmental Justice* 11, no. 2 (April 2018): 89–94, https://doi.org/10.1089/env.2017.0043.

12. Alison Mathie and Gord Cunningham, "From Clients to Citizens: Asset-Based Community Development as a Strategy for Community-Driven Development," *Development in Practice* 13, no. 5 (2003): 474–86; Andrew Crane, Dirk Matten, and Jeremy Moon, "Stakeholders as Citizens? Rethinking Rights, Participation, and Democracy," *Journal of Business Ethics* 53, no. 1–2 (2004): 107–22; Stanley A. Deetz and Lisa Irvin, "Governance, Stakeholder Involvement and New Communication Models," in *Governance Reform under Real-World Conditions: Citizens, Stakeholders, and Voice*, ed. Sina Odugbemi and Thomas Jacobson (Washington, DC: World Bank Publications, 2008); Terry L. Cooper, Thomas A. Bryer, and Jack W. Meek, "Citizen-Centered Collaborative Public Management," *Public Administration Review* 66 (2006): 76–88; Chris Ansell and Alison Gash, "Collaborative Governance in

Chapter 4

Theory and Practice," *Journal of Public Administration Research and Theory: J-PART* 18, no. 4 (2008): 543–71.

13. Eric Rhenman, *Industrial Democracy and Industrial Management* (London: Tavistock Publication Ltd., 1968); Deetz, *Democracy in an Age of Corporate Colonization: Developments in Communication and the Politics of Everyday Life*; Stanley A. Deetz, *Transforming Communication Transforming Business: Building Responsive and Responsible Workplaces* (Cresskill, NJ: Hampton Press Inc, 1995); Stanley A. Deetz, "Generative Democracy and the Collaborative Turn: The Hope for Quality Public and Organizational Decision Making" (New Jersey Communication Association Annual Conference, Lakewood, NJ, March 2017); Crane, Matten, and Moon, "Stakeholders as Citizens?"; Divya Chandrasekhar, Yang Zhang, and Yu Xiao, "Nontraditional Articipation in Disaster Recovery Planning: Cases from China, India, and the United States," *Journal of the American Planning Association* 80, no. 4 (October 2, 2014): 373–84, https://doi.org/10.1080/01944363.2014.989399.

5

Hyperlocal Organizing
after Hurricane Sandy

The View from Coastal New Jersey
and Staten Island, New York

Solomon [executive in disaster response, national Faith Based Organization] explained: "we may perform several types of identifiable tasks, but never know every 'knowable' fact. In many cases, we will not know how many cases, or the scope of needs of the individuals or the individuals who will be applying until we begin the work and intake."

(Coastal New Jersey LTRG executive committee meeting
minutes, January 2013)

In the midst of all this, we joined the Long-Term Recovery Group.

(Author Interview with Staten Island Pop-up Organization
Co-Founder Staten Island, New York, July 2014)

Hyperlocal organizing has two important responsibilities, one in the early days of response and recovery, and the second in the latter stages of long-term recovery. Hyperlocal organizing efforts are especially crucial in the early days of recovery before the federal and national plural sector responses are fully mobilized, programs and contracts are in place, and congressional funding is authorized. In the latter stages of long-term recovery, hyperlocal organizing can keep the focus on unrecovered communities and residents and advocate for the resources needed to finish recovery and get people home.

Long-term recovery after disaster opens historical, longitudinal, and comparative possibilities for understanding hyperlocal organizing and how it can meet the challenges of sustainability and resilience. Particular processes of hyperlocal organizing shape organizational relationships and communication practices that manifest in disaster and crisis. Solving complex problems such as long-term recovery after disaster or pandemic response requires interactions among the community and regional stakeholders who are invested in community problem-solving. While established humanitarian relief organizations are usually viewed as the primary response organizations in partnership with government agencies, their capabilities and capacities may not meet community needs. This chapter focuses on the organizations and interorganizational relationships that comprised the hyperlocal organizing efforts and post-disaster recovery networks in coastal New Jersey between 2012 and 2020.

When confronted by crises, people and organizations mobilize and act collectively even if they aren't part of the official, planned response efforts. Like emergent behaviors, community collaboration is a necessary and ordinary part of a response to crisis and disaster. Community collaboration may be initiated through top-down protocols and organizing frameworks or through the efforts of neighborhood and community organizations spontaneously organizing to aid friends, neighbors, and fellow residents. Citizen and grassroots organizations will often connect with established disaster relief organizations and formal institutional response protocols to share information and access material or financial resources. Regardless of how community collaboration is organized, hyperlocal processes of citizen response and grassroots organizing should be fully incorporated into disaster preparedness and mitigation.

HYPERLOCAL ORGANIZING IN THE AFTERMATH OF DISASTER

Hyperlocal organizing is a community-run process of disaster response and recovery that meets specific community needs often unaddressed by institutional responses. Hyperlocal organizing may include emergent and existing community organizations, which are loosely or tightly connected to a community's existing civic networks and social capital. Hyperlocal organizing expands the stakeholder universe of organizations engaged in response and recovery and may increase the capacity of civic networks to meet local needs. While personal ties are critical for immediate survival, rebuilding, and recovery, organizational relationships enable access to the necessary people, information, and resources needed for short-term and long-term recovery.

Hyperlocal organizations are often an outcome of the emergent response. Citizen volunteers scan the environment, make sense of existing organizational capacity, self-organize, and create new organizational and interorganizational processes. In these ways, citizen organizing activities unite people, places, local knowledge, and insights in a process of discovery. In this process, community organizations seek out material or financial resources that meet the specific needs of a particular disaster-impacted community. Emergent responses, however, are distinct from hyperlocal organizations. Just as hyperlocal media is a distinct subset of a broader set of civic media processes, hyperlocal organizations are part of a broader process of communicating and organizing and are driven by interactions ranging from microprocesses of interpersonal communication to macroprocesses of interorganizational relationships.

Emergent response tends to be ad-hoc, self-organized responses reliant upon a community's social ties and organizational capacities. Emergent organizing is the result of self-organizing processes of spontaneous volunteers. By contrast, hyperlocal organizations are not exclusively outcomes of recently enacted emergent processes; they may represent a broad array of existing community organizations with different roles, purposes, missions, and institutional logics.

A significant challenge for hyperlocal organizing is attaining clarity in structure, roles, operational focus, and relationships with other organizations. Hyperlocal organizing connects grassroots and community responses with institutional responses in disaster-impacted communities but may not always have integrated their knowledge and insights with the recovery process. Dialogue and media coverage about disaster response and recovery is dominated by federal frameworks, traditional and humanitarian and disaster relief organizations, and established faith-based organizations. Hyperlocal organizations may seem redundant or lacking in requisite expertise from experienced disaster professionals and formal institutions. However, they are crucial for providing real-time response and information and on-the-ground knowledge of the disaster-impacted community.

HYPERLOCAL ORGANIZING IN COASTAL NEW JERSEY AND STATEN ISLAND AFTER SANDY

In the New York City Borough of Staten Island, "pop-up" organizations emerged across the island right after Hurricane Sandy's landfall across the harbor in coastal New Jersey. Despite New York's highly professional and experienced emergency services agencies and post-9/11 reforms to the city's emergency management processes, many Staten Island residents felt abandoned. The extended shutdown of the bridges and ferries isolated them from city and state agencies. Residents of Staten Island self-organized in yards and on street corners and began collecting information on neighborhood needs. Many of these "pop-up" organizations later became part of the founding teams and leadership of the Staten Island Long-Term Recovery Organization (SILTRO), a collaboration of emergent, parish, and neighborhood recovery groups engaged in long-term recovery across the island.

In New Jersey, many bayside communities felt the media's attention was unjustifiably focused on seasonal beachside towns and iconic boardwalks that represented the cultural life of summertime New Jersey. Frustrated, these residents and communities turned to hyperlocal community and pop-up organizations, local community foundations, and collaborative activities with social entrepreneurial and movement-based organizations such as SBP, Burners without Borders, and Occupy Sandy. Partnering with larger organizations that differ from more traditional humanitarian assistance and disaster relief organizations allows communities that may be overlooked in the larger response efforts to directly connect with organizations able to provide the expertise, resources, and coordinating or operating capacity for a community or region's recovery:

So it became clear that there was need beyond Sea Bright. New Jersey has been a different recovery for SBP in that in the past and really since then we've partnered with a local grassroots organization that sprouted up after the disaster and focused on one community and how one community has recovered. New Jersey is just different. You know, there's lots of towns who were affected. And they're spread across hundreds of miles of terrain. And just recovering one community is very different than it is in Joplin, Missouri, or New Orleans, for that matter. So there was need beyond just Sea Bright. So we kind of, I think, tried to mirror the need of the community. So we moved into Monmouth. And then we did some investigation of Ocean and found that Ocean County, the need was as great or greater than Monmouth and income is a little bit lower than Monmouth. It seemed like there was a lot of data that supported our moving to Ocean County as well.

(Author Interview, SBP Regional Leader, Coastal New Jersey, February 2017)

The SBP regional leaders' statement that "New Jersey is just different" illustrates the intensely local nature of a disaster. A state that prides itself on home rule, New Jersey has 585 municipalities and over 600 different school districts and fire districts across the state. The state includes 121 municipalities along its 135 miles of coastline, and 4 coastal counties were significantly impacted by the storm. Each municipality has its own characteristics and political dynamics that needed to be negotiated separately. The dynamics of a home rule state are different than a large city with a single jurisdiction such as New York City (8.2 million residents in 2012) or New Orleans (437,186 residents in 2005 prior to Hurricane Katrina). New Jersey is different still from a large metropolitan area like Houston, Texas, where there are only two overarching jurisdictions—The City of Houston (2.3 million residents in 2017 at the time of Harvey's impact) and Harris County, Texas (4.7 million residents)—with superseding jurisdiction over disaster response and recovery issues.

The SBP regional leader's perspective on what constituted the community response of coastal New Jersey is instructive. In 2013, SBP was initially invited into a small beach community of 1,412 year-round residents. For perspective, 630,480 residents resided in Monmouth County, the county Sea Bright is in, as of 2010. Ocean County, Monmouth's neighbor to the south, had 577,574 residents as of 2010. Once they began operations, SBP found a broader need throughout the two-county coastal region and entered into regional partnerships with the long-term recovery groups (LTGRs) in the two counties. They also worked closely with existing community organizations and later expanded operations into Atlantic County (265,498 residents as of 2017) when other organizations ended operations and withdrew from the recovery network. For SBP, the community they operated in initially was a very small beach town in a highly hazardous coastal area wedged between the Atlantic Ocean and the confluence of the Shrewsbury and Navesink rivers. However, coastal New Jersey had outsized needs that went far beyond the boundaries of that hard-hit community. The operating area for SBP was then extended over time to a three-county area that included the heart of coastal New Jersey—the primary impact area of Hurricane Sandy. Community then, should be defined regionally, as a particular geography with shared social, cultural, ecological, and economic concerns.[1]

The locally intensive nature of disasters shapes hyperlocal organizing responses. In coastal New Jersey, fire services are mainly volunteer based and organized by fire companies and fire districts in specific municipalities. Since these are not city-owned and operated facilities, local volunteer firehouses in New Jersey were able to serve as staging and gathering places for information and supplies—and in at least one instance a short-term residence. By contrast, in New York City, firehouses were strictly under city control and lacked the flexibility to meet on-the-ground neighborhood and community needs. Instead, neighborhood residents and grassroots organizations in Staten Island turned to parish and VFW Halls, church basements, street corners, and their own yards. One union leader whose home was destroyed moved an RV into his side yard to live in and pitched a large tent right next to it to serve as a supply depot for the neighborhood. These spontaneous, pop-up efforts filled in or mitigated some of the gaps between the top-down response of government agencies and national disaster relief organizations and the on-the-ground needs, knowledge, and situational awareness of residents.[2]

"Talking in the neighborhoods," as a New Jersey Grassroots Advocacy Organization Founder put it, played a major role in connecting people, communities, and organizations. Talk also helped organizers identify unmet needs and troubleshoot the Sandy-impacted communities of the mid-Atlantic in the immediate aftermath of the disaster and during the much-longer recovery period. This recovery organization estimated that they were able to assist 800 homeowners in one county alone who encountered problems with the state's primary assistance program, the Reconstruction, Rehabilitation, and Mitigation Program (RREM). Those 800 homeowners represented approximately 10 percent of the RREM grantee total.

The state RREM program was particularly problematic because it supported only a very small number of state residents with storm damage. The actual number of residents in the program fluctuated, particularly within the first two years of the long-term recovery period. The highly restricted nature of the grant required plural sector response from nonprofit organizations to address the unmet needs of disaster-impacted residents across a wide geographic area. However, the widespread need identified by SBP was exacerbated by the restrictive nature of the state grant program. The state RREM program also ran into problems with the Federal Flood Insurance Program impacting homeowner eligibility, changing deadlines, and projected increases in insurance rates based on new flood zone maps. During the primary long-term recovery process, a county LTRG expanded its role outside of case management and coordination. It also engaged in advocacy through work with a U.S. Senator's state office and the Senator's Washington DC-based policy staff to craft revisions to federal flood insurance laws and extend filing deadlines for impacted residents.

The unfamiliarity of the public, plural, and private sectors with response to a large-scale disaster in New Jersey resulted in a scramble to find recovery funds and establish new philanthropic efforts to fund long-term recovery efforts. The following interview exchange in July 2017 between the author and the executives and program managers of a large regional nonprofit illustrates the challenges of post-Sandy recovery in New Jersey facing homeowners and communities:

> *Q:* Okay. Okay. So most of the work was New York City, Long Island, and New Jersey. Would you say . . .
> *P1:* The majority of our work was in New Jersey.
> *Q:* Okay. Oh, really? Okay. I guess in a sense, why was that? Why did the majority of the work end up happening in New Jersey given your New York City focus?
> *P1:* Partly because of the way—partly because New York City was structured to do a little bit more of a—repair itself . . . and New Jersey wasn't and partly because of the path of the storm and the devastation of the storm.
> *P1:* The Governor's Fund that—that sort of—as they were trying to get . . . funded in many places they were trying to get this all started. We had a little bit more experience of grantmakers and also having done disaster relief.

> (Author Interview with Leadership of a Regional Nonprofit,
> Mid-Atlantic United States, July 2017)

This organization was not a traditional disaster relief organization and operated in a different city. Although it was concerned with that city's socioeconomic issues, they played a central role in post-disaster recovery in New Jersey, mainly by connecting directly with hard-hit communities and their associated organizations. The exchange continues about their role in the broader post-Sandy recovery network in coastal New Jersey:

> *Q:* Okay. Okay. Interesting. So . . . I'm certainly going to stay with this for a little bit because one of the issues that has come up in some of the research that I've been doing so far is that some people felt that the Long-Term Recovery Groups in New Jersey spent a long time or a lot of time on rulemaking, coming up with guidelines and rules... as opposed to distributing the money right away. What's . . . your perspective or your take on that?
> *P1:* So put it this way. After Katrina, it took about 10 days to get a federal omnibus bill. After Sandy, it took about 10 weeks and then it got tied up in sequester.
> *Q:* Okay.
> *P1:* And so for the federal dollars, right, so FEMA comes but in terms of the large-scale rebuilding dollars, they were . . . very delayed and so . . .
> *Q:* Okay.
> *P1:* But when you . . . the Long-Term Recovery Groups needed to get themselves organized and needed to figure out how to work . . . the purpose of FEMA is to do the emergency and the Red Cross. Frankly, it's to do the emergency dollars. I don't know whether it was disproportionately long or not. They were . . . as you remember from that time . . . there were efforts to try to figure things out and try to both quickly and we actually

worked with a lot of organizations and many that you've already mentioned, which was about how do we get dollars to people as quickly as possible? Sonnie . . . remembering a trip that we took the weekend after Sandy struck we . . . Sonnie is from New Jersey and we met her and as we drove into was it Sea Bright?

P3: Um-hmm (yes).

P1: Where the road is still closed and Sonnie says to the police, the trooper who was standing there. . . . Sonnie says, oh, we're talking to [Sea Bright Local Leader] and so that was the magic word and got us into the town and we were able to both effect and therefore also give funds that the Long-Term Recovery Groups . . . had the responsibility of really doing this long-term.

Q: Um-hmm (yes).

P1: And so . . . even we as funders said oh, this is what we would like to see in terms of how we know the balance between speed and efficiency and security, right, because . . . there were some we knew . . . the large to do dollars and so you also want to make sure that they're going to the right places and that they're not being misdirected.

P2: And it's obviously complicated the situation with federal payments, with insurance payments, they don't necessarily become clear immediately and no one likes to think about fraud, but there's opportunity for fraud whenever we send some of these large . . .

Q: Right.

P2: . . . so much giving out large amounts available so we had this sort of need to put caution to that risk in long-term recovery.

Q: Okay.

P1: And for us we were not interested in seeing our dollars go to help somebody rebuild their second home.

These exchanges highlight the complexity of disaster recovery and the interrelated issues of access, connections, policy, funding, and interorganizational relationships required to establish long-term recovery processes. Long-term recovery after disaster requires multiple types of organizations with different expertise, skills, and roles, all staging at different times. Immediately after the disaster, short-term needs emerge as people, communities, and organizations gather their thoughts, survey the situation, and assess their needs. Long-term needs usually center on rebuilding and recovery, often in the same place, regardless of risk and new opportunities to rebuild livelihoods and heal from disaster-inflicted traumas. While the central roles of reconstruction and case management receive the most funding and are essential to rebuilding homes and communities, reconstruction and individual assistance efforts depend on interrelated programmatic, legislative appropriations, and rule-making activities that create the informational and financial flows that provide the knowledge and resources needed for residents and communities to recover. These network flows, in turn, depend on interorganizational networks and healthy stakeholder relationships.

Networks of Recovery

In coastal New Jersey, the number of organizations active in the post-storm recovery networks declined over an eight-year recovery period (2012 and 2020), moving from 178 to 4 organizations. Network density shows how well every organization is connected to every other organization in a particular network. During this time period, the network evolved from a sparsely connected network (3.5 percent network density) to a tight, closely connected network of 100 percent network density, where all four remaining organizations were connected with one another. In sparsely connected networks, very few participating organizations in the network are connected to the others. In a dense network with 100 percent density—such as the 2017 post-Sandy recovery—all remaining organizations are connected with one another. Of the two active remaining organizations in 2020, one organization announced plans to end operations by the summer of 2021. Analysis of this coastal New Jersey recovery network showed that 36 percent of the network were planned response organizations, 36 percent were existing community organizations, and 28 percent of the organizations active in the network were emergent organizations that had not existed prior to the storm.

What this network composition tells us about long-term recovery after disaster is (a) the post-recovery network declined dramatically over time, (b) these networks become more connected over time, and (c) there is an equal balance between traditional disaster response organizations, existing community organizations, and emergent organizing in these networks. What is also important to note is that hyperlocal organizing is evident in all aspects of the network composition. Locally based organizations take on increasing responsibility as the recovery network declines and funding organizations move on. Most significantly, most of the emergent organizations folded up shop within two years of the disaster, just as the most complex problems of the recovery began to emerge.

Findings from these analyses support Bosworth and Kreps' (1986, 1993) classification of disaster response roles as well as the broader literature on emergence during disaster response. Earlier research by Harris and Doerfel (2017) analyzed the recovery networks of a single municipality in the coastal New Jersey recovery area. They documented how existing community organizations took on new roles, and new organizations were formed out of interactions between volunteers, the office of emergency management, and the mayor's office. The initial study by Harris and Doerfel only looked at the three-month transition from emergency response to the start of long-term recovery. Although limited, network analysis of organizational centrality in this study found shifts in organizational role and importance at four time points in that three-month period. Analysis of both the single municipality's recovery networks immediately after Hurricane Sandy and the multiyear coastal New Jersey recovery network make the case for understanding networks of recovery after disaster as dynamic processes in which organizational roles and importance will shift over time. Most importantly, these analyses support the importance of "whole community" response after disaster. What needs to be considered, however, is what combination of local and institutional responses is most connective and effective.

Hyperlocal Organizing and Institutional Response

We don't have clients that need to be served.
We have Sandy survivors that need to help themselves.

(Author Interview with New Jersey Organizing Project
Leadership, March 14, 2017)

On October 29, 2020—the eighth anniversary of Hurricane Sandy—state government and media reports[3] reported that 93 percent of homes funded through the state grant program had completed the post-Sandy rebuilding process. This is a misleading number, however, as numerous nonprofit and LTRG directors reported throughout the five years of field research that the state grant program enrolled only a small portion of impacted homeowners, due to confusing eligibility requirements and complicated participation processes. Impacted residents continually expressed confusion over recovery programs and processes.

County LTRGs often had to navigate clients through the recovery process and help them transition from one nonprofit to other nonprofits better equipped to serve their specific needs. LTRGs often picked up the slack or took responsibility for residents who had a nonprofit organization or case worker withdraw from the recovery network, or who had unmet needs. Community and grassroots organizations active in the post-recovery network over the long haul often supplemented these LTRG activities with their own case managers and processes. For example, the new advocacy organization, the New Jersey Organizing Project (NJOP), mobilized impacted residents to challenge state and federal programs and the slow pace of recovery. The NJOP had a connection with the federal lobbying efforts of the Ocean County LTRG to close and reform loopholes in the Federal Flood Insurance Program. However, the NJOP continued to play a more peripheral role in the recovery network and weren't consistent participants in the state Voluntary Organizations Active in Disaster (VOAD) during the most active periods of the post-disaster recovery network between 2012 and 2015. Instead, NJOP (founded in 2014) tackled the tough problems of long-haul recovery after other nonprofits and funders withdrew in the later stages of the recovery.

Organizations that activate after long-term recovery starts are vital, yet often overlooked parts of the recovery network. As organizations and their members burn out, exceed operational capacity, or run out of funding, they withdraw from the recovery networks. Grassroots organizations like the NJOP often pick up the slack. Some organizations with disaster and humanitarian relief missions move on to other disasters while other community organizations revert to their primary missions. Supporting organizations that remain in the latter stages of recovery remains a challenge for state and federal disaster planning and philanthropic organizations. Burnout is very real as the executive director of a Monmouth County nonprofit explained in a 2017 interview with the author.

No, listen, you're in long-term recovery, you're in it for a couple years, and you're in it full-time, you're burnt out. You are. You've done enough. Let the next crew come in and worry about the real—because those real estate projects they started for Sandy, how many of them are really going on right now? That takes years of studies, environmental studies. Long-term recovery is about raising funds quickly, utilizing volunteers to reduce the cost. It's about getting people home. You have enough issues dealing with the local building codes and FEMA and elevations. And the reality of it is that most of the flood affected communities are your low-income communities. So they don't have the resources to manage their recovery. They need a lot of help.

(Author Interview with Executive Director of a Monmouth
County Nonprofit Coalition Builder, March 2017)

The executive director of this nonprofit emphasizes the number of different types of organizations needed at different points in time in long-term recovery. What he also makes clear is that the decisions needed for rebuilding peoples' lives and communities after disaster are short term and by necessity may ignore longer-term issues related to community storm-readiness and resilience-building, especially in low-income communities. This highlights the tensions between recovery and mitigation. The mayor of a hard-hit beach community expressed frustration in multiple interviews with the author about media and environmental organizations constant queries about climate change and long-term mitigation measures to address sea level rise, beach erosion, and back bay flooding. The mayor was clear that those were not their priorities, and the immediate goal was to rebuild public infrastructure to facilitate residents return home and individual rebuilding processes.

This mayor's decision-making was replicated throughout coastal New Jersey. The most visible tradeoff between rebuilding, mitigation, and long-term planning could be seen in the rapid closing of ocean breaches in Long Branch, Spring Lake/Sea Girt, and Mantoloking. Decisions were made to quickly close breaches and rebuild bridges and roads in areas where long closed historic ocean inlets were reopened by Sandy's storm surge. The long-term implications of those decisions to close the breaches in a time of rising seas and increasingly intense storms remain to be seen. What these decisions highlight is the need for rebuilding and recovery to operate as parallel processes drawing from robust cross-sector networks that address both short-term rebuilding and long-term recovery needs. Long-term recovery needs to be about more than just rebuilding homes, roads, and municipal buildings. It needs to balance the immediate needs of residents and municipal officials with longer-term considerations of the regional ecologies within which disaster-impacted communities are located.

Hyperlocal Organizing: Undervalued and Underappreciated?

Overall, community and grassroots organizations emphasizing advocacy were not engaged in regular collaboration with traditional disaster relief organizations. As organizations withdrew from recovery over the past eight years, the NJOP remained one of the few organizations attentive to unrecovered communities and residents. Given their role as an advocacy organization—rather than an organization focused on rebuilding, case management, or funding—NJOP's direct impact on the broader recovery network has been limited. Rather than directly moving people home, NJOP's primary focus was on stakeholder engagement and community mobilization efforts for policy reform rather than specific rebuilding and human services activities. They often used media and lobbying to try to directly influence lawmakers and were less connected to the Sandy recovery network than many of the organizations focused on rebuilding, case management, mental health services, and philanthropy. NJOP's activities were important but provided only indirect benefits through legislation and policy reform.

The NJOP's peripheral involvement in the post-Sandy disaster recovery network raises interesting questions about the role of advocacy, class, and race in post-disaster response and recovery networks. An open question remains as to how well organizations engaged in advocacy and representation of marginalized groups may be received in post-disaster recovery and crisis response networks led by traditional disaster response and community organizations. The Ironbound Community Corporation in Newark is a widely recognized leader in neighborhood advocacy, offering resources and services for community members, and is a leader in environmental justice organizing. During the COVID-19 response, the organization helped pass state legislation addressing the housing dimensions of the crisis and in organizing food assistance and access to city and state resources for residents of New Jersey's largest city. However, while part of the State VOAD, they were absent from almost all the 2020 Monday morning weekly coordinating calls that brought nonprofit organizations and food banks together with state and federal government agencies in the first six months of the pandemic. This award-winning organization had significant policy impacts and was a major contributor to community well-being during the COVID-19 pandemic. However, it was only peripherally connected to the broader plural sector networks of disaster and humanitarian assistance in New Jersey grappling with the provision of support and services to people and communities during COVID-19.

Grassroots vs. Institutional Coordination in Staten Island

Differences between grassroots organizations and more traditional humanitarian assistance and disaster relief organizations were evident in the post-disaster recovery processes on Staten Island. Two different coordinating groups were operating in the New York Borough of Staten Island after Hurricane Sandy. The SILTRO was mainly composed of emergent, grassroots, and faith-based organizations. It took a "boots on the ground" perspective from the neighborhoods, churches, and parishes gathering information and providing assistance. The Staten Island Coalition of Organizations Active in Disaster (SI COAD) was sponsored by the Staten Island Nonprofit Association (SINPFA). SI COAD represented the more formal organizational and interorganizational processes of disaster recovery in Staten Island. Mostly composed of organizations in the nonprofit sector—including human services organizations, educational institutions, hospitals, and the broader healthcare system—SI COAD was formally linked to the Staten Island Borough President's Office and the New York City Office of Emergency Management.

SI COAD currently describes themselves as "a coalition managed by SINFPA," whereas SILTRO describes themselves as "A Coalition of Nonprofit Organizations, Houses of Worship, and Grassroots Groups on Staten Island." The descriptors point to important distinctions. SI COAD is a program of the SINFPA, meaning they represent a more centralized or bureaucratic version of networked organizing, with program management and governance administered by a single entity. SILTRO is managed by the members of the coalition themselves, and the eight different organizations represented on their board of directors highlight a more grassroots model of networked organizing. SILTRO was created following Hurricane Sandy within the parameters of FEMA's National Disaster Recovery Framework. SI COAD had been in operation since 2005 and would be the logical locus for the LTRG, with SINFPA serving as fiscal agent. However, the early exclusion of grassroots groups and Occupy Sandy from the post-Sandy recovery coalitions resulted in a new hyperlocal organizing process that united disparate groups, people, and emergent efforts, which transitioned into the Staten Island Long-Term Recovery Organization, or SILTRO.

Staten Island was a hotbed of "pop-up" organizations after Hurricane Sandy. These emergent efforts were initially loosely organized and sparsely connected with other emergent efforts and institutional responses. They were ad-hoc and could initially operate outside the bounds of FEMA, state, and city protocols and guidelines. However, as a coalition of established organizations of core health and human services nonprofits and government agencies, SI COAD was constrained by their members' primary missions and state and federal rules and regulations governing their services and operations. Strict guidelines established under FEMA frameworks cover post-disaster mass shelter and feeding operations. Failure to adhere to these guidelines could jeopardize existing or future federal funding and reimbursement. Emergent groups are not constrained by those issues and can act in the moment to meet neighborhood and community needs. When federal shelters were shut down by agency leaders in Monmouth County, New Jersey, and food wasn't delivered by national nonprofits in both Staten Island and New Jersey after Hurricane Sandy, local volunteers gathered. They cooked in parking lots, fired up school kitchens, set up field kitchens, and procured supplies from local bakeries, restaurants, and locally owned regional supermarkets. These measures supplemented—and in some cases completely replaced—the national nonprofits' responsible for mass sheltering and feeding as outlined in the Recovery Support Functions (RSFs) of the federal disaster recovery frameworks.

Also overlooked in post-disaster recovery is the canvassing and data collection that emergent organizers and organizations conduct in their neighborhoods and local communities. Both spontaneous volunteers and emergent organizations began collecting hyperlocal information on the extent and types of damage impacting residents in the days and weeks after the storm. Clipboards and legal pads were liberally deployed in the early days after disaster to ensure impacted residents could be located and contacted once the post-storm FEMA assessments began and the insurance adjusters rolled into town. In many instances, emergency responders, government agencies, and the nonprofits that comprised the formal institutional response turned to these local data collection efforts to support their own data collection. Hyperlocal data collection also provided a way for emergent organizations to direct impacted residents to programs and services that they may not have been aware of, or thought they weren't eligible for. Support frameworks for ad-hoc hyperlocal data collection are overlooked as critical components of post-disaster response and recovery. The next iterations of the National Disaster Recovery Frameworks and the RSFs should provide guidance and a loose framework for supporting hyperlocal data collection and management in the early days and weeks of a major disaster. The co-founder of a Staten Island pop-up stated in a 2014 interview with the author that "we should have a setup so that police, OEM, FEMA should come to us the day after a storm." What this co-founder was emphasizing was the role that these pop-up organizations play in collecting data on damage to peoples' home and the needs of different neighborhoods. Simple clipboards and Excel spreadsheets created by volunteers and managed by hyperlocal organizations often provide a first look into the extent of damage in a community and the different needs of residents in these communities.

Hyperlocal organizations active in neighborhoods and communities after disaster conduct a range of partnership activities and take on different roles. They work in concert with, but independently of, the formal disaster relief efforts of the LTRGs and VOAD-affiliated organizations. Hyperlocal organizing often involves big-tent collaborations that include activist organizations and foundations, hyperlocal pop-up organizations, and well-established community organizations. Together they create a foundational civic network focused on disaster relief and recovery. Hyperlocal networks of recovery are not just emergent and grassroots organizations and the activities of spontaneous volunteers engaged in random activities in a disaster-impacted community. Rather, hyperlocal networks are forged between organizations with varying sizes, capabilities, missions, and motivations. They share a common interest in helping a particular community recover from disaster and can establish shared goals to achieve these interests through hyperlocal organizing.

Accessing Local Resources after Disaster

People were helping out the neighborhood they grew up in.

(Author Interview with Co-Founders of Staten Island
Pop-up Organization, July 2014)

How and when people turn to local resources after disaster and during crisis is an enduring question. Survey data from a 2014 Rutgers Eagleton Institute of Politics and National Opinion Research Center survey indicated that 37 percent of residents in waterfront Brooklyn[4] turned to local faith-based organizations after Sandy, with 19 percent of residents turning to local community organizations. Only 25 percent of these residents turned to National Nonprofits, with 51 percent of Brooklyn residents turning to federal agencies such as FEMA. The higher response rates for FEMA may be reflective of (a) the role that FEMA adjusters play in initial contact with impacted homeowners and (b) FEMA's role as the initial spigot of recovery dollars in federally declared disasters. For those encountering a disaster for the first time, the expectation is that FEMA is responsible for and will manage all facets of the disaster and make people and communities whole. This expectation is widespread despite extensive institutional messaging that FEMA's role is to support state and local response, and not to manage the recovery or make residents and business owners whole. In Staten Island, 43 percent of impacted residents turned to local faith-based organizations, with 17 percent turning to local community-based organizations. Some 31 percent of these residents turned to National Nonprofits, while only 29 percent of impacted Staten Island residents turned to federal agencies for assistance. The finding that only 29 percent of impacted Staten Islanders turned to federal agencies reflected similar findings from focus groups and interviews in which participants talked of feeling isolated, cut off, and abandoned in the initial days and weeks after Sandy. Residents' confusion led them to seek local solutions and locally led recovery and disaster assistance efforts typified by "pop-ups" and SILTRO. Similar sentiments of abandonment by the institutional response were expressed by impacted residents interviewed in more remote bayside regions of coastal New Jersey.

Citizen volunteers and grassroots organizing—whether pop-up organizations, national, or international organizations that work with local communities and grass-roots organizers—play crucial roles in connecting people to information and aid, and in assessing the on-the-ground realities and needs of disaster-impacted communities. They bridge between national response efforts and the local realities of the post-disaster recovery. These collaborations between institutional response and hyperlocal organizing are a critical part of post-disaster recovery and an important part of ensuring community survivability in an era of increased intensity and frequency of storms and disasters. Current federal disaster frameworks require the establishment of coordinating organizations such as LTRGs under the auspices of the American Red Cross and the National VOAD. In reality, other organizations like local faith-based organizations, community organizations, and emergent groups like Occupy Sandy are more likely to take on the role of convening LTRGs after disaster.

Disaster is a dynamic event situated in the particular socioeconomic and historic contexts of the impacted community or region. It requires ongoing sensemaking efforts by impacted communities, residents, and organizations to understand the scope of the disaster and the resources available for recovery. Citizens in impacted communities may turn to grassroots and neighborhood organizations to aid their sensemaking efforts and begin the process of post-disaster recovery. These grass-roots organizing efforts, in turn, may create new emergent organizations that play important roles in a community's response and recovery efforts. Citizen response and emergent (or "pop-up" organizations) play multiple roles in community collaborations after disaster. These organizations serve as conveners and temporary backbone organizations until LTRGs or other more expansive coordinating entities are established. Emergent organizations serve as resource providers and case managers or provide social support to their impacted community.

The multifaceted role that hyperlocal organizations play is often overlooked and even seen as a conflicting process by the institutionalized humanitarian assistance and disaster relief community. However, the on-the-ground reality is that short- and long-term recovery efforts cannot be effectively launched without the local knowledge and information that hyperlocal organizations provide. It is the relationship between organizations with different roles, missions, identities, and capacities that enables long-term recovery after disaster. These organizational relationships may be planned or emergent, and vary widely in scale and scope, depending on the breadth and severity of the disaster. It is through these relationships that problems are identified, solutions formulated, decisions made, and resources allocated.

Analysis of long-term recovery in the mid-Atlantic region of the United States after Hurricane Sandy has suggested that grassroots organizing plays numerous roles. Grassroots organizing may be especially important for neighborhoods and communities overlooked in media coverage, neglected by formal disaster response and recovery agencies, or overshadowed by wealthier neighbors with more capital. Grassroots organizations, in turn, are part of broader hyperlocal organizing processes that enable different activities of recovery and connect different grassroots, faith-based and community organizations, each engaging in different roles in impacted communities. Hyperlocal organizations serve ancillary roles, such as to collect donations and provide resources, identify immediate or unmet needs, and organize information. They serve as ad-hoc caseworkers, develop expertise about funding programs, connect residents to larger organizations with resources, and provide local or tacit knowledge of the community. In these ways, hyperlocal organizations serve as conveners, coordinators, and participants of LTRGs and organizations.

Community collaboration after disaster takes many forms, from the informal and ad-hoc to formal and planned frameworks such as the Stafford Act and the National Response and Recovery Frameworks that detail obligations and relationships. However, federal disaster planning has yet to make space for the role of citizen response and grassroots organizing. All too often, it cedes control of decision-making and agenda setting to national organizations with limited insight into conditions on the ground. The reality is that community collaborations can help people and communities recover.

NOTES

1. Frank Rennie, *The Changing Outer Hebrides: Galson and the Meaning of Place* (Stornoway, Isle of Lewis: Acair Books, 2020); Judith Ennew, *The Western Isles Today* (Cambridge: Cambridge University Press, 1980); John Charles Morris et al., *The Case for Grassroots Collaboration: Social Capital and Ecosystem Restoration at the Local Level* (Lanham, MD: Lexington Books, 2013).

2. Alan J. Karcher, *New Jersey's Multiple Municipal Madness* (Piscataway, NJ: Rutgers University Press, 1998); Sara Bondesson, "Vulnerability and Power: Social Justice Organizing in Rockaway, New York City after Hurricane Sandy" (Dissertation, Uppsala, Sweden, Uppsala University, 2017), http://uu.diva-portal.org/smash/record.jsf?pid=diva2%3A1084218&dswid=8530.

3. The most recent annualized data available as of this writing.

4. Residents in Brooklyn neighborhoods within one mile of the water.

6

Hyperlocal Organizing

Implications for Democratic Governance and Resilience

Trauma is both personal and communal.

Laura Greenstone, M.S., L.P.C., ATR-BC

Hyperlocal organizing democratizes governance and improves resilience. While hyperlocal communication and organizing processes build upon the capacities of networked stakeholders, they also rely upon individual citizens dedicated to the response, relief, and recovery process. When disaster strikes, residents turn to other residents and organizations to make sense of the event, seek information, find help, and aid other impacted residents. We can think of these activities as driven by associational and communal ties. Associational ties are connections between organizations, while communal ties are connections between neighbors, friends, and families. Both types of ties are important for building resilience and sustainability over time, and for solving complex public problems such as climate change. They also are crucial to disaster response and recovery.

Communal and associational ties are the building blocks of resilience and generate social capital. However, associational and communal ties are important not just for building and deploying social capital in the hopes that it will insulate people from crisis and disaster; they also form the civic networks essential for civic life and democratic governance. The wide range of associations citizens engage in have traditionally been an important part of U.S. social and political life. While an argument has been made over the past two decades that Americans are increasingly "bowling alone," a counterargument can be made that Americans simply have more diffuse associational and communal ties than before. The presidential election of 2004, the organizing efforts of Obama for America in 2008 and 2012, the experiences of Katrina, the Tea Party, the Occupy movements, Puerto Rican community responses to Hurricane

Maria, and Mutual Aid and nonprofit organizing during COVID-19 show more diffuse forms of volunteering and civic engagement in action.[1]

Emergent organizing, spontaneous volunteering, and Mutual Aid all emerge out of associational and communal ties. These same ties are crucial for hyperlocal organizing and are necessary for repairing governance and building resilience. To some degree, the notions of governance and resilience may seem contradictory. If the government is working, institutional and transnational governance remain effective. In a world of sound governance, policy solutions to ecological challenges would be created, and adequate resources would become available during crisis and disaster. Institutional responses to post-disaster and post-crisis recovery would work, and marginalized communities would receive the resources they need for recovery and be treated as equal partners in recovery. Instead, resilience is celebrated at the personal and communal levels; the ability to "bounce back" is lauded rather than seen as an institutional failure.

HYPERLOCAL ORGANIZING AND SOCIAL RESILIENCE

Often associated with the hardening of coastlines and physical infrastructure after natural disaster, resilience is also defined as an individual psychological trait. It contributes to individual "hardiness" and the ability to recover from disruption or dislocation. However, resilience is more than engineering solutions, planning paradigms, and psychological toughness. Resilience has social and communicative dimensions, which maximize the utility of social ties and organizational relationships that undergird communities and nations. These social ties form a social infrastructure that shapes the social relations of a community, similar to how networks of roads and utilities help shape the physical dimensions of a community.

Social resilience integrates the social interactions and work activities that underly hyperlocal organizing. These organizing processes connect people and groups with networks of social support and recovery activities after disaster. Like social capital, social resilience can often be hard to pin down. Social capital has a long tradition in the social and organizational sciences and can be simply defined as the social and organizational ties that unite people and organizations. Multiple models of social capital exist, and it can be framed as an individual, communal, or networked resource. Small (2009) uses the term "organizational capital" in his study of networked inequalities. He found that how well early childhood centers were connected to other educational and human service organizations was a better predictor of access to services by families than their personal networks, regardless of socioeconomic background. Other models of social capital include elements as diverse as trust, communal forms of association, inherited resources, and social ties that contain or transmit financial, informational, and reputational resources. Such definitions also capture the horizontal and vertical linkages that connect people and groups within and across their social and organizational networks.[2]

Disaster research provides opportunities to explore how social resilience and social capital function in communities where traditional social and organizational relationships have been disrupted and need to be reconfigured or reconstructed. Social capital is not simply synonymous with social resilience, however. Social resilience is hyperlocal organizing that unites existing and emergent organizations in a community response to crisis and disaster. It integrates the communication and organizing activities generated in response and recovery into a singular organizing process centered on community survivability and social well-being. In contrast, social capital is a networked resource existing within a community that may contribute to community survivability and social well-being, especially in times of disruption or disaster. The dynamic processes of hyperlocal organizing, however, present opportunities for even communities with weak social capital and frayed social ties to rapidly remix emerging and existing organizations with spontaneous volunteering and outside support into a robust civic network focused on disaster response and recovery. Both social resilience and social capital are built through the communicating and organizing processes that help a community bounce back from crisis. As a process of social well-being, social resilience integrates existing individual, community, and organizational coping mechanisms into a process of social interaction. Personal ways of coping with disruption and trauma are transformed into communal activities that benefit from hyperlocal organizing processes. In these ways, social resilience connects organizations and people with the requisite knowledge, capabilities, and capacity to survive.

Understanding How Social Resilience Works

Social resilience differs from ordinary conceptions of resilience. It emphasizes the social and organizational ties of a community and the patterns of interaction that connect community members through organizing processes. Its emphasis on social organizing differs from the physical, engineering, planning, and policy dimensions that are typically thought of when resilience is discussed as part of disaster planning and recovery. It is also separate from individual attributes of "toughness" or "grit." Communities with strong elements of social resilience are better able to coordinate tasks and collaborate on post-disaster recovery than communities with weaker social resilience. Social resilience is also an important facet of community survivability and can support individuals trying to recover from crisis or disaster. While social resilience is a net positive for communities with strong social and organizational infrastructures, a history of civic engagement, or traditions of solidarity and Mutual Aid, it is no replacement for adequate and timely resources, competent governance, and functioning governments.[3]

The Role of Communication in Social Resilience

Social resilience relies upon the communicative capacities of communities. As a relational process, communication between individuals, organizations, and communities is the building block of the social infrastructure that binds communities, regions, and nations together. Social infrastructure is created through the communication of these civil society actors and relies upon trust between partnering organizations. Trust between community and organizational partners helps create the social capital that is activated during times of crisis. That is, hyperlocal organizing activates relationships between existing community organizations and emergent organizing activities. These organizing processes may, in turn, prompt organizations to seek new partnerships. Having a broader range of organizations available after disaster provides impacted people and communities with more resources, and robust information sharing and sensemaking capabilities. These partnership processes are both fixed and dynamic, as they rely on existing community ties but can rapidly evolve and incorporate new entrants as circumstances change.

Communicative management facilitates these partnering opportunities and organizing processes by promoting shared interests and goals. It balances organizational power and interests to increase social well-being through shared governance and strategic cooperation, ultimately achieving shared goals. Specific communication activities that build social resilience include face-to-face and mediated interactions, communication channels, and meetings. Social resilience can be fostered through mass communication technologies such as radio, broadcast, and cable TV, and niche or limited technologies like Meshnet Wireless and ham radios. Crowdsourced technologies also play a role in post-disaster communication and have been extensively utilized for mapping impacted communities and procuring supplies. Like most new media technologies, social media and distributed peer-to-peer technologies help reveal social networks and facilitate communication within and between disaster-impacted communities and organizations providing assistance.

Communication studies of rebuilding after Katrina by Doerfel and her colleagues have identified organizational networks as driving short and long-term recovery processes. Recovery after disaster proceeded in phased periods, each of which presented different organizing opportunities for organizations dislocated or disrupted by Katrina. The "Urgent," "Transitional," and "Rebuilding" phases identified by Doerfel and her collaborators are similar to the time-based disaster planning framework established by the Federal Emergency Management Agency. The communication activities central to organizational rebuilding after Katrina ranged from face-to-face interactions with known trusted partners to mediated interactions enabled by weak ties. These weak ties were activated as organizations sought to make sense of the totality of Katrina's impact and identify paths to recovery. Organizations used organizational and social capital to mobilize the resources they needed for survival. They operated at interpersonal, intergroup, organizational, and interorganizational levels to identify and secure needed resources. The organizations that rapidly activated their networks moved more quickly out of the emergency response phase and into the transitional and rebuilding phases. Communities organizing for recovery after disaster can provide insight into the interactions between grassroots and institutional efforts to solve complex public problems. In turn, they can create new ways of understanding the communication and organizing processes of democratic governance.[4]

SOCIAL RESILIENCE AND
DEMOCRATIC GOVERNANCE

Social resilience is composed of both associational and communal ties. Associational and communal ties are social ties that enable the civic and political life of communities to unfold. These ties integrate social relationships and governance and are crucial to disrupted communities and civic networks rebuilding and reconnecting. Associational and communal ties are traditionally found within the United States in the township system of governance. Most famously, Tocqueville describes voluntary associations as crucial parts of the landscape of American civic and political life. Building off of Tocqueville, an established tradition in American politics emphasizes that communal ties are key to American political relations, civic engagement, and governance. Politics and political life are an outcome of communal ties that reflect the close relationships of family, neighborhood, and community. Communal ties also reflect the private self and patterns of homophily that give shape to the social relationships that organize community life and civic networks. Often exclusive, communal ties emphasize the private self of the individual and community but remain important components of the public sphere and public life. In crisis and disaster, the exclusivity of communal ties can be overcome through a form of "greater love" that transcends individual self-interest. In these instances, communal ties become social ties that bind the community through shared grief, solidarity, and public action.[5]

Governance that emerges from these social relationships reflects a push and pull between formal institutions and the social relationships of civic life. At a basic level, associational ties represent the voluntary and membership organizations that have played significant roles in American civic and political life since the early nineteenth century. These associational ties often sit outside the formal institutional frameworks of government and policymaking and are fostered by plural sector organizations sitting in the space often referred to as "civil society" or third sector." The plural sector includes a much broader variety of organizations that are traditionally defined as civil society organizations and include alternative forms of organizing such as social enterprises and cooperatives, as well as labor unions.[6]

Democratic governance is ultimately about commitment to the people. It is about the ties that bind and a greater love that recognizes a common humanity across differences. Democratic governance centers on people and is fiercely focused on economic and social well-being that can only come from centering people's voices and participation in agenda-setting and decision-making processes. It relies on associational and communal ties and fosters, as the late Senator Paul Wellstone has said, "the fullest development of human capabilities." The old-fashioned bowling leagues of which my grandmother was a Catholic parish league champion, the Catholic Workers' Movement, Catholic Charities, and Burners without Borders are all associations through which common values are expressed. Here is where social ties are created that foster collaborative actions to improve social and political life. They represent an associational politics that drives social welfare in the neighborhood and across the globe and are often an expression of communal ties that transcend geographic and temporal boundaries in a commitment to service and the common good.

Social resilience and democratic governance both rely upon robust social and organizational infrastructures that enable the pursuit of shared goals, joint interests, and the overall common good. Hyperlocal organizing is how communities coalesce to achieve collective goals and connect with a broader set of institutions in which power and resources are typically concentrated. Hyperlocal organizing, then, lays a pathway people and communities can walk to bypass unresponsive institutions and failed institutional response efforts. As disaster increases and long-term recovery efforts multiply, the hyperlocal organizing processes that underly social resilience and democratic governance become increasingly important.

Hyperlocal Organizing: The New Normal?

Resilience may appear to be a negative externality resulting from institutional responses to disaster that failed communities. Governments gaze longingly backward toward outdated policies, segregated communities, limited social mobility, and strictly enforced class, ethnic, and racial hierarchies that ostensibly simplify disaster response and limit collaboration to a set of homogenous partners. The wealthy and connected are resourced, while the poverty-stricken, working and middle classes, and vulnerable and marginalized populations see their bank accounts emptied and credit cards maxed out as they try and "bounce back" from disaster. Clean water, food, or least nutritious food, and adequate shelter may also be difficult to access after disaster. However, I have argued in this book that the resilience fostered by hyperlocal organizing is a communicative process that empowers grassroots groups, neighborhoods, communities, and local organizations. By remixing existing and emergent organizing processes, hyperlocal organizing charts a democratic path for the voices of people and their communities to be heard and gain a seat at the recovery table. Hyperlocal organizing mobilizes resources for communities impacted by disaster and enables residents to envision new ways forward. It opens opportunities for volunteering, organizing, leading, and strategic cooperation, which link local need and knowledge with institutional patterns of response and recovery. In processes of hyperlocal organizing, resilience is activated through communication practices that emphasize joint interests, shared goals, cooperative leadership, and a recognition of community and organizational interests.

We collectively need hyperlocal organizing. Institutions and governments are stretched to their breaking point wrestling with climate change, mass migration, and the aftermaths of disaster. Intense storms, fires, flooding, and tornadoes are happening more frequently in places where there were previously few and far between. In the final stages of manuscript preparation, Hurricane Ida, a Category 4 Hurricane with sustained wind speeds of 150 miles per hour, came ashore on the Gulf Coast of Louisiana. It knocked out power for almost two weeks to the City of New Orleans after Entergy, the primary electrical utility for the region, resisted upgrading energy infrastructure for years. Ida then blasted through the Mississippi and Ohio Valleys before tearing through the mid-Atlantic states of Pennsylvania, New Jersey, and New York, spawning record-setting tornadoes and river flooding before heading out to sea over the Northeastern Atlantic Ocean.

Storms and disasters such as Hurricane Ida spawn recovery operations across multiple states, demanding recurring commitments from disaster relief and humanitarian assistance organizations. Afterward, communities wait days, weeks, and years for federal assistance, which often never comes. If it does arrive, financial support is so low that many middle-class, vulnerable, and marginalized populations are unable to fully recover. Burnout is real, and volunteer coordination has become tricky because of the pandemic. It is through the local chapters of national voluntary associations that community and institutional responses have traditionally emerged. But national voluntary associations have become hollowed out as they consolidate and downsize local chapters. As a result, staff with operational expertise in disaster relief and humanitarian assistance have become scarce.

Hyperlocal organizing after disaster replaces older traditions of voluntary association in the United States. It is an organizational remix of locally based and loosely organized collectives, grassroots groups, emergent and community organizations, and spontaneous volunteers. They partner with nontraditional disaster relief organizations and new philanthropic players to promote a speedy recovery in disaster-impacted regions. Hyperlocal organizing is both associational and communal, as it relies on both organizational ties and the bonds between friends, families, and neighbors who become volunteer leaders. Hyperlocal organizing can be both an outcome of resilience and an enactment of resilience. Communities or regions with little to no experience with catastrophic disaster may have never needed to be socially resilient. However, with the advent of a catastrophic disaster, communities that remix and organize may yet build resilience through repeated patterns of communication, collaboration, and interorganizational interactions that result in enduring relationships among stakeholders.

The stakeholder relationships that emerge from hyperlocal organizing make recovery possible. They embed social resilience in communities and provide possibilities for more democratic governance. Yet, successful disaster recovery requires balancing social and organizational interests. Power plays are counterproductive, as is tasking just one or two large institutional players with the task of making communities whole. Disaster recovery should be understood as an entanglement of social, economic, and political interests with shared goals or joint interests in the recovery of people and communities. Leaders at all levels should adopt this definition and become sensitized to the importance of strategic cooperation and communicative management in disaster recovery. Hyperlocal organizing is ultimately the process through which grassroots and community stakeholders engage with institutionalized disaster response and recovery to rebuild communities and reestablish economic and social well-being after disaster.

We are overdue for a comprehensive review of national disaster recovery in the United States, and hyperlocal organizing could take center stage. Great strides were made in the post-Katrina era from 2005 to 2015 to center whole community approaches to disaster recovery. However, the complexity, frequency, and intensity of disaster and complexity of recovery have only increased since then. New iterations of the Stafford Act should account for emergence, and the United States' national disaster recovery frameworks must be updated to tap into the power of hyperlocal organizing processes. An outline of communicative management processes for integrating hyperlocal organizing and whole community response should be reflected in future government approaches to disaster recovery. Long-term recovery after disaster requires multiyear collaboration, clear cooperation among stakeholders enacting the recovery, and a balancing of social and organizational interests through communicative management practices. This is the bedrock of disaster management. Only by understanding and integrating hyperlocal organizing processes can we improve social well-being and make democratic governance more effective in addressing grand challenges and wicked problems.

NOTES

1. Robert D. Putnam, *Bowling Alone: The Collapse and Revival of American Community* (New York: Simon & Schuster, 2000); J. Katz, M. Barris, and A. Jain, *The Social Media President: Barack Obama and the Politics of Digital Engagement* (Springer, 2013); Chris Wells, *The Civic Organization and the Digital Citizen: Communicating Engagement in a Networked Age* (Oxford University Press, 2015); James R. Elliot and Jeremey Pais, "Race, Class, and Hurricane Katrina: Social Differences in Response to Disaster," *Social Science Research* 35, no. 2006 (2006): 295–321; Christopher A. Airriess et al., "Church-Based Social Capital, Networks and Geographical Scale: Katrina Evacuation, Relocation, and Recovery in a New Orleans Vietnamese American Community," *Geoforum* 39, no. 3 (May 2008): 1333–46, https://doi.org/10.1016/j.geoforum.2007.11.003; Emily Chamlee-Wright and Virgil Henry Storr, "'There's No Place Like New Orleans': Sense of Place and Community Recovery in the Ninth Ward After Hurricane Katrina," *Journal of Urban Affairs* 31, no. 5 (December 2009): 615–34, https://doi.org/10.1111/j.1467-9906.2009.00479.x; Jessica M. Mulligan and Adriana Garriga-López, "Forging *Compromiso* after the Storm: Activism as Ethics of Care among Health Care Workers in Puerto Rico," *Critical Public Health* 31, no. 2 (March 15, 2021): 214–25, https://doi.org/10.1080/09581596.2020.1846683; Adriana Maí Garriga-López, "Compounded Disasters: Puerto Rico Confronts COVID-19 under US Colonialism," *Social Anthropology* (June 3, 2020): 1469-8676.12821, https://doi.org/10.1111/1469-8676.12821; Isa Rodríguez Soto, "Mutual Aid and Survival as Resistance in Puerto Rico: Faced with an Onslaught of Disasters, Government Mismanagement of Life-Threatening Crises, and the Injustices of Colonialism, Puerto Rican Communities Have Bet on Their Own Survival. Their Mutual Aid Efforts Testify to Both the Power of Grassroots Organizing and the Scale of State Neglect," *NACLA Report on the Americas* 52, no. 3 (July 2, 2020): 303–8, https://doi.org/10.1080/10714839.2020.1809099; Daniela G. Domínguez et al., "Leveraging the Power of Mutual Aid, Coalitions, Leadership, and Advocacy during COVID-19," *American Psychologist* 75, no. 7 (October 2020): 909–18, https://doi.org/10.1037/amp0000693.

2. James S. Coleman, "Social Capital in the Creation of Human Capital," *American Journal of Sociology* 94 (January 1, 1988): S95–120, https://doi.org/10.1086/228943; Ronald S. Burt, "The Network Structure of Social Capital," *Research in Organizational Behavior* 22 (2000): 345–423; Nan Lin, "Building a Network Theory of Social Capital," in *Social Capital: Theory and Research*, ed. Nan Lin, Karen Cook, and Ronald S. Burt, Sociology And

Economics: Theory and Research (Hawthorne, NY: Aldine de Gruyter, 2001), 3–29; Marya L Doerfel, Chih-Hui Lai, and Lisa V Chewning, "The Evolutionary Role of Interorganizational Communication: Modeling Social Capital in Disaster Contexts," *Human Communication Research* 36, no. 2 (2010): 125–62, https://doi.org/10.1111/j.1468-2958.2010.01371.x; Daniel P. Aldrich, *Building Resilience: Social Capital in Post-Disaster Recovery* (Chicago, IL: University of Chicago Press, 2012); Daniel P. Aldrich and Michelle A. Meyer, "Social Capital and Community Resilience," *American Behavioral Scientist* 59, no. 2 (February 2015): 254–69, https://doi.org/10.1177/0002764214550299.

3. George A. Bonanno, "Loss, Trauma, and Human Resilience: Have We Underestimated the Human Capacity to Thrive after Extremely Aversive Events?," *American Psychologist* 59, no. 1 (2004): 20–28, https://doi.org/10.1037/0003-066X.59.1.20; George A. Bonanno et al., "What Predicts Psychological Resilience after Disaster? The Role of Demographics, Resources, and Life Stress," *Journal of Consulting and Clinical Psychology* 75, no. 5 (2007): 671–82, https://doi.org/10.1037/0022-006S.75.5.671; Isabel Cuervo, Les Leopold, and Sherry Baron, "Promoting Community Preparedness and Resilience: A Latino Immigrant Community–Driven Project Following Hurricane Sandy," *American Journal of Public Health* 107, no. S2 (September 2017): S161–64, https://doi.org/10.2105/AJPH.2017.304053; Patrice Buzzanell, "Resilience: Talking, Resisting, and Imagining New Normalcies into Being," *Journal of Communication* 60, no. 1 (2010): 1–14; Marya L. Doerfel and Jack L. Harris, "Resilience Processes," in *The International Encyclopedia of Organizational Communication*, ed. C.R. Scott and Laurie Lewis (Hoboken, NJ: Wiley-Blackwell, 2017); Chih-Hui Lai and Ying-Chia Hsu, "Understanding Activated Network Resilience: A Comparative Analysis of Co-Located and Co-Cluster Disaster Response Networks," *Journal of Contingencies and Crisis Management* 27, no. 1 (January 2019): 14–27, https://doi.org/10.1111/1468-5973.12224; Minkyung Kim et al., "Serving the Vulnerable While Being Vulnerable: Organizing Resilience in a Social Welfare Sector," *Nonprofit and Voluntary Sector Quarterly*, Online First (2021), https://doi.org/0.1177/0899764021103912; Nathan E Busch and Austen D. Givens, "Achieving Resilience in Disaster Management: The Role of Public-Private Partnerships," *Journal of Strategic Security* 6, no. 2 (2013): 1–19.

4. Doerfel, Lai, and Chewning, "The Evolutionary Role of Interorganizational Communication: Modeling Social Capital in Disaster Contexts"; Marya L Doerfel, Lisa V Chewning, and Chih-Hui Lai, "The Evolution of Networks and the Resilience of Interorganizational Relationships after Disaster," *Communication Monographs* 80, no. 4 (2013): 533–59, https://doi.org/10.1080/03637751.2013.828157; Marya L Doerfel and Muge Haseki, "Networks, Disrupted: Media Use as an Organizing Mechanism for Rebuilding," *New Media & Society* 17, no. 3 (2013): 432–52, https://doi.org/10.1177/1461444813505362; Lisa V. Chewning, Chih-Hui Lai, and Marya L. Doerfel, "Organizational Resilience and Using Information and Communication Technologies to Rebuild Communication Structures," *Management Communication Quarterly* 27, no. 2 (2013): 237–63, https://doi.org/10.1177/0893318912465815.

5. Wilson Carey McWilliams, *The Idea of Fraternity in America* (Berkeley, CA: University of California Press, 1973); Wilson Carey McWilliams, "Toward Genuine Self-Government," in *The Democratic Soul: A Wilson Carey McWilliams Reader*, ed. Patrick J. Deneen and Susan J McWilliams (Lexington: The University Press of Kentucky, 2011), 353–60; Wilson Carey McWilliams, "Democracy and the Citizen: Community, Dignity, and the Crisis of Contemporary Politics in America," in *Redeeming Democracy in America*, ed. Patrick J. Deneen and Susan J. McWilliams (Lawrence, KS: University Press of Kansas, 2011), 9–28; Wilson Carey McWilliams, "In Good Faith: On the Foundations of American Politics," in *Redeeming*

Democracy in America, ed. Patrick J. Deneen and Susan J. McWilliams (Lawrence, KS: University Press of Kansas, 2011), 107–26; Patrick J. Deneen and Susan J. McWilliams, "A Better Sort of Love," in *The Democratic Soul: A Wilson Carey McWilliams Reader*, ed. Patrick J. Deneen and Susan J. McWilliams (Lexington: The University Press of Kentucky, 2011), 1–18; Alexis de Tocqueville, *Democracy in America*, ed. Harvey C. Mansfield and Winthrop (Chicago, IL: University of Chicago Press, 2000).

    6. Henry Mintzberg et al., "The Invisible World of Association," *Leader to Leader* 2005, no. 36 (2005): 37–45, https://doi.org/10.1002/ltl.126; Henry Mintzberg, "Time for the Plural Sector," *Stanford Social Innovation Review* 13, no. 3 (summer 2015): 28–33; Bruce Nissen and Paul Jarley, "Unions as Social Capital: Renewal through a Return to the Logic of Mutual Aid?," n.d., 26; Stanley Deetz, "Corporate Governance, Communication, And Getting Social Values Into The Decisional Chain," *Management Communication Quarterly* 16, no. 4 (May 2003): 606–11, https://doi.org/10.1177/0893318902250236; Rong Wang et al., "Is Collective Impact the Destination? A Typology of Interorganizational Collaboration," 2018; Rong Wang, Katherine R Cooper, and Michelle Shumate, "Alternatives to Collective Impact: The Community Systems Solutions Framework," *Stanford Social Innovation Review*, Winter 2020, https://ssir.org/articles/entry/community_system_solutions_framework_offers_an_alternative_to_collective_impact_model.

Appendix A

Social science disciplines have called for transparency in the research process over the past several years. However, full elucidation of qualitative methods is often hard to articulate in scholarly journals given page constraints. Reflexive qualitative approaches are particularly difficult to fully detail through journal publication, yet their multilayered process—combining thick data with researcher positionality, interpretation, and perspective—makes the need for deeper accounting of methodology and methods particularly important. Any discussion of methodology and research process should make clear the data generated, analytical decisions made, and reasons for relying on different types of analysis. It should also develop an understanding of the interplay between local knowledge, researcher positionality, and observable phenomena in complex multiyear studies.

THEORY CONSTRUCTION

Abductive theorizing generated new ideas related to hyperlocal organizing and community collaboration from the observable empirical data collected through the three studies described below. Abductive theorizing uses empirical data to generate concepts and ideas about observed phenomena identified during the research process. The role of emergent organizing and spontaneous volunteers is well documented in the disaster literature. What is less well documented are the relationships between different types of organizations, and their collaborative efforts to guide response and recovery activities. Understanding organizing over a multiyear period of disaster recovery following a natural hazards event can generate new insights into the organizational roles and relationships that foster the social and organizational infrastructure for disaster response and recovery. Insights generated from this theorizing guided interview questions and helped determine which subsequent interviews would best shed light on the concepts and ideas generated from the collected data.

Like Small's work on how neighborhood childcare centers generated organizational and social capital, my primary study of long-term recovery and networked stakeholders began with a hunch. I suspected, given my volunteer roles in response and recovery in New Jersey, that grassroots organizing played a much larger role in response and recovery than typically given credit for by nonprofit and disaster relief professionals. I suspected that their activities were complementary rather than duplicative, and that collaborative efforts often excluded or marginalized grassroots and neighborhood-level organizing efforts. By marginalizing grassroots and neighborhood organizations in community collaborations, local and tacit knowledge is often lost and opportunities to develop organizational capital are missed. After a disaster, interorganizational relationships (IORs) include a wide range of behaviors and interactions in a disrupted environment, making them particularly suitable for reflexive multi-methods research that analyzes both the organizational landscape of recovery and processes of long-term recovery. I also discovered that hyperlocal organizing is not simply synonymous with emergent organizing and spontaneous volunteers, though there was plenty of evidence of emergent and pop-up organizations in both field study sites. Rather, what emerged was that emergent behaviors and organizing were integrated—sometimes seamlessly and at other times jaggedly—with grassroots, neighborhood, and community organizations. In turn, these organizations connected with regional and national plural, public, and private sector organizations that had access to a broader range of resources and expertise. It appeared that hyperlocal organizing, played two roles. It was (1) a stopgap measure where institutions were absent or formal response and recovery efforts failed, and (2) a translator or connector between the institutional architecture of recovery and the local needs of neighborhoods and communities.

As the project developed, I began to see disaster response and recovery as a problem of civic association as well as a problem of communication, logistics, and funding. The findings and frameworks generated through these studies enabled me to frame a multilevel process of collaboration that was about more than the flow of funding and materials in storm-impacted regions. Organizational infrastructure and organizational capital enable the financial, informational, and material flows necessary for rebuilding and recovery. However, they require civic associations and networks to generate organizational infrastructure and capital.[1]

RESEARCH PROCESS AND SITES

Hyperlocal Organizing: Collaborating for Recovery over Time is organized around five years of multi-methodological field research on long-term recovery after Hurricane Sandy in the mid-Atlantic region of the United States. Data collection extended beyond the original 2013 to 2017 time period analyzed in this book. It also continued into the summer of 2021, as I collected media reports and government documents while having ongoing conversations with leaders and community members about recovery in coastal New Jersey. Data from 2012 was collected from participation in response and recovery activities in my community, which I captured in notes as events unfolded, and organizational relationships and tensions emerged. Data from this year was also collected from local documents and files with the permission of my volunteer colleagues and collaborators, as we served in leadership roles. This timeframe provided an almost eight-year overview of long-term recovery after disaster, in this case, a late-season hurricane that merged with an early winter storm, commonly called a Nor'easter, in October of 2012.

Over these eight years, I informed both participants and volunteer colleagues of my dual roles as an academic and community member engaged in recovery. Two separate field studies of Hurricane Sandy response and recovery, a five-year study of long-term recovery in coastal New Jersey (2012–2017), and a three-month study of information ecosystems in the New York City Boroughs of Brooklyn and Staten Island during and after Hurricane Sandy's landfall were integrated to develop a framework of hyperlocal organizing. The author's personal field notes from a study of organizational resilience in Houston, Texas, following Hurricane Harvey were used to identify similar hyperlocal organizing processes and issues in Houston, Texas.

Hurricane Harvey field research was conducted in the Spring of 2018 as part of a study on organizational resilience organized by Dr. Marya L. Doerfel, the Principal Investigator, (NSF RAPID Grant# 1765012 "Hurricane Harvey and Organizational Resilience"), to explore the elements of organizational resilience during crisis and disaster. The author of this book worked as a Research Associate on the project and the five years of fieldwork in coastal New Jersey was supervised by Dr. Doerfel as part of the author's dissertation research. Three months of field research in the New York City Boroughs of Staten Island and Brooklyn were conducted as part of a project sponsored by Internews, Embracing Change the Critical Role of Information (http://wp.comminfo.rutgers.edu/mpii-new/embracing-change-the-critical-role-of-information/), which was funded by the Rockefeller Foundation. Dr. Phil Napoli was the principal investigator, and the author of this book was one of four research assistants and was primarily responsible for the Staten Island field research. The primary goal of the project was to explore the role of information ecosystems in promoting resilience. Disaster response in New York City after Hurricane Sandy was developed as a case to explore the role of information in resilience. As part of the author's field research in Staten Island, he uncovered the extensive role that "pop-up" and hyperlocal organizations were playing in the borough's recovery.

These baseline studies were further informed by recent scholarship on Hurricanes Maria and Michael, and research on mutual aid activities during the COVID-19 pandemic. Mutual Aid research was conducted as part of participation in the Hyper-Local and Emergent Mutual-Aid Responses to COVID-19 working group, part of the CONVERGE COVID-19 Working Groups for Public Health and Social Sciences Research sponsored by the National Science Foundation's Social Science Extreme Events Research network and housed at the Natural Hazards Research Center at the University of Colorado Boulder. Additional secondary research on

Mutual Aid was conducted after 2021's Winter Storm Uri in Texas by the author to assess hyperlocal versus institutional response. Together, these experiences provided eight years of empirical evidence on the role of grassroots and neighborhood-level organizing in crisis and disaster, with a particular focus on the processes of long-term recovery following a disaster.

Information on the organizational landscape of Scotland's Isle of Jura was drawn from a trip there in July 2019. While on a personal retreat, I noticed installations signed as joint development projects through regional, national, and transnational agencies. I began taking pictures and asking questions in the stores and pubs. One stormy night, I settled into the hotel sitting room across the entrance foyer from the pub with a pint and discovered *Jura Jottings* on the bookshelf—a series of newsletters bound in blue binders detailing community life on the island of Jura, Scotland. I settled in and began to read about the community enterprises, struggles to find a permanent doctor and nurse for the island, church events, and recruitment for staff positions to support the civil and voluntary sector on Islay and Jura. As I had done after Sandy, I began taking notes that I later combined with my photos to paint a picture of the connection between national and transnational policies on Jura. My research was supplemented with information from the Jura Community Trust's website, and analysis of Scottish land reform legislation and policy, and desk (or secondary) research.

There are two units of analysis in this study: the organization and the IOR—the aggregation of organizations engaged in response and recovery in a particular community or region. This book has taken a reflexive, multi-methods approach to discovery and analysis by combining data from participant observation, interviews, focus groups, surveys, organizational documents, websites, blogs, and the media. Qualitative, quantitative, and network analysis techniques were used to reconstruct networks and identify patterns through which impacted residents and communities sought assistance and engaged in recovery. However, my research and analysis was also conducted reflexively through a lens of social constructivist grounded theory and abductive theorizing, in which insights generated from the field at one point in time guide subsequent iterations of field research and interview questions.

Both the research and the book sought a "middle way" through postpositivist and interpretive frameworks of social science research by integrating researcher positionality, local knowledge, and analytic techniques drawn from qualitative inquiry, descriptive statistics, and network analysis. In my multi-methods fieldwork research that defined the study at the heart of the book, there were no clearly defined entry and exit points to the field. As a resident of the impacted region, I engaged as a volunteer and community leader, I never officially entered the field, nor did I ever officially exit the field. In fact, my understanding of the processes and dynamics of long-term recovery continued to evolve long after the field research ended. In his study of network inequalities, Mario Small writes that his study began with a hunch. The genesis of this research also began with a hunch.

On October 30, 2012, I drove to the middle school in Oceanport, New Jersey, where a microshelter was being set up. My partner, Laura Greenstone, was a Disaster

Response Crisis Counselor, one of the first trained in New Jersey after 9/11. As an art therapist and licensed counselor, she worked with people impacted by trauma and grief and worked extensively with the families of 9/11 victims. We were headed over to the middle school so that she could check in with the local incident commander since county-wide communications were spotty and formal organizational systems overwhelmed. A tall woman came out of the gym and asked what I did. After a short conversation, I replied that I was a Boy Scout a long time ago. She said, "come with me." Within an hour, I was reorganizing the intake desk in the middle school gym and recruiting other volunteers as they came into the shelter. Nine years later, I'm still involved with disasters through community organizations and my academic research. While helping to organize disaster assistance in my community after Hurricane Sandy, it rapidly became clear that I was witnessing organizing processes driven by the needs and exigencies of the situation, resulting in new interpersonal and IORs. Even the formal Office of Emergency Management (OEM) framework and organizational relationships were rapidly shifting within a very compressed time frame. I began taking notes that later became the genesis of my field research, dissertation, and this book.

REFLEXIVE METHODOLOGY AND MULTI-METHODS FIELDWORK

Reflexive fieldwork integrates the researcher's localized position in a community or organization with their knowledge of the phenomena under investigation and their own disciplinary expertise. In reflexive fieldwork, there are no clearly defined entry and exit points to the field, and the researcher is immersed in the social, cultural, and historical context of the event or process being examined. The researcher uses their vantage point to generate empirical evidence through a variety of sources and methods, and evaluates the data being generated through a set of criteria. By generating robust empirical evidence while engaged in the field, the reflexive researcher moves beyond issues of researcher positionality and intersectionality to considerations of perspective. This is how the researcher's personal knowledge of the situation connects to a broader set of empirical evidence gathered through multi-methods field research.

Personal perspectives and knowledge gained from immersion in the site—either through participant observation or simple observation—helps guide the development of research questions in the initial phases of the study and informs the interview process. In short, prior personal knowledge is used to develop lines of inquiry and research questions, while the generation of data from empirical sources allows for personal, community, or organizational perspectives. Ultimately, reflexive fieldwork eschews both postpositivist and interpretive ways of knowing in favor of a middle path through which both personal position and independent inquiry is balanced. Empirical evidence is generated through clearly articulated methodologies and methods that can be adapted by other researchers within other communities and organizations.

The Research Setting

Defining Community and Place

The study area includes New Jersey coastal counties between the Raritan Bay in the north and the Delaware Bay in the southwest—137 miles of Atlantic Ocean —coastline encompassing four counties and 121 separate municipalities. Parts of two additional counties encompassing another ten municipalities were included as part of the networks of recovery, as organizations active in the core coastal areas also engaged in recovery activities in other counties.

The New York City Borough of Staten Island was also included in the conceptual development of hyperlocal organizing. Through data generated from the Staten Island field research, I first generated the concept of hyperlocal organizing. Staten Island research was conducted as part of research commissioned by Internews as part of a global study of information ecosystems. Research in New York City after Hurricane Sandy was conducted by a team of Rutgers researchers under the direction of Dr. Phil Napoli, the principal investigator with a focus on Brooklyn and Staten Island. Brooklyn research was concentrated in neighborhoods within one mile of the water, while Staten Island research was conducted across the entire borough. I coordinated the Staten Island part of the study. Staten Island sits across the Raritan Bay from Monmouth County, New Jersey, where the study originated. New Jersey's northern Bayshore region was one of the hardest-hit areas and had one of the longest recoveries. Both Staten Island and the Northern part of Monmouth County and the adjacent southeastern towns of Middlesex County encompass the New York Harbor Complex and include significant numbers of communities adjoining multiple bays, rivers, and estuaries.

Despite New York City's position as a global city and a global hub for finance, media, fashion, and publishing, New York is a city of neighborhoods. It is in the neighborhoods of Staten Island where hyperlocal organizing processes were most pronounced. New Jersey, by comparison, is a state of small towns and home rule, despite its position as the most urbanized and densely populated state in the United States. These communities and neighborhoods all have their own distinct identities, cultures, and rhythms, which enabled the exploration of long-term recovery after disaster across multiple geographic and political boundaries and in different sociohistorical and cultural contexts. However, given the small size of these communities, a singular organizational study of a community at a particular point in time—such as the post-Katrina studies and analyses of Houston post-Harvey—was not feasible. Also, defining community boundaries through census data would have led to improper bounding. Many of the municipalities in the coastal New Jersey region analyzed contained only a single census tract and had a population of 8,000 people or less. Other communities of 6,000 or less residents might be included in census tracts with adjoining communities of widely varying demographics. In many of these communities, block-level data was nonexistent due to their small size, or they crossed one or more municipal boundaries. Census data in the coastal New Jersey region often diverged from census best practices, which stipulate that tracts and blocks correspond with jurisdictional or geographic boundaries, to enable comparisons over time.

These data challenges made it difficult to identify hidden pockets of residents and neighborhoods with high levels of unmet needs that could be correlated with demographic data to more precisely identify hyperlocal boundaries using the socio-economic characteristics of the community. In some instances, smaller communities did not qualify for nonprofit grants or interventions because the census data identified these communities as wealthy or upper-middle income, despite large pockets of senior citizens and middle-income first-time home buyers whose needs were obscured by wealthy neighborhoods across the river or bay. Local community and nonprofit leaders would then work on a case-by-case, neighborhood-by-neighborhood basis to meet resident, neighborhood, and community needs. These organizing activities might start in one community but would typically cross multiple political jurisdictions and geographic boundaries as the recovery processed.[2]

BOUNDING THE STUDY

Geographic bounding rather than a sampling frame was used to bound the study. Geographic bounding situates the study within a region undergoing complex environmental change. It provides a way of linking salient communication, organizing, and geographic phenomena with impacted communities, organizations, and residents across political and administrative jurisdictions. This type of bounding is especially important when it comes to suburban, exurban, and rural regions in which organizational density may be much lower than what would be found in more densely populated areas impacted by disaster. In a place like New Jersey, with highly decentralized political and administrative jurisdictions and a tradition of home rule, geographic bounding more accurately captures nongovernmental organizational processes.

Community or place is not just an administrative jurisdiction or a location with shared cultural norms and history. Traditional notions of the community may often isolate a study to a specific place and time. New Orleans in 2005, Joplin, Missouri, in 2011, Houston in 2017, Lake Charles, Louisiana, in 2020–2021 all represent specific geographic and political entities that can be economically, socially, politically, culturally, and organizationally analyzed as discrete units impacted by a particular disaster. Neighborhood-level studies may also follow this approach where the characteristics and social behaviors of the neighborhood may be the focal point of an ethnographic study or survey analysis. However, overlapping political and social processes may be lost and broader patterns of IORs missed by the granular focus of these types of studies. Placing singular communities within a broader region with common geographic features and boundaries makes it possible to explore a larger set of government-society relationships that shape the organizational processes and landscapes of post-disaster recovery. Geographic bounding does not exclude the importance of political and administrative processes in a post-disaster study or a study of complex environmental change. Rather, it highlights the salience of social and political processes in economic and organizational life.[3]

DATA COLLECTION

Sequential interviewing complements geographic bounding since both methods help avoid false inferences that can be made through random sampling frames that may draw artificial boundaries that may not be truly representative of the community or organizing processes under study. Sequential interviewing allows unknown social and organizational processes to emerge, rather than predefining these processes through artificial boundaries. It provides a way of directly connecting participants' insights, experiences, and knowledge to emerging theories generated from the empirical data. Sequential interviewing also attends to the local histories and cultures participants may be embedded in, or knowledge they hold. In sequential interviewing, data and insights generated from one interview guide the development of subsequent interviews throughout the study.[4]

What makes sequential interviewing specifically compelling for multi-methods disaster research is that the insights generated from interviews can be combined with organizational data such as rosters, agendas, meeting minutes, media reporting, and observations collected throughout the study to shape insights and research questions. Sequential interviewing can also help with the collection and management of perishable data, a significant challenge in disaster research. In the social sciences, "perishable data" refers to information and insights generated by a disaster that are accessible only for a limited period. Originally framed as issues relating to physical processes disrupted by storms, earthquakes, and fire, perishable data is also an issue in the social and organizational sciences. Emergent behaviors and hyperlocal organizing are rapidly moving processes in which only traces of organizational data may be physically or digitally left behind. Focused, semi-structured interviews can play an important role in piecing together data from documents, observation, news stories, social media, and websites to build a conceptual map of organizing and long-term recovery processes after disaster.[5]

Interview participants in sequential interviewing are selected based on their ability to provide new information and geographic perspectives, or to deepen knowledge related to a salient concept or theory in disaster research. Each interview equals one case, and interviews are sequentially linked over time and in a bounded geographic space. Just as one Hardy Boys or Nancy Drew book equals one case in an extended series of cases that can be rooted locally in Bayport or River Heights and extend to far-flung places (and over time from 1927 to the present day), sequential interviews are treated as a series of cases that comprise a unified story about a process, event, or location. In this study, the story was about how long-term recovery after a disaster unfolded over time (a temporal event), in coastal New Jersey (location or place), and the role that hyperlocal organizing (a process) plays in post-disaster recovery.

Interview participants were chosen based on their ability to (a) identify new organizations or municipalities, (b) identify new processes or mechanisms of post-disaster organizing, (c) identify new data or data sources and/or make them accessible, and (d) engage with participants whose knowledge may be useful for exploring theoretical concepts such as emergence or organizing. The Staten Island interviews, focus groups, and observations, though representing a separate study with distinct goals, provided insights for developing interview questions that addressed the concept of emergence and hyperlocal organizing in coastal New Jersey. There were two differences in the studies, though the concept of hyperlocal organizing became visible in each of them. The Staten Island study examined information ecosystems in disaster response and short-term recovery, while the coastal New Jersey study focused on networked stakeholders in long-term recovery. While neither study was designed to look at emergence or grassroots organizing, let alone hyperlocal organizing, a theory of hyperlocal organizing began to emerge from my analysis of the data and interviews.

Theoretical development is a strength of sequential interviewing, like other strands of qualitative inquiry that use data generation and empirical evidence to build explanations and theories. Similar to grounded theory (or more specifically, socially constructivist grounded theory), sequential interviewing attains theoretical saturation at both the end point of a study and the beginnings of theory construction. Theoretical saturation is the point at which a concept, idea, or data has been exhausted and there are no new insights to be mined. With sequential interviewing, insights, knowledge, and inferences gained from one interview are laid down as a stepping stone. Slowly, the path toward conceptualizing and understanding hyperlocal organizing was built across years, cases, and studies.[6]

Theoretical saturation in this study was reached when data and stories about emergent and pop-up organizations from interview participants began covering the same ground as previous interviews. At the point of saturation, no new or unique patterns of organizational partnering or IORs could be identified. In the field study of long-term recovery in coastal New Jersey, issues related to the allocation and sequencing of funding, organizational entrance and exit, conflict over case management processes, and types of organizational relationships were raised in earlier participant-observer activities and interviews. These earlier findings were used to guide the final round of interviews in 2017 and extend the field research into the southernmost counties in the study area in 2016 and 2017.

Sequential interviewing proved particularly fruitful in the latter stages of the study, as new organizations were interviewed and the study pushed further south. These late-stage interviews confirmed previous research that revealed the patterns and heterogeneity of the IORs enacting post-disaster recovery after Hurricane Sandy. These interviews and related organizational documents (at least, what were still available and accessible five years or more after the storm) told a similar story. They highlighted the slow and then rapid withdrawal of organizations from the recovery network, leading to the disappearance of emergent, pop-up organizations from long-term recovery. Final stage interviews in the southern region of the study area also confirmed previous findings; the organizational partnerships and recovery networks extended across multiple municipal and county jurisdictions. Certain organizations operated throughout the region or expanded operations into new areas of as other organizations withdrew.

COASTAL NEW JERSEY DATA COLLECTION

Organizations and municipalities were selected for inclusion in interviews (*n* = 38, 1,855.43 minutes of audio recording; M = 51.5, SD = 25.8) through a combination of participant-observation, archival research, web research, and sequential interviewing. Organizational leaders were asked to identify organizations with which they interacted during long-term recovery and to suggest additional organizations to include in this project. The interviews and information obtained from volunteer meetings and activities guided each subsequent set of interviews to develop a broader picture of organizations operating at different levels within the research site. Organizations were also identified from rosters, meeting minutes and agendas, as well as participation in meetings and workshops. Documents collected included binders of organizational materials from fiscal agents involved in the recovery, and personal and organizational notebooks from the lead organizer for a networked grassroots organization with regional and national reach. I also obtained agendas, rosters, and meeting minutes from different organizations interviewed, and communication and marketing collateral collected at different events.

Interviews can be categorized into first and second waves. First-wave interviews included interviews with businesses and Chamber of Commerce leaders in Asbury Park, New Jersey, and Southern Ocean County, as part of a pilot investigation into business and community response and recovery after Hurricane Sandy. Most of these interviews took place between December 2012 and March 2013 and built on findings from previous post-Katrina research in New Orleans by Dr. Marya L. Doerfel. Asbury Park and Southern Ocean County were chosen because they could be categorized as distinct communities in hard-hit areas. During this first round of interviews, communities like Sea Bright, Ortley Beach, and the northern barrier beaches of Ocean County were mostly closed due to the physical and geological devastation of the storm. A New Jersey National Guardsmen returning from a post-storm mission to evacuate terminally ill and immobile patients from Sea Bright to nearby hospitals likened the navigation of Sea Bright in the first days after the storm to navigating in Iraq during the Second Gulf War.

Questions in this round of interviews focused mainly on emergency response and short-term recovery. A total of 567 minutes of audio were recorded (n = 16, M = 35.4, SD = 18.8). Initial interview participants were identified through canvassing business districts, attending recovery meetings, name generator questionnaires, and snowball sampling. After this first wave of interviews, subsequent interviews took place mostly within the plural and public sectors. Second-wave interview questions related to organizational relationships, communication practices, and processes of long-term recovery within the plural and public sectors. Second-round interviews took place in 2016 and 2017 in the coastal New Jersey area, and a total of 1,288 minutes of interviews were recorded (n = 22, M = 64.4, SD = 23.3). The first set of second-wave interviews was conducted in 2016 with two alternative disaster relief organizations. The first round of questions was about the relationships between municipalities and alternative disaster relief organizations. Data from those two interviews helped shape subsequent interviews and guide my thinking on the loose connections between different organizations and organizational roles engaged in recovery.

First-wave interviews provided a framework from which to think about geographically bounding all or part of the coastal New Jersey area as a unit of analysis. Except for extended power outages and heavy damage to the boardwalk and adjacent buildings, Asbury Park escaped relatively unscathed compared to adjoining communities. The Southern Ocean County interviews revealed the difficulty of bounding a community study in New Jersey. Just a few smaller communities were impacted, and there were stark differences in impact, visibility, and media coverage of bayside and oceanside communities. These findings guided me to move on from Asbury Park as a possible community-level unit of analysis and to start thinking of Southern Ocean County as embedded within a larger unit of recovery. The Southern Ocean findings paralleled my observations as a volunteer and community leader in Monmouth County. These data and observations then led to the framing of the primary study as a geographic unit of analysis centered on coastal New Jersey.

New York City

Staten Island and Brooklyn Data Collection

Field and survey research was conducted in Brooklyn and Staten Island between May and August 2014 as part of a study of information and media ecosystems sponsored by Internews. Four focus groups in total were held (two each in Brooklyn and Staten Island, n = 36 participants), five interviews were held with New York City policymakers, and ten interviews (five in each borough) were held with community leaders. The author led the Staten Island portion of the study and interviewed five community leaders and six leaders active in hyperlocal organizing in the borough. Focus group participants were selected from the survey through a question about whether participants were willing to be contacted for further research. Interview participants were organizational leaders (from both established and emergent organizations) suggested by the project sponsor, organizations identified in the focus groups, and snowball sampling.

A survey (n = 749) of all Staten Island residents and of Brooklyn residents who lived within one mile of the water's edge was conducted by Rutgers Eagleton Institute of Politics in spring of 2014, before the field research team entered the communities. The survey and field research project was funded by Internews and the field research team did not have an opportunity to participate in survey design or question development. Four questions directly related to organizational assistance were included in the survey, and those questions are listed below.

Given the low (16.18 percent) response rate of participants answering survey questions related to organizational information (n = 121), survey data related to sources of organizational information cannot be used to make statistically valid inferences. Rather, the survey data was used to guide question development for focus groups and interviews. Comparatively, questions related to trust in media and information sources had a near 100 percent response rate (use and trust of media and information in Hurricane Sandy response was the primary purpose of the study). The higher response rates for these questions may be due to the design of the survey, as survey fatigue may have suppressed response rates to questions about organizational assistance. The trust questions were in the first third of the survey, immediately after participant qualification and questions about sources of information accessed by participants after Sandy. Questions about sources of assistance came toward the end of the survey, just before a broad set of demographic questions. The survey designers also didn't distinguish between material, financial, and informational assistance when asking about assistance received or requested. Specific questions asking residents what sources of assistance they received from which types of organizations included the following:

- Help was received from local faith-based organizations like churches, synagogues, or charities.
- Help was received from local grassroots or citizen organizations such as human services, local welfare agencies, or small community-led groups.
- Help was received from national nonprofit organizations like the American Red Cross or the Salvation Army.

While the survey was not designed to ask about local sources of assistance, the questions related to sources of local assistance provided an opportunity to explore how impacted residents drew on organizations for information and assistance in their neighborhoods and boroughs. Combined with data from focus groups and interviews, a picture of local and hyperlocal assistance on Staten Island began to emerge that complemented the field research underway in coastal New Jersey.

NOTES

1. Stefan Timmermans and Iddo Tavory, "Theory Construction in Qualitative Research: From Grounded Theory to Abductive Analysis," *Sociological Theory* 30, no. 3 (September 2012): 167–86, https://doi.org/10.1177/0735275112457914; Mario Luis Small, *Unanticipated Gains: Origins of Network Inequality on Everyday Life* (Oxford: Oxford University Press, 2009); Greg Oulahen, Brennan Vogel, and Chris Gouett-Hanna, "Quick Response Disaster Research: Opportunities and Challenges for a New Funding Program," *International Journal*

of Disaster Risk Science 11, no. 5 (October 2020): 568–77, https://doi.org/10.1007/s13753
-020-00299-2.

2. Alan J. Karcher, *New Jersey's Multiple Municipal Madness* (Piscataway, NJ: Rutgers
University Press, 1998); "Glossary: Census Tract," *United States Census Bureau* (blog), n.d.,
https://www.census.gov/programs-surveys/geography/about/glossary.html#par_textimage
_13.

3. Judith Ennew, *The Western Isles Today* (Cambridge: Cambridge University Press,
1980); Tom Piazza, *Why New Orleans Matters* (New York: HarpersCollins Publishers, 2005);
John Charles Morris et al., *The Case for Grassroots Collaboration: Social Capital and Ecosystem
Restoration at the Local Level* (Lanham, MD: Lexington Books, 2013).

4. Mario Luis Small, "'How Many Cases Do I Need?': On Science and the Logic of Case
Selection in Field-Based Research," *Ethnography* 10, no. 1 (March 2009): 5–38, https://doi
.org/10.1177/1466138108099586; Small, *Unanticipated Gains.*

5. Jc Gaillard and Christopher Gomez, "Post-Disaster Research: Is There Gold Worth the
Rush?," *Jàmbá: Journal of Disaster Risk Studies* 7, no. 1 (February 27, 2015): 6pp, https://doi
.org/10.4102/jamba.v7i1.120; Jc Gaillard and Lori Peek, "Disaster-Zone Research Needs a
Code of Conduct," *Nature* 575, no. 7783 (November 21, 2019): 440–42, https://doi.org/10
.1038/d41586-019-03534-z.

6. Kathy Charmaz, "Grounded Theory as an Emergent Method," *Handbook of Emergent Methods* (2008): 155–70; Kathy Charmaz, "Teaching Theory Construction with Initial
Grounded Theory Tools: A Reflection on Lessons and Learning," *Qualitative Health Research*
25, no. 12 (2015): 1610–22; Kathy Charmaz, "The Power of Constructivist Grounded
Theory for Critical Inquiry," *Qualitative Inquiry* (July 25, 2016), https://doi.org/10.1177
/1077800416657105.

Appendix B

CODING AND ANALYSIS

Data was combined from three different studies to develop a picture of an organizational landscape of recovery between 2012 and 2020, following a natural hazards event in the mid-Atlantic region of the United States. Two of the studies included field research with interviews (n = 38, n = 10), focus groups (n = 4), and participant observation, while the third study analyzed web-based communication to categorize the organizational activities of disaster recovery organizations activities in the region. Organizational documents, website descriptions, government, and media reports were collected, and descriptive survey results were provided for the second, limited-scope field research project. The analysis involved qualitative, network, and quantitative approaches.

Qualitative approaches included first and cycle second coding to analyze interview and focus group data, which was used to guide subsequent interview questions and data analysis over the course of the field research. Network analysis used interview, observational, and archival data, including organizational documents from participating individuals and organizations. These networks mapped interorganizational relationships between response and recovery organizations active in the region. Analytical and theoretical memos were developed at multiple stages of the research process and incorporated qualitative, quantitative, and network data from the field research. These memos then guided empirical analysis and theory construction over the course of the projects.[1]

Coding of Qualitative Data

A three-column table was created in Microsoft Word for each typed transcript (n = 38). The transcript language was arranged in rows in the first column. The second column contained in vivo codes representing the specific language used by participants to describe organizational activities, processes, and relationships, as well as ideas or reflections about the organization's participation in post-Sandy response and recovery partnerships. Process codes used gerunds to describe actions that people, and organizations used for communication, organizing, and other necessary activities. Process coding is particularly useful for organizational and interorganizational analysis because it identifies actions or activities engaged in by the organization.

Coding was lumped—rather than assigning a code for every line in a transcript as would be done in a classic grounded theory study, multiple codes were developed for the communication and organizing activities associated with long-term recovery after a disaster. Code lumping is particularly suited for process coding as it captures the cyclical nature of the coding process and facilitates the linking of ideas and activities across interviews, data sets, organizations, and communities. Second cycle coding used analytic and theoretical memos to support the abductive theorizing and sequential interviewing parts of the research process. It also explored themes, processes, ideas, and codes raised during field research and qualitative coding. Themes developed with these memos include Bayside vs. Oceanside, Hidden Pockets [of recovery], Isolation, and Abandonment, Timelines and Processes of Recovery, and Networks of Recovery.

Coding of Organizations

Throughout my fieldwork, organization names were extracted from the interview data and added to a list of organizations previously identified through fieldwork, archival data, and media sources. This aggregation process created a more rigorously bounded network. Early conversations and interviews provided anecdotal information of 240 different organizations participating in the initial long-term recovery meetings in the coastal New Jersey study area. However, I was able to confirm only 178 organizations through multisource data collection and interviews. Only organizations that were named in interviews, rosters, sign-up sheets, agendas, meetings, or organizational documents were included as part of the coastal New Jersey recovery network.

Organizations were initially coded as plural- (e.g., nonprofits, nongovernmental organizations, unions, social enterprises), public- (e.g., government agencies and public-sector organizations), and private-sector (i.e., for-profit firms) organizations. Organizations were then coded by type based on their mission and institutional logic, and by organizational activities. Assigned organizational typologies included Fiscal Agent, Coordinating Agency, Faith-Based Organization, National Government Agency, State Government Agency, County Government Agency, Foundation, Funding Agency, National-Nonprofit, International NGO, Nonprofits-Housing &

Rebuilding, Nonprofits-Mental Health & Human Services, Nonprofits-Arts, and Emergent. Codes for organizational activities included coordination, community-based resource coordination, case management, emotional and spiritual support, shelter, and rebuilding. Finally, organizations were coded as having a primary disaster response and recovery phase, or a secondary response and recovery phase. Within these categories, organizations were coded as emergency response (1) or long-term recovery (2). This coding also served as the basis for network analysis. These organizations and their associated codes were used to create network matrixes in Excel that were analyzed in UCINET.[2]

NETWORK ANALYSIS (COASTAL NEW JERSEY)

Network analysis was conducted for organizations active in long-term recovery in coastal New Jersey between 2012 and 2017 (*n* = 178) in UCINET by using the list of organizations and their associated roles identified through the data collection and coding process. Network analysis relied on the geographic bounding of the coastal New Jersey region, consisting of all or parts of six counties between New York Harbor in the North and Delaware Bay to the southwest. Network ties were undirected and measured as simple connections based on meeting attendance, shared event participation, and resource or information provision and coded as a one or zero (the presence or absence of network ties). Strong and weak ties were not measured because consistent data on the frequency of meetings or the importance of ties between organizations was not able to be collected. Network density and centrality and degree of centrality were the main network measures that resulted from this network analysis.[3]

I defined the project's analysis through the lens of reflexive methodology and qualitative inquiry because, while a significant amount of empirical evidence was collected over the five-year field research period and the broader eight-year study period, data was not collected through a random sampling frame in a bounded or unbounded network related to the post-Sandy recovery process, or through a traditional network survey using name generation. Data collection occurred in waves, rather than at specific time intervals over the five-year period. So, while the data revealed significant changes in the coastal New Jersey recovery period over time, measurement of these changes at precise moments in time in order to analyze the network longitudinally and confirm statistical significance was not feasible.

SURVEY ANALYSIS

Exploratory data analysis of the Eagleton Institute of Politics and Associated Press-National Opinion Research (AP-NORC) post-Sandy surveys commissioned by Internews was conducted in SPSS using univariate and multivariate analysis. Additive indexes were constructed to create four independent variables and one dependent variable. Indexes were constructed that represented hyperlocal organizing at the associational level (combining questions on assistance from local organizations and faith-based organizations), and the communal level (combining questions on neighborhood level assistance, assistance from friends and family, and emergent organizing). The community recovery index—the dependent variable—represented questions concerning respondents' perceptions of the state and level of recovery in their homes and neighborhoods.[4]

The AP-NORC data set is nationally representative, drawn from 2,025 residents impacted by Hurricane Sandy in all five boroughs of New York City and impacted areas of New Jersey and Long Island. The AP-NORC survey had two main goals: (1) assess the impact of Sandy and the state of recovery six months after impact, and (2) understand the relationship of neighborhood and social characteristics to recovery and resilience. The EIP data set of 749 individuals included residents of Staten Island and those who lived within one mile of the water in Brooklyn.

A FINAL NOTE ON FINDINGS AND MULTI-METHODS, REFLEXIVE RESEARCH

Findings from the survey data did not provide statistical support for the salience of associational (R^2 = .36) or communal (R^2 .53) ties in community recovery. Empirical data from field research, however, supported the salience of communication and organizing activities in community response and recovery. Network analysis showed a loosely connected network in coastal New Jersey in 2012; 178 organizations with a 3.5 percent network density evolved into a tightly connected network in 2017 of only four organizations with 100 percent network density, meaning that all organizations still active in 2017 were connected to each other. Of the top twenty-five organizations by network degree centrality—importance of the organization to the network in terms of connections to other organizations—seven were emergent organizations.

The divergence between the surveys conducted by Eagleton and AP-NORC, the empirical data generated from the field research, and the network analysis point to the importance of immersive multi-methods field research for studying organizations after a disaster. Disasters disrupt and reconfigure social systems and interorganizational relationships. Recovery processes unfold over years, meaning organizational and fiscal data from hyperlocal organizations and long-term recovery groups are typically not archived or centralized. Post-disaster data management is sorely lacking at the local and county levels and remains an important area of future exploration for possible policy reform.[5]

NOTES

1. Jonny Saldaña, *The Coding Manual for Qualitative Researchers* (London: SAGE Publications Ltd, 2016); Betina Hollstein, "Mixed Methods Social Networks Research: An

Introduction," in *Mixed Methods Social Network Research: Design and Application*, ed. Silvia Dominguez and Betina Hollstein, Structural Analysis in the Social Sciences (New York: Cambridge University Press, 2014), 373.

2. S.P. Borgatti and L.C. Freeman, *Ucinet for Windows: Software for Social Network Analysis* (Harvard, MA: Analytic Technologies, 2002).

3. Betina Hollstein, "Qualitative Approaches," in *The SAGE Handbook of Social Network Analysis* (London: SAGE Publications LTD, 2011), 404–16.

4. Rebecca M. Warner, *Applied Statistics: From Bivariate Through Multivariate Techniques: From Bivariate Through Multivariate Techniques* (SAGE, 2013).

5. Jc Gaillard and Christopher Gomez, "Post-Disaster Research: Is There Gold Worth the Rush?," *Jàmbá: Journal of Disaster Risk Studies* 7, no. 1 (February 27, 2015): 6pp, https://doi.org/10.4102/jamba.v7i1.120; Jc Gaillard and Lori Peek, "Disaster-Zone Research Needs a Code of Conduct," *Nature* 575, no. 7783 (November 21, 2019): 440–42, https://doi.org/10.1038/d41586-019-03534-z; Ann L. Cunliffe and Geetha Karunanayake, "Working Within Hyphen-Spaces in Ethnographic Research: Implications for Research Identities and Practice," *Organizational Research Methods* 16, no. 3 (July 2013): 364–92, https://doi.org/10.1177/1094428113489353; Paul Hibbert et al., "Relationally Reflexive Practice: A Generative Approach to Theory Development in Qualitative Research," *Organizational Research Methods* 17, no. 3 (July 2014): 278–98, https://doi.org/10.1177/1094428114524829; Andreas Wald, "Triangulation and Validity of Network Data," in *Mixed Methods Social Network Research*, ed. Silvia Dominguez and Betina Hollstein (New York: Cambridge University Press, 2014), 373.

REFERENCES

Borgatti, S. P., and L.C. Freeman. *Ucinet for Windows: Software for Social Network Analysis*. Harvard, MA: Analytic Technologies, 2002.

Cunliffe, Ann L., and Geetha Karunanayake. "Working Within Hyphen-Spaces in Ethnographic Research: Implications for Research Identities and Practice." *Organizational Research Methods* 16, no. 3 (July 2013): 364–92. https://doi.org/10.1177/1094428113489353.

Gaillard, Jc, and Christopher Gomez. "Post-Disaster Research: Is There Gold Worth the Rush?" *Jàmbá: Journal of Disaster Risk Studies* 7, no. 1 (February 27, 2015): 6 pages. https://doi.org/10.4102/jamba.v7i1.120.

Gaillard, Jc, and Lori Peek. "Disaster-Zone Research Needs a Code of Conduct." *Nature* 575, no. 7783 (November 21, 2019): 440–42. https://doi.org/10.1038/d41586-019-03534-z.

Hibbert, Paul, John Sillince, Thomas Diefenbach, and Ann L. Cunliffe. "Relationally Reflexive Practice: A Generative Approach to Theory Development in Qualitative Research." *Organizational Research Methods* 17, no. 3 (July 2014): 278–98. https://doi.org/10.1177/1094428114524829.

Hollstein, Betina. "Mixed Methods Social Networks Research: An Introduction." In *Mixed Methods Social Network Research: Design and Application*, edited by Silvia Dominguez and Betina Hollstein, 373. Structural Analysis in the Social Sciences. New York: Cambridge University Press, 2014.

———. "Qualitative Approaches." In *The SAGE Handbook of Social Network Analysis*, 404–16. London: SAGE Publications LTD, 2011.

Saldaña, Jonny. *The Coding Manual for Qualitative Researchers*. London: SAGE Publications Ltd, 2016.

Wald, Andreas. "Triangulation and Validity of Network Data." In *Mixed Methods Social Network Research*, edited by Silvia Dominguez and Betina Hollstein, 373. New York: Cambridge University Press, 2014.

Warner, Rebecca M. *Applied Statistics: From Bivariate Through Multivariate Techniques: From Bivariate Through Multivariate Techniques*. SAGE, 2013.

References

"2019 Trade Statistics." New York: Port Authority of New York and New Jersey, 2020.

"2020 U.S. Billion-Dollar Weather and Climate Disasters in Historical Context | NOAA Climate.Gov." Accessed September 27, 2021. https://www.climate.gov/news-features/blogs/beyond-data/2020-us-billion-dollar-weather-and-climate-disasters-historical.

"2022–2026 FEMA Strategic Plan Building the FEMA Our Nation Needs and Deserves." Washington D.C.: Federal Emergency Management Agency, 2021. 2022–2026 FEMA Strategic Plan Building the FEMA our Nation Needs and Deserves.

Aakhus, Mark, and Michael Bzdak. "Stakeholder Engagement as Communication Design Practice: Stakeholder Engagement." *Journal of Public Affairs* 15, no. 2 (May 2015): 188–200. https://doi.org/10.1002/pa.1569.

Adams, James Luther. *Voluntary Associations.* Chicago: Exploration Press; Chicago Theological Association, 1986.

Agarwal, Sheetal D., W. Lance Bennett, Courtney N. Johnson, and Shawn Walker. "A Model of Crowd Enabled Organization: Theory and Methods for Understanding the Role of Twitter in the Occupy Protests." *International Journal of Communication* 8 (February 14, 2014): 27.

Airriess, Christopher A., Wei Li, Karen J. Leong, Angela Chia-Chen Chen, and Verna M. Keith. "Church-Based Social Capital, Networks and Geographical Scale: Katrina Evacuation, Relocation, and Recovery in a New Orleans Vietnamese American Community." *Geoforum* 39, no. 3 (May 2008): 1333–46. https://doi.org/10.1016/j.geoforum.2007.11.003.

Aldrich, Daniel P. *Black Wave: How Networks and Governance Shaped Japan's 3/11 Disasters.* Chicago and London: University of Chicago Press, 2019.

———. *Building Resilience: Social Capital in Post-Disaster Recovery.* Chicago, IL: University of Chicago Press, 2012.

Aldrich, Daniel P., and Michelle A. Meyer. "Social Capital and Community Resilience." *American Behavioral Scientist* 59, no. 2 (February 2015): 254–69. https://doi.org/10.1177/0002764214550299.

"American Red Cross Governance for the 21st Century: A Report to the Board of Governors." Washington, DC: The American Red Cross, October 2006.

Ansell, Chris, and Alison Gash. "Collaborative Governance in Theory and Practice." *Journal of Public Administration Research and Theory: J-PART* 18, no. 4 (2008): 543–71.

Atkins, Katie. "Nearly 1,200 Buildings in the Keys Were Destroyed by Hurricane Irma." *Miami Herald.* December 3, 2017, sec. Florida Keys. http://www.miamiherald.com/news/local/community/florida-keys/article187816479.html.

Banerjee, Bobby, and Diane-Laure Arjaliès. "Celebrating the End of Enlightenment: Organization Theory in the Age of the Anthropocene and Gaia (and Why Neither Is the Solution to Our Ecological Crisis)." *Organization Theory*, 2021. https://doi.org/10.1177/26317877211036714

Bennett, W. Lance, and Alexandra Segerberg. *The Logic of Connective Action: Digital Media and the Personalization of Contentious Politics.* Cambridge University Press, 2013.

Bimber, Bruce, Andrew J. Flanagin, and Cynthia Stohl. *Collective Action in Organizations: Interaction and Engagement in an Era of Technological Change.* New York: Cambridge University Press, 2012.

Bliss, Laura. "After Florence, the Gullah Could Face New Threats." *Bloomberg CityLab* (blog), September 15, 2018. https://www.bloomberg.com/news/articles/2018-09-15/hurricane-florence-threatens-the-gullahs-of-south-carolina.

Bonanno, George A. "Loss, Trauma, and Human Resilience: Have We Underestimated the Human Capacity to Thrive after Extremely Aversive Events?" *American Psychologist* 59, no. 1 (2004): 20–28. https://doi.org/10.1037/0003-066X.59.1.20.

Bonanno, George A., Sandrao Galea, Angela Bucciarelli, and David Vlahov. "What Predicts Psychological Resilience after Disaster? The Role of Demographics, Resources, and Life Stress." *Journal of Consulting and Clinical Psychology* 75, no. 5 (2007): 671–82. https://doi.org/10.1037/0022-006S.75.5.671.

Bondesson, Sara. "Vulnerability and Power: Social Justice Organizing in Rockaway, New York City after Hurricane Sandy." Dissertation, Uppsala University, 2017. http://uu.diva-portal.org/smash/record.jsf?pid=diva2%3A1084218&dswid=8530.

Borgatti, S. P. "Centrality and Network Flow." *Social Networks* 27, no. 1 (January 2005): 55–71. https://doi.org/10.1016/j.socnet.2004.11.008.

Borgatti, S. P., Martin G. Everett, and Jeffrey C. Johnson. *Analyzing Social Networks.* SAGE, 2013.

Borgatti, S. P., and L.C. Freeman. *Ucinet for Windows: Software for Social Network Analysis.* Harvard, MA: Analytic Technologies, 2002.

Borgatti, S. P., and Daniel S. Halgin. "On Network Theory." *Organization Science* 22, no. 5 (2011): 1168–81. https://doi.org/10.1287/orsc.1110.064.

Bosworth, Susan Lovegren, and Gary A. Kreps. "Structure as Process: Organization and Role." *American Sociological Review* 51, no. 5 (October 1986): 699. https://doi.org/10.2307/2095494.

Brinkley, Douglas. *The Great Deluge Hurricane Katrina, New Orleans, and the Mississippi Gulf Coast.* New York: Harper Perennial, 2006.

Browne, Katherine E. *Standing in the Need: Culture, Comfort, and Coming Home after Katrina.* Austin, TX: University of Texas Press, 2015.

Brunsma, David L., David Overfelt, and J. Steven Picou, eds. *The Sociology of Katrina: Perspectives on a Modern Catastrophe.* New York: Rowan & Littlefield Publishers Inc., 2007.

Bullard, Robert D., and Beverly Wright. "The Legacy of Bias: Hurricanes, Droughts, and Floods." In *The Wrong Complexion for Protection: How the Government Response to Disaster*

Endangers African American Communities, 47–72. New York and London: New York University Press, 2012.

Byrkjeflot, Haldor. "Nordic Management: From Functional Socialism to Shareholder Value?" In *The Northern Lights: Organization Theory in Scandinavia*, 471. Herndon, VA: Copenhagen Business School Press, 2003.

———. "The Nordic Model of Democracy and Management." In *The Democratic Challenge to Capitalism: Management and Democracy in the Nordic Countries*, edited by Haldor Byrkjeflot, Sissel Myklebust, Christine Myrvang, and Francis Sejersted. Bergen: Fagbokforlager Vigmostad & Bjorke AS, 2001.

Browne, Katherine E. *Standing in the Need: Culture, Comfort, and Coming Home after Katrina.* Austin, TX: University of Texas Press, 2015.

Bullard, Robert D., and Beverly Wright. "The Legacy of Bias: Hurricanes, Droughts, and Floods." In *The Wrong Complexion for Protection: How the Government Response to Disaster Endangers African American Communities*, 47–72. New York and London: New York University Press, 2012.

Burt, Ronald S. "The Network Structure of Social Capital." *Research in Organizational Behavior* 22 (2000): 345–423.

Busch, Nathan E, and Austen D. Givens. "Achieving Resilience in Disaster Management: The Role of Public-Private Partnerships." *Journal of Strategic Security* 6, no. 2 (2013): 1–19.

Buzzanell, Patrice. "Resilience: Talking, Resisting, and Imagining New Normalcies into Being." *Journal of Communication* 60, no. 1 (2010): 1–14.

CAL FIRE August 22, 2022 Stats and Events, https://www.fire.ca.gov/stats-events/

Capelotti, P.J. Chief Petty Officer. *Rouge Wave: The U.S. Coast Guard on and after 9/11.* Washington, DC: U.S. Coast Guard Historians Office, 2003.

Carley, Kathleen. "Extracting Culture through Textual Analysis." *Poetics* 22, no. 4 (June 1994): 291–312.

Carley, Kathleen, and Michael Palmquist. "Extracting, Representing, and Analyzing Mental Models." *Social Forces* 70, no. 3 (March 1992): 601. https://doi.org/10.2307/2579746.

Carley, Kathleen M., and David S. Kaufer. "Semantic Connectivity: An Approach for Analyzing Symbols in Semantic Networks." *Communication Theory* 3, no. August (1993): 183–213.

Carlson, Elizabeth J., Marshall Scott Poole, Natalie J. Lambert, and John C. Lammers. "A Study of Organizational Reponses to Dilemmas in Interorganizational Emergency Management." *Communication Research* 44, no. 2 (January 6, 2016): 0093650215621775. 287–315. https://doi.org/10.1177/0093650215621775.

Chamlee-Wright, Emily, and Virgil Henry Storr. "'There's No Place Like New Orleans': Sense of Place and Community Recovery in the Ninth Ward After Hurricane Katrina." *Journal of Urban Affairs* 31, no. 5 (December 2009): 615–34. https://doi.org/10.1111/j.1467-9906.2009.00479.x.

Charmaz, Kathy. "Grounded Theory as an Emergent Method." In *Handbook of Emergent Methods*, 155–70, 2008.

———. "Teaching Theory Construction with Initial Grounded Theory Tools: A Reflection on Lessons and Learning." *Qualitative Health Research* 25, no. 12 (2015): 1610–22.

———. "The Power of Constructivist Grounded Theory for Critical Inquiry." *Qualitative Inquiry* 23, no. 1 (2017). https://doi.org/10.1177/1077800416657105.

Chandrasekhar, Divya, Yang Zhang, and Yu Xiao. "Nontraditional Participation in Disaster Recovery Planning: Cases from China, India, and the United States." *Journal of the*

American Planning Association 80, no. 4 (October 2, 2014): 373–84. https://doi.org/10.1080/01944363.2014.989399.

Chewning, Lisa V., Chih-Hui Lai, and Marya L. Doerfel. "Organizational Resilience and Using Information and Communication Technologies to Rebuild Communication Structures." *Management Communication Quarterly* 27, no. 2 (2013): 237–63. https://doi.org/10.1177/0893318912465815.

Clarkson, Max B. E. "A Stakeholder Framework for Analyzing and Evaluating Corporate Social Performance." *The Academy of Management Review* 20, no. 1 (January 1995): 92. https://doi.org/10.2307/258888.

Coleman, James S. "Social Capital in the Creation of Human Capital." *American Journal of Sociology* 94 (January 1, 1988): S95–120. https://doi.org/10.1086/228943.

Collins, Thomas H. "Change and Continuity—The U.S. Coast Guard Today." *Naval War College Review* 57, no. 2 (Spring 2004): 2–19.

Community Empowerment (Scotland) Act 2015 (2015). https://www.legislation.gov.uk/asp/2015/6/contents/enacted.

"Community Energy: State of the Sector Report 2021." Community Energy England, Wales, and Scotland, 2021.

Cooper, Terry L., Thomas A. Bryer, and Jack W. Meek. "Citizen-Centered Collaborative Public Management." *Public Administration Review* 66 (2006): 76–88.

Cooren, Francois, Timothy R. Kuhn, J. P. Cornelissen, and T. Clark. "Communication, Organizing and Organization: An Overview and Introduction to the Special Issue." *Organization Studies* 32, no. 9 (September 1, 2011): 1149–70. https://doi.org/10.1177/0170840611410836.

Cornelissen, Joep P., Rodolphe Durand, Peer C. Fiss, John C. Lammers, and Eero Vaara. "Putting Communication Front and Center in Institutional Theory and Analysis." *Academy of Management Review* 40, no. 1 (January 1, 2015): 10–27. https://doi.org/10.5465/amr.2014.0381.

Crane, Andrew, Dirk Matten, and Jeremy Moon. "Stakeholders as Citizens? Rethinking Rights, Participation, and Democracy." *Journal of Business Ethics* 53, no. 1–2 (2004): 107–22.

Cuervo, Isabel, Les Leopold, and Sherry Baron. "Promoting Community Preparedness and Resilience: A Latino Immigrant Community–Driven Project Following Hurricane Sandy." *American Journal of Public Health* 107, no. S2 (September 2017): S161–64. https://doi.org/10.2105/AJPH.2017.304053.

Cunliffe, Ann L., and Geetha Karunanayake. "Working Within Hyphen-Spaces in Ethnographic Research: Implications for Research Identities and Practice." *Organizational Research Methods* 16, no. 3 (July 2013): 364–92. https://doi.org/10.1177/1094428113489353.

Czarniawska, Barbara. "Complex Organizations Still Complex." *International Public Management Journal* 10, no. 2 (2007): 137–51.

———. "Organizations as Obstacles to Organizing." In *Organizations and Organizing: Materiality, Agency, and Discourse*, edited by Daniel Robichaud and Francois Cooren, 4–22. New York: Routledge, 2013.

Dahlen, Øystein Pedersen, and Helge Skirbekk. "How Trust Was Maintained in Scandinavia through the First Crisis of Modernity." *Corporate Communications: An International Journal* 26, no. 1 (January 1, 2021): 23–39. https://doi.org/10.1108/CCIJ-01-2020-0036.

Deetz, Stanley A. "Corporate Governance, Communication, And Getting Social Values into The Decisional Chain." *Management Communication Quarterly* 16, no. 4 (May 2003): 606–11. https://doi.org/10.1177/0893318902250236.

———. *Democracy in an Age of Corporate Colonization: Developments in Communication and the Politics of Everyday Life.* Albany, NY: State University of New York Press, 1992.

———. "Generative Democracy and the Collaborative Turn: The Hope for Quality Public and Organizational Decision Making." Presented at the New Jersey Communication Association Annual Conference, Lakewood, NJ, March 2017.

———. *Transforming Communication Transforming Business: Building Responsive and Responsible Workplaces.* Cresskill, NJ: Hampton Press Inc, 1995.

Deetz, Stanley A., and Lisa Irvin. "Governance, Stakeholder Involvement and New Communication Models." In *Governance Reform under Real-World Conditions: Citizens, Stakeholders, and Voice*, edited by Sina Odugbemi and Thomas Jacobson. Washington, DC: World Bank Publications, 2008.

Deneen, Patrick J., and Susan J. McWilliams. "A Better Sort of Love." In *The Democratic Soul: A Wilson Carey McWilliams Reader*, edited by Patrick J. Deneen and Susan J. McWilliams, 1–18. Lexington: The University Press of Kentucky, 2011.

Diani, Mario. *The Cement of Civil Society: Studying Networks in Localities.* New York: Cambridge University Press, 2015.

Dickman, Kyle. "The Future of Disaster Relief Isn't the Red Cross," August 25, 2016. https://www.outsideonline.com/2106556/team-rubicon-takes-red-cross.

DiMaggio, Paul J., and Walter W. Powell. "Introduction." In *The New Institutionalism in Organizational Analysis*, 1–38. Chicago: University of Chicago Press, 1991.

"Disaster Recovery: FEMA Needs to Assess Its Effectiveness in Implementing the National Disaster Recovery Framework." U.S. Government Accountability Report, May 2016.

Doerfel, Marya L, Chih-Hui Lai, and Lisa V Chewning. "The Evolutionary Role of Interorganizational Communication: Modeling Social Capital in Disaster Contexts." *Human Communication Research* 36, no. 2 (2010): 125–62. https://doi.org/10.1111/j.1468-2958.2010.01371.x.

Doerfel, Marya L., and Jack L. Harris. "Resilience Processes." In *The International Encyclopedia of Organizational Communication*, edited by C.R. Scott and Laurie Lewis. Hoboken, NJ: Wiley-Blackwell, 2017.

Doerfel, Marya L, Lisa V. Chewning, and Chih-Hui Lai. "The Evolution of Networks and the Resilience of Interorganizational Relationships after Disaster." *Communication Monographs* 80, no. 4 (2013): 533–59. https://doi.org/10.1080/03637751.2013.828157.

Doerfel, Marya L., and Maureen Taylor. "The Story of Collective Action: The Emergence of Ideological Leaders, Collective Action Network Leaders, and Cross-Sector Network Partners in Civil Society." *Journal of Communication* 67, no. 1 (2017): 920–43. https://doi.org/10.1111/jcom.12340.

Doerfel, Marya L, and Muge Haseki. "Networks, Disrupted: Media Use as an Organizing Mechanism for Rebuilding." *New Media & Society* 17, no. 3 (2013): 432–52. https://doi.org/10.1177/1461444813505362.

Domínguez, Daniela G., Dellanira García, David A. Martínez, and Belinda Hernandez-Arriaga. "Leveraging the Power of Mutual Aid, Coalitions, Leadership, and Advocacy during COVID-19." *American Psychologist* 75, no. 7 (October 2020): 909–18. https://doi.org/10.1037/amp0000693.

Drabek, Thomas E. "Community Processes: Coordination." In *Handbook of Disaster Research*, 217–33, 2007.

Drabek, Thomas E., and David A. McEntire. "Emergent Phenomena and the Sociology of Disaster: Lessons, Trends, and Opportunities from the Research Literature." *Disaster Prevention and Management* 12, no. 2 (2003): 97–112. https://doi.org/10.1108/09653560310474214.

Dunham, Laura, R. Edward Freeman, and Jeanne Liedtka. "Enhancing Stakeholder Practice: A Particularized Exploration of Community." *Business Ethics Quarterly* 16, no. 1 (2006): 23–42.

Elliot, James R., and Jeremey Pais. "Race, Class, and Hurricane Katrina: Social Differences in Response to Disaster." *Social Science Research* 35 (2006): 295–321.

Elliott, Justin, and Jesse Eisinger. "How Fear of Occupy Wall Street Undermined the Red Cross' Sandy Relief Effort." *ProPublica.* December 11, 2014. https://www.propublica.org/article/how-fear-of-occupy-wall-street-undermined-the-red-cross-sandy-relief-effort.

Elliot, Justin, and Justin Eisinger. "PR Over People: The Red Cross' Secret Disaster." *Pro Publica*, October 29, 2014. https://www.propublica.org/article/the-red-cross-secret-disaster.

Elliott, Justin, Jessica Huseman, and Decca Muldowney. "Texas Official After Harvey: The 'Red Cross Was Not There.'" *ProPublica*, October 2017. https://www.propublica.org/article/texas-official-after-harvey-the-red-cross-was-not-there.

Ennew, Judith. *The Western Isles Today.* Cambridge: Cambridge University Press, 1980.

Federal Emergency Management Agency (FEMA). *Lessons from Community Recovery: Seven Years of Emergency Support Function #14, Long-Term Recovery from 2004 to 2011.* Washington, DC: Department of Homeland Security, April 2012.

———. *National Disaster Recovery Framework.* Washington, DC: Department of Homeland Security, September 2011.

———. *National Disaster Recovery Framework*, 2nd ed. Department of Homeland Security, June 2016.

———. *National Response Framework.* Washington, DC: Department of Homeland Security, January 2008.

———. *National Response Framework*, 2nd ed. Washington, DC: Department of Homeland Security, May 2013. http://www.fema.gov/media-library-data/20130726-1914-25045-1246/final_national_response_framework_20130501.pdf.

———. "Recovery Federal Interagency Operational Plan," August 2016.

Feuer, Alan. "Where FEMA Fell Short, Occupy Sandy Was There." *The New York Times*, November 9, 2012. http://www.nytimes.com/2012/11/11/nyregion/where-fema-fell-short-occupy-sandy-was-there.html.

Freeman, John H., and Pino G. Audia. "Community Ecology and the Sociology of Organizations." *Annual Review of Sociology* 32, no. 1 (August 2006): 145–69. https://doi.org/10.1146/annurev.soc.32.061604.123135.

Freeman, R. Edward. *Strategic Management: A Stakeholder Approach.* Marshfield, MA: Pitman Publishing, 1984.

Freeman, R. Edward, Jeffrey S. Harrison, Andrew C. Wicks, Bidhan L. Parmar, and Simone de Colle. *Stakeholder Theory: The State of the Art.* Cambridge, UK: Cambridge University Press, 2010.

Freeman, R. Edward, Robert Phillips, and Rajendra Sisodia. "Tensions in Stakeholder Theory." *Business & Society* 59, no. 2 (February 2020): 213–31. https://doi.org/10.1177/0007650318773750.

Freeman, R. Edward, and Sergiy Dmytriyev. "Corporate Social Responsibility and Stakeholder Theory: Learning From Each Other." *Symphonya. Emerging Issues in Management* 1 (2017): 7–15. https://doi.org/10.4468/2017.1.02freeman.dmytriyev.

Friedland, Lewis A. "Networks in Place." *American Behavioral Scientist* 60, no. 1 (2016): 24–42. https://doi.org/10.1177/0002764215601710.

Gaillard, Jc, and Lori Peek. "Disaster-Zone Research Needs a Code of Conduct." *Nature* 575, no. 7783 (November 21, 2019): 440–42. https://doi.org/10.1038/d41586-019-03534-z.

Gaillard, Jc, and Christopher Gomez. "Post-Disaster Research: Is There Gold Worth the Rush?" *Jàmbá: Journal of Disaster Risk Studies* 7, no. 1 (February 27, 2015): 6pp. https://doi.org/10.4102/jamba.v7i1.120.

Gaillard, Jc, and Lori Peek. "Disaster-Zone Research Needs a Code of Conduct." *Nature* 575, no. 7783 (November 21, 2019): 440–42. https://doi.org/10.1038/d41586-019-03534-z.

Ganesh, Shiv, and Cynthia Stohl. "Community Organizing, Social Movements, and Collective Action." In *The SAGE Handbook of Organizational Communication*, 3rd ed., 743–66. Thousand Oaks, CA: Sage, 2014.

García-López, Gustavo A. "The Multiple Layers of Environmental Injustice in Contexts of (Un)Natural Disasters: The Case of Puerto Rico Post-Hurricane Maria." *Environmental Justice* 11, no. 3 (June 2018): 101–8. https://doi.org/10.1089/env.2017.0045.

Garriga-López, Adriana Maí. "Compounded Disasters: Puerto Rico Confronts COVID-19 under US Colonialism." *Social Anthropology* (June 3, 2020): 1469-8676.12821. https://doi.org/10.1111/1469-8676.12821.

Goffman, E. *Behavior in Public Places: Notes on the Social Organization of Gathering*. New York: Free Press, 1963.

Graff, Garret M. "Escape From New York the Great Maritime Rescue of Lower Manhattan on 9/11." *New York Magazine*, September 11, 2021. https://nymag.com/intelligencer/2021/09/the-great-maritime-rescue-of-lower-manhattan-on-9-11.html.

Hagen, Ryan. "Acts of God, Man, and System: Knowledge, Technology, and the Construction of Disaster." In *Critical Disaster Studies*, edited by Jacob A.C. Remes and Andy Horowitz, 32–50. University of Pennsylvania Press, 2021.

Harris, Jack L., and Marya L. Doerfel. "Interorganizational Resilience: Networked Collaboration in Communities after Disasters." In *Social Network Analysis of Disaster Response, Recovery, and Adaptation*, edited by E.C. Jones, and A.J. Faas, 1st ed. London: Elsevier, 2017.

Harris, Margaret, Duncan Shaw, Judy Scully, Chris M. Smith, and Graham Hieke. "The Involvement/Exclusion Paradox of Spontaneous Volunteering: New Lessons and Theory From Winter Flood Episodes in England." *Nonprofit and Voluntary Sector Quarterly* 46, no. 2 (April 2017): 352–71. https://doi.org/10.1177/0899764016654222

Hartman, Chester, and Gregory D. Squires, eds. *There Is No Such Thing As A Natural Disaster: Race, Class, and Hurricane Katrina*. New York: Routledge; Taylor & Francis Group, 2006.

Herr, Alexandria. "'Solidarity, Not Charity': Mutual Aid Groups Are Filling Gaps in Texas' Crisis Response." *Grist*, February 26, 2021. https://grist.org/justice/solidarity-not-charity-mutual-aid-groups-are-filling-gaps-in-texas-crisis-response/.

Hibbert, Paul, John Sillince, Thomas Diefenbach, and Ann L. Cunliffe. "Relationally Reflexive Practice: A Generative Approach to Theory Development in Qualitative Research." *Organizational Research Methods* 17, no. 3 (July 2014): 278–98. https://doi.org/10.1177/1094428114524829.

Hoffman, Matthew. "Why Community Ownership? Understanding Land Reform in Scotland." *Land Use Policy* 31, no. March (2013): 289–97.

Hollstein, Betina. "Mixed Methods Social Networks Research: An Introduction." In *Mixed Methods Social Network Research: Design and Application*, edited by Silvia Dominguez and Betina Hollstein, 373. Structural Analysis in the Social Sciences. New York: Cambridge University Press, 2014.

———. "Qualitative Approaches." In *The SAGE Handbook of Social Network Analysis*, 404–16. London: SAGE Publications LTD, 2011.

Homeland Security Operational Analysis Center. "Hurricanes Irma and Maria: Impact and Aftermath." Accessed September 27, 2021. https://www.rand.org/hsrd/hsoac/projects/puerto-rico-recovery/hurricanes-irma-and-maria.html.

hooks, bell. *Belonging: A Culture of Place*. New York: Routledge, 2009.

Horowitz, Andy. *Katrina: A History, 1915-2015*. Harvard University Press, 2020.

"Hurricane Sandy Rebuilding Strategy." Hurricane Sandy Rebuilding Task Force (U.S. Department of Housing and Urban Development), August 2013.

IDMC. "Behind the Numbers: The Shadow of 2010's Earthquake Still Looms Large in Haiti." Accessed September 27, 2021. https://www.internal-displacement.org/expert-opinion/behind-the-numbers-the-shadow-of-2010s-earthquake-still-looms-large-in-haiti.

Internews. "Information Ecosystems in Action: New York." *Internews*, November 2014. http://www.internews.org/sites/default/files/resources/Internews_Information_Ecosystems_in_Action-NewYork.pdf.

Islands (Scotland) Act 2018 (2018). https://www.legislation.gov.uk/asp/2018/12/contents.

Jackson, Gregory, and Richard Deeg. "From Comparing Capitalisms to the Politics of Institutional Change." *Review of International Political Economy* 15, no. 4 (October 27, 2008): 680–709. https://doi.org/10.1080/09692290802260704.

Kaltenbrunner, Katharina, and Birgit Renzl. "Social Capital in Emerging Collaboration Between NPOs and Volunteers: Performance Effects and Sustainability Prospects in Disaster Relief." *VOLUNTAS: International Journal of Voluntary and Nonprofit Organizations* 30, no. 5 (October 2019): 976–90. https://doi.org/10.1007/s11266-019-00123-6.

Kapucu, Naim, Tolga Arslan, and Matthew Lloyd Collins. "Examining Intergovernmental and Interorganizational Response to Catastrophic Disasters: Toward a Network Centered Approach." *Administration & Society* 42, no. 2 (April 2010): 222–47. https://doi.org/10.1177/0095399710362517.

Kapucu, Naim, and Qian Hu. "Understanding Multiplexity of Collaborative Emergency Management Networks." *The American Review of Public Administration* 46, no. 4 (October 23, 2014): 399–417. https://doi.org/10.1177/0275074014555645.

Karcher, Alan J. *New Jersey's Multiple Municipal Madness*. Piscataway, NJ: Rutgers University Press, 1998.

Karunarathne, Ananda Y. and Douglas R. Gress. "The Role of Organizational Networks in Ameliorating Flood Disaster Impacts: A Case Study of Flood Inundated Rural and Urban Areas in Sri Lanka." *International Journal of Risk Reduction* 71, no. 2022 (2022): 1–15. https://doi.org/10.1016/j.ijdrr.2022.102819.

Katz, J., M. Barris, and A. Jain. *The Social Media President: Barack Obama and the Politics of Digital Engagement*. Springer, 2013.

Katz, Vikki S., and Keith N. Hampton. "Communication in City and Community: From the Chicago School to Digital Technology." *American Behavioral Scientist* 60, no. 1 (2016): 3–7.

Kendra, James, and Tricia Wachtendorf. *American Dunkirk: The Waterborne Evacuation of Manhattan on 9/11*. Philadelphia, PA: Temple University Press, 2016.

Kim, Minkyung, Melanie Kwestel, Hyunsook Youn, Justine Quow, and Marya L. Doerfel. "Serving the Vulnerable While Being Vulnerable: Organizing Resilience in a Social Welfare Sector." *Nonprofit and Voluntary Sector Quarterly*, Online First (2021). https://doi.org/0.1177/0899764021103912.

Kishore, Nishant, Domingo Marqués, Ayesha Mahmud, Mathew V. Kiang, Irmary Rodriguez, Arlan Fuller, Peggy Ebner, et al. "Mortality in Puerto Rico after Hurricane Maria." *New England Journal of Medicine* 379, no. 2 (July 12, 2018): 162–70. https://doi.org/10.1056/NEJMsa1803972.

Kluckow, Richard. "The Impact of Heir Property on Post-Katrina Housing Recovery in New Orleans." Thesis, Colorado State University, 2014.

Knowles, Scott Gabriel, and Zachary Loeb. "The Voyage of the Paragon: Disaster as Method." In *Critical Disaster Studies*, edited by Jacob A.C. Remes and Andy Horowitz, 11–31. University of Pennsylvania Press, 2021.

Kosar, Kevin R. "The Congressional Charter of the American National Red Cross: Overview, History, and Analysis." Congressional Research Service, The Library of Congress, March 15, 2006. http://oai.dtic.mil/oai/oai?verb=getRecord&metadataPrefix=html&identifier =ADA462052.

Kranich, Nancy. "Civic Partnerships: The Role of Libraries in Promoting Civic Engagement." *Resource Sharing & Information Networks* 18, no. 1–2 (August 10, 2005): 89–103. https:// doi.org/10.1300/J121v18n01_08.

Kranich, Nancy, and Jorge Reina Schement. "Information Commons." *Annual Review of Information Science and Technology* 42, no. 1 (2008): 546–91.

Kravitz, Derek. "Red Cross 'Failed for 12 Days' After Historic Louisiana Floods." *ProPublica*, October 3, 2016. https://www.propublica.org/article/red-cross-failed-for-12-days-after -historic-louisiana-floods.

Kreps, Gary A. "Disaster, Organizing, and Role Enactment: A Structural Approach." *American Journal of Sociology* 99, no. 2 (September 1993): 428–63.

———. "Sociological Inquiry and Disaster Research." *Annual Review of Sociology* 10 (1984): 309–30.

Kreps, Gary A., and Susan Lovegren Bosworth. "Organizational Adaptation to Disaster." In *Handbook of Disaster Research*, 297–315. New York: Springer-Verlag, 2007.

Kroll-Smith, Steve, Vern Baxter, and Pam Jenkins. *Left to Chance: Hurricane Katrina and the Story of Two New Orleans Neighborhoods*. Austin, TX: University of Texas Press, 2015.

Kroll-Smith, Steve, Vern Baxter, and Pam Jenkins. *Left to Chance: Hurricane Katrina and the Story of Two New Orleans Neighborhoods*. Austin, TX: University of Texas Press, 2015.

Kuhn, Timothy R. "A Communicative Theory of the Firm: Developing an Alternative Perspective on Intra-Organizational Power and Stakeholder Relationships." *Organization Studies* 29, no. 8–9 (August 1, 2008): 1227–54. https://doi.org/10.1177/0170840608094778.

Kvasny, Lynette, Nancy Kranich, and Jorge Reina Schement. "Communities, Learning, and Democracy in the Digital Age." In *Learning in Communities*, 41–44. Springer, 2009. http://link.springer.com/chapter/10.1007/978-1-84800-332-3_9.

Lai, Chih-Hui, Chen-Chao Tao, and Yu-Chung Cheng. "Modeling Resource Network Relationships between Response Organizations and Affected Neighborhoods after a Technological Disaster." *Voluntas* 28, 2145–2175 (2017). https://doi.org/10.1007/s11266 -017-9887-4.

Lai, Chih-Hui, and Ying-Chia Hsu. "Understanding Activated Network Resilience: A Comparative Analysis of Co-Located and Co-Cluster Disaster Response Networks." *Journal of Contingencies and Crisis Management* 27, no. 1 (January 2019): 14–27. https://doi.org/10 .1111/1468-5973.12224.

Lammers, John C. "How Institutions Communicate: Institutional Messages, Institutional Logics, and Organizational Communication." *Management Communication Quarterly* 25, no. 1 (February 1, 2011): 154–82. https://doi.org/10.1177/0893318910389280.

Lammers, John C., and Joshua B. Barbour. "An Institutional Theory of Organizational Communication." *Communication Theory* 16, no. 3 (2006): 356–77. https://doi.org/10.1111/j .1468-2885.2006.00274.x.

Laplume, André O., Karan Sonpar, and Reginald A. Litz. "Stakeholder Theory: Reviewing a Theory That Moves Us." *Journal of Management* 34, no. 6 (December 2008): 1152–89. https://doi.org/10.1177/0149206308324322.

Lin, Nan. "Building a Network Theory of Social Capital." In *Social Capital: Theory and Research*, edited by Nan Lin, Karen Cook, and Ronald S. Burt, 3–29. Sociology and Economics: Theory and Research. Hawthorne, NY: Aldine de Gruyter, 2001.

Logan, Nneka. "A Theory of Corporate Responsibility to Race (CRR): Communication and Racial Justice in Public Relations." *Journal of Public Relations Research* 33, no. 1 (February 16, 2021): 6–22. https://doi.org/10.1080/1062726X.2021.1881898.

MacDonald, Adriane, Amelia Clarke, and Lei Huang. "Multi-Stakeholder Partnerships for Sustainability: Designing Decision-Making Processes for Partnership Capacity." *Journal of Business Ethics* 160, no. 2 (2019): 409–426.

Majchrzak, A., S. L. Jarvenpaa, and A. B. Hollingshead. "Coordinating Expertise among Emergent Groups Responding to Disasters." *Organization Science* 18, no. 1 (2007): 147–61.

Marques, José Carlos, and Henry Mintzberg. "Why Corporate Social Responsibility Isn't a Piece of Cake." *MIT Sloan Management Review* 56, no. 4 (2015): 7–11.

Mathie, Alison, and Gord Cunningham. "From Clients to Citizens: Asset-Based Community Development as a Strategy for Community-Driven Development." *Development in Practice* 13, no. 5 (2003): 474–86.

Maxouris, Christina. "Here's Just How Bad the Devastating Australian Fires Are -- by the Numbers." *CNN*, January 6, 2020. https://www.cnn.com/2020/01/06/us/australian-fires -by-the-numbers-trnd/index.html.

McCambridge, Ruth. "As Storm Season Looms, Miami Drops Reliance on the Red Cross." *Nonprofit Quarterly*, June 6, 2018. https://nonprofitquarterly.org/2018/06/06/as-storm -season-looms-miami-drops-reliance-on-red-cross/.

McCarthy, Amy. "When Government Could Not, Mutual Aid Kept Texans' Needs Met Through Winter Storm Uri," February 22, 2021. https://houston.eater.com/22293485/ mutual-aid-groups-disaster-relief-texas-winter-storm-uri.

McWilliams, Wilson Carey. "Democracy and the Citizen: Community, Dignity, and the Crisis of Contemporary Politics in America." In *Redeeming Democracy in America*, edited by Patrick J. Deneen and Susan J. McWilliams, 9–28. Lawrence, KS: University Press of Kansas, 2011.

———. "In Good Faith: On the Foundations of American Politics." In *Redeeming Democracy in America*, edited by Patrick J. Deneen and Susan J. McWilliams, 107–26. Lawrence, KS: University Press of Kansas, 2011.

———. *The Idea of Fraternity in America*. Berkeley, CA: University of California Press, 1973.

———. "The Search for a Public Philosophy." In *The Democratic Soul: A Wilson Carey McWilliams Reader*, 336–52. Lexington: The University Press of Kentucky, 2011.

———. "Toward Genuine Self-Government." In *The Democratic Soul: A Wilson Carey McWilliams Reader*, edited by Patrick J. Deneen and Susan J. McWilliams, 353–60. Lexington: The University Press of Kentucky, 2011.

Mesure, Herve. "A Liberal Critique of the Corporation as Stakeholders." In *Stakeholder Theory: A European Perspective*, edited by Maria Bonnafous-Boucher and Yvon Pesquex, 185. New York: Palgrave MacMillan, 2005.

Miles, Samantha. "Stakeholder: Essentially Contested or Just Confused?" *Journal of Business Ethics* 108, no. 3 (July 2012): 285–98. https://doi.org/10.1007/s10551-011-1090-8.

———. "Stakeholder Theory Classification: A Theoretical and Empirical Evaluation of Definitions." *Journal of Business Ethics* 142 (2017): 437–59. https://doi.org/10.1007/s10551-015-2741-y.

Mintzberg, Henry. *Rebalancing Society: Radical Renewal beyond Left, Right, and Center.* Oakland, CA: Berrett-Koehler Publishers, 2015.

———. "Time for the Plural Sector." *Stanford Social Innovation Review* 13, no. 3 (2015): 28–33. https://doi.org/10.48558/0WX6-ZG74.

Mintzberg, Henry, Dror Etzion, and Saku Mantere. "Worldly Strategy for the Global Climate." *Stanford Social Innovation Review* 16, no. 4 (2018): 42–47.

Mintzberg, Henry, and Guilherme Azevedo. "Fostering 'Why Not?' Social Initiatives – beyond Business and Governments." *Development in Practice* 22, no. 7 (September 2012): 895–908. https://doi.org/10.1080/09614524.2012.696585.

Mintzberg, Henry, Rick Molz, Emmanuel Raufflet, Pamela Sloan, Chahrazed Abdallah, Rick Bercuvitz, and C. H. Tzeng. "The Invisible World of Association." *Leader to Leader* 2005, no. 36 (2005): 37–45. https://doi.org/10.1002/ltl.126.

Monge, Peter R., and Noshir S. Contractor. *Theories of Communication Networks.* New York: Oxford University Press, 2003.

Montano, Samantha. *Disasterology: Dispatches from the Frontlines of the Climate Crisis.* Toronto: Park Row Books, 2021.

Montano, Samantha, and Amanda Savitt. "Not All Disasters Are Disasters: Pandemic Categorization and Its Consequences." Social Science Research Council. *Items Insights from the Social Sciences* (blog), September 10, 2020. https://items.ssrc.org/covid-19-and-the-social-sciences/disaster-studies/not-all-disasters-are-disasters-pandemic-categorization-and-its-consequences/.

Morris, John Charles, William Allen Gibson, William Marshall Leavitt, and Shana Campbell Jones. *The Case for Grassroots Collaboration: Social Capital and Ecosystem Restoration at the Local Level.* Lanham, MD: Lexington Books, 2013.

Morris, Zachary A., R. Anna Hayward, and Yamirelis Otero. "The Political Determinants of Disaster Risk: Assessing the Unfolding Aftermath of Hurricane Maria for People with Disabilities in Puerto Rico." *Environmental Justice* 11, no. 2 (April 2018): 89–94. https://doi.org/10.1089/env.2017.0043.

Mulligan, Jessica M., and Adriana Garriga-López. "Forging *Compromiso* after the Storm: Activism as Ethics of Care among Health Care Workers in Puerto Rico." *Critical Public Health* 31, no. 2 (March 15, 2021): 214–25. https://doi.org/10.1080/09581596.2020.1846683.

National Voluntary Organizations Active in Disaster. "About Us." Organizational, November 13, 2018. https://www.nvoad.org/about-us/.

New Jersey Voluntary Organizations Active in Disaster (NJVOAD). "New Jersey Non-Profit Long-Term Recovery Assessment: Hurricane Sandy Recovery," October 28, 2016. http://www.njvoad.org/wp-content/uploads/2017/01/NJ-Non-Profit-Long-Term-Recovery-Assessment-print-version.pdf.

Nissen, Bruce, and Paul Jarley. "Unions as Social Capital: Renewal through a Return to the Logic of Mutual Aid?" *Labor Studies Journal* 29, no. 4 (2005): 1–26.

NOAA National Centers for Environmental Information (NCEI). "U.S. Billion-Dollar Weather and Climate Disasters (2021)," January 8, 2021. https://www.ncdc.noaa.gov/billions/.

Norman, Jesse. *Adam Smith: What He Thought and Why It Matters.* Milton Keynes, UK: Allen Lane, 2018.

"No Title? No Easy Access to Post-Katrina Aid." *All Things Considered*. NPR, April 28, 2008. https://www.npr.org/templates/story/story.php?storyId=90005954.

Ocasio, William, Jeffrey Loewenstein, and Amit Nigam. "How Streams of Communication Reproduce and Change Institutional Logics: The Role of Categories." *Academy of Management Review* 40, no. 1 (January 1, 2015): 28–48. https://doi.org/10.5465/amr.2013.0274.

Otsuyama, Kensuke, and Rajib Shaw. "Exploratory Case Study for Neighborhood Participation in Recovery Process: A Case from the Great East Japan Earthquake and Tsunami in Kesennuma, Japan." *Progress in Disaster Science* 9, no. January (2021). https://doi.org/10.1016/j.pdisas.2021.100141.

Oulahen, Greg, Brennan Vogel, and Chris Gouett-Hanna. "Quick Response Disaster Research: Opportunities and Challenges for a New Funding Program." *International Journal of Disaster Risk Science* 11, no. 5 (October 2020): 568–77. https://doi.org/10.1007/s13753-020-00299-2.

Palser, B. "The Hazards of Hyperlocal: Why Neighborhood News Online Is a Dicey Proposition." *American Journalism Review* 32, no. 32 (2010): 68–69.

Peck, Jamie, and Nik Theodore. "Variegated Capitalism." *Progress in Human Geography* 31, no. 6 (December 2007): 731–72. https://doi.org/10.1177/0309132507083505.

Perrow, Charles. "A Society of Organizations." *Theory and Society* 20, no. 6 (December 1991): 725–62. https://doi.org/10.1007/BF00678095.

Pfeffer, Jeffrey, and Gerald R. Salancik. *The External Control of Organizations*. New York: Harper & Row, 1978.

Phillips, Robert, R. Edward Freeman, and Andrew C. Wicks. "What Stakeholder Theory Is Not." *Business Ethics Quarterly* 13, no. 4 (October 2003): 479–502. https://doi.org/10.5840/beq200313434.

Piazza, Tom. *Why New Orleans Matters*. New York: HarpersCollins Publishers, 2005.

Porter, A. J. "Emergent Organization and Responsive Technologies in Crisis: Creating Connections or Enabling Divides?" *Management Communication Quarterly* 27, no. 1 (February 1, 2013): 6–33. https://doi.org/10.1177/0893318912459042

Porter, Michael E., and Mark Kramer. "Creating Shared Value." *Harvard Business Review* 89, no. 1/2 (January-February 2011): 62–77.

Presser, Lizzie. "Their Family Bought Land One Generation After Slavery: The Reels Brothers Spent Eight Years in Jail for Refusing to Leave It." *ProPublica*, July 15, 2019. https://features.propublica.org/black-land-loss/heirs-property-rights-why-black-families-lose-land-south/.

Putnam, Linda L., and Robert D. McPhee. "Theory Building: Comparisons of CCO Orientations." In *Building Theories of Organization: The Constitutive Role of Communication*, 187–205. New York: Routledge, 2009.

Putnam, Robert D. *Bowling Alone: The Collapse and Revival of American Community*. New York: Simon & Schuster, 2000.

Rhenman, Eric. *Industrial Democracy and Industrial Management*. London: Tavistock Publication Ltd., 1968.

Quarantelli, Enrico L. "Catastrophes Are Different from Disasters: Some Implications for Crisis Planning and Managing Drawn from Katrina." Social Science Research Council. *Items Insights from the Social Sciences* (blog), June 11, 2006. https://items.ssrc.org/understanding-katrina/catastrophes-are-different-from-disasters-some-implications-for-crisis-planning-and-managing-drawn-from-katrina/.

———. "Conventional Beliefs and Counterintuitive Realities." *Social Research* 75, no. 3 (Fall 2008): 873–904.

————. "The Earliest Interest in Disasters and Crises, and the Early Social Science Studies of Disasters, as Seen in a Sociology of Knowledge Perspective," 2009. http://udspace.udel.edu/handle/19716/5745.

Quarantelli, Enrico L., and Russell R. Dynes. "Response to Social Crisis and Disaster." *Annual Review of Sociology* 3, no. 1 (1977): 23–49.

Rennie, Frank. *The Changing Outer Hebrides: Galson and the Meaning of Place.* Stornoway, Isle of Lewis: Acair Books, 2020.

Rescue at Water's Edge: The U.S. Merchant Marine Response to 9/11. New York: U.S. Department of Transportation, 2011. https://youtu.be/yc66PsnXPoA.

Robert T. Stafford Disaster Relief and Emergency Assistance Act, Pub. L. No. 93–288, as amended, 42 42 U.S.C. 5121 et. seq., and Related Authorities (1988).

Rosenstein, Eddie. *BOATLIFT: An Untold Tale of 9/11 Resilience.* Brooklyn, NY: Eyepop Productions, 2011. https://www.youtube.com/watch?v=18lsxFcDrjo.

Rowe, Stephen C. "Toward a Postliberal Liberalism: James Luther Adams and the Need for a Theory of Relational Meaning." *American Journal of Theology & Philosophy* 17, no. 1 (January 1996): 51–70.

Rubin, Claire B. "Long Term Recovery from Disasters -- the Neglected Component of Emergency Management." *Journal of Homeland Security and Emergency Management* 46, no. 6 (2009): 1.

———— "Reflections on 40 Years in the Hazards and Disasters Community." *Journal of Homeland Security and Emergency Management* 12, no. 4 (January 1, 2015). https://doi.org/10.1515/jhsem-2015-0050.

————. "The Community Recovery Process in the United States after a Major Natural Disaster." *International Journal of Emergencies and Mass Disaster* 3, no. 2 (1985): 9–28.

Rubin, Claire B., and Susan L. Cutter. *U.S. Emergency Management in the 21st Century: From Disaster to Catastrophe.* New York: Routledge, 2020.

Saldaña, Jonny. *The Coding Manual for Qualitative Researchers.* London: SAGE Publications Ltd, 2016.

Sampson, Robert J. *Great American City: Chicago and the Enduring Neighborhood Effect.* University of Chicago Press, 2012.

Sanial, Gregory J. "The Response to Hurricane Katrina: A Study of the Coast Guard's Culture, Organizational Design & Leadership in Crisis." Masters of Management, Massachusetts Institute of Technology, 2007.

Saunders, Sarah Lee, and Gary A. Kreps. "The Life History of Emergent Organization in Times of Disaster." *The Journal of Applied Behavioral Science* 23, no. 4 (1987): 443–62.

Schenk, G. J. "Historical Disaster Research. State of Research, Concepts, Methods, and Case Studies." *Historical Social Research* 2007 (2007): 9–31.

Schoeneborn, Dennis, Timothy R. Kuhn, and Dan Kärreman. "The Communicative Constitution of Organization, Organizing, and Organizationality." *Organization Studies* 40, no. 4 (April 2019): 475–96. https://doi.org/10.1177/0170840618782284.

Scott, Dianne, and Catherine Oelofse. "Social and Environmental Justice in South African Cities: Including 'Invisible Stakeholders' in Environmental Assessment Procedures." *Journal of Environmental Planning and Management* 48, no. 3 (May 2005): 445–67. https://doi.org/10.1080/09640560500067582.

Selznick, Philip. "Institutionalism 'Old' and 'New.'" *Administrative Science Quarterly* 41, no. 2 (June 1996): 270. https://doi.org/10.2307/2393719.

Shier, Micheal L., and Femida Handy. "From Advocacy to Social Innovation: A Typology of Social Change Efforts by Nonprofits." *VOLUNTAS: International Journal of Voluntary and*

Nonprofit Organizations 26, no. 6 (December 2015): 2581–2603. https://doi.org/10.1007/s11266-014-9535-1.

Shumate, Michelle, and Katherine R. Cooper. *Networks for Social Impact.* New York: Oxford University Press, 2022.

Sillince, J. A. A. "Can CCO Theory Tell Us How Organizing Is Distinct from Markets, Networking, Belonging to a Community, or Supporting a Social Movement?" *Management Communication Quarterly* 24, no. 1 (February 1, 2010): 132–38. https://doi.org/10.1177/0893318909352022.

Simsa, Ruth, Paul Rameder, Anahid Aghamanoukjan, and Marion Totter. "Spontaneous Volunteering in Social Crises: Self-Organization and Coordination." *Nonprofit and Voluntary Sector Quarterly* 48, no. 2_suppl (April 2019): 103S–122S. https://doi.org/10.1177/0899764018785472.

Small, Mario Luis. "'How Many Cases Do I Need?': On Science and the Logic of Case Selection in Field-Based Research." *Ethnography* 10, no. 1 (March 2009): 5–38. https://doi.org/10.1177/1466138108099586.

———. *Unanticipated Gains: Origins of Network Inequality on Everyday Life.* Oxford: Oxford University Press, 2009.

Smith, Adam B. "U.S. Billion-Dollar Weather and Climate Disasters, 1980 - Present (NCEI Accession 0209268)." NOAA National Centers for Environmental Information, 2020. https://doi.org/10.25921/STKW-7W73.

Smith, Julian. "The Untold Story of Hurricane Harvey's First Urban Air Rescue Mission." *Esquire*, September 1, 2020. https://www.esquire.com/news-politics/a33611137/hurricane-harvey-coast-guard-rescue/.

"Social Enterprise in Scotland: Census 2017." Community Enterprise in Scotland, 2017. https://socialenterprise.scot/files/4de870c3a3.pdf.

Son, Joonmo, and Nan Lin. "Social Capital and Civic Action: A Network-Based Approach." *Social Science Research* 37, no. 1 (March 2008): 330–49. https://doi.org/10.1016/j.ssresearch.2006.12.004.

Soto, Isa Rodríguez. "Mutual Aid and Survival as Resistance in Puerto Rico: Faced with an Onslaught of Disasters, Government Mismanagement of Life-Threatening Crises, and the Injustices of Colonialism, Puerto Rican Communities Have Bet on Their Own Survival. Their Mutual Aid Efforts Testify to Both the Power of Grassroots Organizing and the Scale of State Neglect." *NACLA Report on the Americas* 52, no. 3 (July 2, 2020): 303–8. https://doi.org/10.1080/10714839.2020.1809099.

Sprain, Leah, and David Boromisza-Habashi. "Meetings: A Cultural Perspective." *Journal of Multicultural Discourses* 7, no. 2 (July 2012): 179–89. https://doi.org/10.1080/17447143.2012.685743.

Springer, Simon. "Caring Geographies: The COVID-19 Interregnum and a Return to Mutual Aid." *Dialogues in Human Geography* 10, no. 2 (July 2020): 112–15. https://doi.org/10.1177/2043820620931277.

Stallings, Robert A., and E. L. Quarantelli. "Emergent Citizen Groups and Emergency Management." *Public Administration Review* 45 (January 1985): 93. https://doi.org/10.2307/3135003.

Starbuck, William H. "Karl E. Weick and the Dawning Awareness of Organized Cognition." *Management Decision* 53, no. 6 (July 13, 2015): 1287–99. https://doi.org/10.1108/MD-04-2014-0183.

Staten Island Advance. "4 Bridges Connect Staten Island to the Rest of The World." March 4, 2019. https://www.silive.com/guide/2012/04/4_bridges_connect_staten_island_to_the_rest_of_the_world.html.

Strand, Robert. "Scandinavian Stakeholder Thinking: Seminal Offerings from the Late Juha Näsi." *Journal of Business Ethics* 127, no. 1 (March 2015): 89–105. https://doi.org/10.1007/s10551-013-1793-0.

Strand, Robert, and R. Edward Freeman. "Scandinavian Cooperative Advantage: The Theory and Practice of Stakeholder Engagement in Scandinavia." *Journal of Business Ethics* 127, no. 1 (March 2015): 65–85. https://doi.org/10.1007/s10551-013-1792-1.

———. *Unanticipated Gains: Origins of Network Inequality on Everyday Life*. Oxford: Oxford University Press, 2009.

Strandh, Veronica, and Niklas Eklund. "Emergent Groups in Disaster Research: Varieties of Scientific Observation over Time and across Studies of Nine Natural Disasters." *Journal of Contingencies and Crisis Management* 26, no. 3 (2017): 1–9.

Taylor, J.R. "Organization as an (Imbricated) Configuring of Transactions." *Organization Studies* 32, no. 9 (September 1, 2011): 1273–94. https://doi.org/10.1177/0170840611411396.

"Texas Organizers Discuss Mutual Aid Responses to Storm." *It's Going Down*. Pacifica Radio Network: 94.1 KPFA, March 12, 2021. https://kpfa.org/episode/its-going-down-march-12-2021/.

The 9/11 Boat Rescue That Saved Half a Million People | I Was There. Vice Productions, 2021. https://youtu.be/XyS-tYoOj6g.

"The Ins and Outs of NYC Commuting: An Examination of Recent Trends and Characteristics of Commuter Exchanges between NYC and the Surrounding Metro Region." New York City Department of Planning, September 2019.

The Land Reform (Scotland) Act 2003 (2003). https://www.legislation.gov.uk/asp/2003/2/contents.

"The Resilient Social Network: @OccupySandy #SuperstormSandy." RP12-01.04.11-01. Falls Church, VA: Department of Homeland Security, Science and Technology Directorate, Homeland Security Studies and Analysis Institute, September 30, 2013. http://homelandsecurity.org/docs/the%20resilient%20social%20network.pdf.

Tierney, Kathleen J. "From the Margins to the Mainstream: Disaster Research at the Crossroads." *Annual Review of Sociology* 33, no. 2007 (2007): 503–25.

Timmermans, Stefan, and Iddo Tavory. "Theory Construction in Qualitative Research: From Grounded Theory to Abductive Analysis." *Sociological Theory* 30, no. 3 (September 2012): 167–86. https://doi.org/10.1177/0735275112457914.

Tocqueville, Alexis de. *Democracy in America*. Edited by Harvey C. Mansfield and Winthrop. Chicago, IL: University of Chicago Press, 2000.

Tufekci, Zeynep. *Twitter and Tear Gas: The Power and Fragility of Networked Protest*. New Haven and London: Yale University Press, 2017.

Twarog, Evan Cadet. "Hurricane Ready: Coast Guard Adapts to the Social Media Storm." *Proceedings of the U.S. Naval Institute* 144, no. 10 (October 2018). https://www.usni.org/magazines/proceedings/2018/october/hurricane-ready-coast-guard-adapts-social-media-storm.

Twigg, John, and Irina Mosel. "Emergent Groups and Spontaneous Volunteers in Urban Disaster Response." *Environment and Urbanization* 29, no. 2 (October 2017): 443–58. https://doi.org/10.1177/0956247817721413.

United States Census Bureau. "Glossary: Census Tract," n.d. https://www.census.gov/programs-surveys/geography/about/glossary.html#par_textimage_13.

Varda, Danielle M., Rich Forgette, David Banks, and Noshir Contractor. "Social Network Methodology in the Study of Disasters: Issues and Insights Prompted by Post-Katrina

Research." *Population Research and Policy Review* 28, no. 1 (February 2009): 11–29. https://doi.org/10.1007/s11113-008-9110-9.

Wailoo, Keith, Karen M. O'Neill, Jeffrey Dowd, and Roland Anglin, eds. *Katrina's Imprint: Race and Vulnerability in America*. New Brunswick, NJ: Rutgers University Press, 2010.

Wald, Andreas. "Triangulation and Validity of Network Data." In *Mixed Methods Social Network Research*, edited by Silvia Dominguez and Betina Hollstein, 373. New York: Cambridge University Press, 2014.

Wan, William. "Haiti's Long, Terrible History of Earthquakes and Disaster." *Washington Post*, August 14, 2021. Accessed September 27, 2021. https://www.washingtonpost.com/history/2021/08/14/haiti-earthquake-last-one/.

Wang, Rong, Katherine R. Cooper, and Michelle Shumate. "Alternatives to Collective Impact: The Community Systems Solutions Framework." *Stanford Social Innovation Review*, Winter 2020. https://ssir.org/articles/entry/community_system_solutions_framework_offers_an_alternative_to_collective_impact_model.

Warner, Rebecca M. *Applied Statistics: From Bivariate Through Multivariate Techniques: From Bivariate Through Multivariate Techniques*. SAGE, 2013.

Wasserman, Stanley, and Katherine Faust. *Social Network Analysis Methods and Applications*. Cambridge: Cambridge University Press, 1994.

Weber, Klaus, and Mary Ann Glynn. "Making Sense with Institutions: Context, Thought and Action in Karl Weick's Theory." *Organization Studies* 27, no. 11 (November 2006): 1639–60. https://doi.org/10.1177/0170840606068343.

Weick, K. "Enacted Sensemaking in Crisis Situations [1]." *Journal of Management Studies* 25, no. 4 (1988): 305–17.

———. *Sensemaking in Organizations*. Thousand Oaks, CA: SAGE Publications, Inc, 1995.

———. "The Collapse of Sensemaking in Organizations: The Mann Gulch Disaster." *Administrative Science Quarterly* 38 (1993): 628–52.

Weick, Karl E., and Kathleen M. Sutcliffe. *Managing the Unexpected: Assuring High Performance in an Age of Complexity*. San Francisco: Jossey-Bass, 2001.

Weick, Karl E., Kathleen M. Sutcliffe, and David Obstfeld. "Organizing and the Process of Sensemaking." *Organization Science* 16, no. 4 (August 2005): 409–21. https://doi.org/10.1287/orsc.1050.0133.

Weiss, Kenneth A. "Clearing Title in Katrina's Wake." *Probate and Property* (October 2006).

Wells, Chris. *The Civic Organization and the Digital Citizen: Communicating Engagement in a Networked Age*. Oxford University Press, 2015.

Wilhoit, Elizabeth D. "Space, Place, and the Communicative Constitution of Organizations: A Constitutive Model of Organizational Space." *Communication Theory* 28, no. 3 (August 1, 2018): 311–31. https://doi.org/10.1093/ct/qty007.

———. "Where Is an Organization? How Workspaces Are Appropriated to Become (Partial and Temporary) Organizational Spaces." *Management Communication Quarterly* 34, no. 3 (August 2020): 299–327. https://doi.org/10.1177/0893318920933590.

Wilhoit, Elizabeth D., and Lorraine G. Kisselburgh. "Collective Action Without Organization: The Material Constitution of Bike Commuters as Collective." *Organization Studies* 36, no. 5 (May 2015): 573–92. https://doi.org/10.1177/0170840614556916.

Index

abandonment, 3, 89, 100
abductive theorizing, 113–14
access, 34–35, 93, 97, 104, 108
Adams, James Luther, 75
adaptability, 57–59
advocacy, 91, 95–97
African Americans/Black people, 2–3, 42–44
Alabama, 58
Amberjack V (boat), 55
analysis, 94, 116, 129–30
Anglo-American. *See* Western society
Annexes, FEMA, 39, 47
AP-NORC. *See* Associated Press-National Opinion Research
Ardolino, Vincent, 55
assessment, 7, 10–11, 25–26, 39, 93, 98–101
Associated Press-National Opinion Research (AP-NORC), 129–30
associational ties, 13, 103–4, 107
Atlantic County, New Jersey, 90

backbone organizations, 48, 100
bike commuters, 29–30, 81
Black people/African Americans, 2–3, 42–44
boats, 9, 55–58, 62–63
Bobbi (faith-based organization leader), 81
"boots on the ground" perspective, 97
Bosworth, Susan Lovegren, 36–38, 47, 94

bounding, geographical, 119–20
Brexit, 35, 65, 83n1
Brooklyn, New York, 55, 66–68, 99–100, 101n4, 115, 123–24
Browne, Katherine E., 10
BurgerBiz (restaurant), 26–27
Burners without Borders, 8, 64, 89
burnout, 95–96
businesses, local, 25–27

Cajun Navy, 62–63
California, 2
Cambridge Analytica, 65
capitalism, 79
case management, 19, 60, 93, 96
CCO. *See* Communication as Organizing/ Communication as Constitutive of Organizing
Census, U.S., 118–19
centralization, 20, 66, 79, 89
Chewning, Lisa V., 25
Chicago, Illinois, 27–28
churches, 8, 24, 77
citizens/individuals, 18–19, 64–65, 88, 103, 107; roles of, 100–101
civic engagement, 12, 65–66, 68, 103–5
civic media, 6, 64–68
civic networks, 22–23, 99
class, 2–3, 97, 108–9
climate change, 13, 43
cloud software, 62–63

COADs (Coalitions of Organizations Active in Disaster), 4, 19, 47–48
coastal New Jersey, 8–9, 24–27, 68–69, 88, 118–19, 129; data collection, 114–15, 122–24; post-Sandy, 18–21, 89–101
Coast Guard, U.S., 9, 56–58
coding of data, 127–29
coffee shops, 23
collaboration, 34–35, 40–41, 80–83, 100, 107–8, 110; community, 88, 101; cross-sector, 47, 79; FEMA and, 46–48; grassroots, 62–66; hyperlocal organizing and, 6–12; multi-stakeholder, 11, 47, 76; organizational, 113–14
communal ties, 13, 103–4, 107
communication, 39, 46, 56, 69, 81–83, 88, 114; face-to-face, 68, 77, 80, 106; hyperlocal, 9–11, 103; interorganizational, 5, 11, 25, 64–65, 68; as organizing, 12, 17–27; role of, 17–18, 79–80, 105–6; technology, 62–68, 106
Communication as Organizing/ Communication as Constitutive of Organizing (CCO), 21–26
communicative management, 13, 77–83, 106, 110
community/communities, 21, 46, 59, 78–79, 81–83, 91, 116, 118–19; collaboration, 88, 101; communicative capacities of, 105–6; disaster impacted, 6–7, 36–38, 66–69, 80, 89, 108–10; empowerment, 33–35; gathering and, 22–26; information, 67–68; leaders, 18–19, 123; maritime, 9, 56, 59; resilience, 53–54; survivability, 7, 25–26, 73–77, 100, 105
Community Empowerment Act of 2015, Scottish, 34
community organizations, existing, 37–38, 62–63, 88–90, 94–95, 99–100
Compass 82 (organization), 4–5, 60
connective logistics, 63–66
consensus, 79–80, 82
Cooper, Katherine R., 54
coordination, 39, 46–48, 100
corporate/corporations, 5, 76–77. *See also* for-profit organizations

costs, 1–2, 76
counseling, 7, 37, 116–17
COVID-19 pandemic, 19, 22, 27–28, 61, 65, 97, 115
cross-sector, 7–8, 12, 19, 34–36, 54, 56, 96; collaboration, 47, 79
crowd-sourced technologies, 62–63, 106
culture, 10, 54, 57–58, 64–66, 68, 82, 109; Scottish, 34–35

data, 98–100, 113, 120–24, 127–29; Census, 118–19
Day, Jack, 56–57
decentralization/decentralized, 6, 57–58, 119
decision-making, 8, 56, 78–79, 96
decline/declining, 20–21, 93–94
Deetz, Stanley A., 79
democracy, 68, 75
density, 119–20; network, 69, 93–94
Department of Commerce, U.S., 58
Department of Defense, U.S., 58
Department of Homeland Security, U.S., 58
Department of Transportation, U.S., 58
Department of Treasury, U.S., 58
dependency/dependencies, 20–21, 76, 79
digital environments, 22, 77
digital technologies, 62–68
disaster: defined, 1–12. *See also specific topics*
disaster relief organizations, 37, 60, 62–63, 87–88, 91, 96–97
disaster research, 11, 105
disaster response crisis counseling, 116–17
diversity/diversification, 42–44
documents, 44, 45, 46, 81, 122
Doerfel, Marya L., 8, 20, 25, 94, 106, 115, 122
domestic violence agency, 7, 37
dynamics/dynamism, 7, 20–21, 27, 35–41, 60, 100, 105

early childhood centers, 104, 114
earthquakes, 2, 8, 63
ecology, organizational, 20–21
economies, 33–35, 42–43, 79
ecosystems, information, 67–68, 115, 118, 121

elected officials, 36, 61, 69, 79, 96
eligibility, disaster assistance, 42–44, 91–93, 95
emergence/emergent, 4–6, 12, 27, 36–38, 54, 97, 120; hyperlocal organizing and, 63–66, 88–89; organizing, 28–29, 59–63, 88–89, 98–99, 113. *See also* organizing, emergent
emergency management, 4–6, 38–41, 43, 89
emergency response, 25, 36–37, 55–58, 60
empirical data, 130
empirical evidence, 117
employment, 25–26, 33–35, 42–44, 76
empowerment, 33–36
Energy Scotland (charity), 34
engagement: civic, 12, 65–66, 68, 103–5; stakeholder, 78–79, 82, 96–97
Entergy (utilities company), 108–9
equity, 41–44
ethics, 75, 77
European Union, 83n1
evacuation, 9–11, 55–58
evidence, empirical, 117
experts/expertise, 10, 56–58, 75–76, 89, 109

Facebook, 28
face-to-face communication, 68, 77, 80, 106
failure, institutional, 9–10, 38, 40, 61–63, 82–83, 114
faith-based organizations, 8, 39, 81, 97, 99–100; coastal New Jersey, 18–19; National VOAD and, 47–48; on Staten Island, 67, 69
federal disaster response/policies, 62–63, 87, 92–93, 109; frameworks, 38–41, 44, 82, 89, 100; funding, 46–48, 98; language of, 44, *45*, 46. *See also specific policies*
Federal Emergency Management Agency (FEMA), U.S., 10, 22, 29, 92–93, 100, 106; National Disaster Recovery Framework, 38–41, 46, 98–99, 101; RSFs, 38–41, 46–48, 98–99; 2022–2026 Strategic Plan, 41–44
Federal Flood Insurance Program, U.S., 91, 95

FEMA. *See* Federal Emergency Management Agency
field research, 23, 114–19, 127
fire services/firehouses, 8, 23, 56, 91
first responders, 36–37, 62–63
first wave interviews, 122–24
501c3 status. *See* nonprofit organizations
flexibility, 91
flooding/flood zones, 1, 3, 7–8, 91, 109
Florida, 60
flotilla, boat, 9, 55–58
focus groups, 100, 116, 121, 124, 127
food assistance, 4, 19, 26, 97, 98
formal disaster relief responses, 19–20, 28–30, 56, 99–100
for-profit organizations, 35–36, 76–77
frameworks, 3–5, 13, 21–26, 33–37, 116, 117; civic media, 64–66; federal disaster, 38–41, 44, 82, 89, 100; FEMA, 40, 98–99; institutional, 41–44, 107; time-based, 106, 114–15
funding, 43, 91–93, 114, 115; federal, 46–48, 98; long-term recovery, 95–96; Scottish, 34–35
A Future with Hope (nonprofit), 18

gathering (post-disaster), 22–27
gender, 34
geographical bounding, 119–20
GIS mapping software, 62–63
goals, 17–18, 26, 41, 76–77, 79–80, 106, 115; shared, 22, 27–28, 30, 82–83
Google Maps, 62–63
governance, democratic, 13, 78–79, 103–4, 106–10
government, U.S. *See* federal disaster response/policies
grant programs, 92–95
grassroots organizations, 4, 9, 11–13, 30, 61, 88, 91, 109; advocacy by, 95–97; collaboration by, 62–66; marginalization of, 36, 114; post-Sandy, 22–26, 89–90, 95; roles of, 2, 101; Staten Island, 97–99
Greenstone, Laura, 103, 116
Gress, Douglas R., 7–8
grounded theory, 121
Guyon Rescue, 19–20

Haiti, 2, 63
Harris, Jack L., 8, 20, 94
HBCUs. *See* Historically Black Colleges and Universities
Health and Social Services Recovery Support Function, National Disaster Recovery Framework, 39–40
healthcare, 35
hi-flex operations, 57–58
high-reliability organizations (HROs), 57–58
Historically Black Colleges and Universities (HBCUs), 42–44
history, 2–3, 42–44, 47, 58
homeowners, 42–43, 78, 99–100; eligibility for disaster assistance for, 91–92, 95
Horowitz, Andy, 2–3
hospitals, 4
housing, 18–19, 39, 42–44, 97
Housing Recovery Support Function, National Disaster Recovery Framework, 39–40
Houston, Texas, 62–63, 90, 115, 119
HROs. *See* high-reliability organizations
humanitarian relief organizations, 88, 89
Hurricane Betsy, 3
Hurricane Harvey, 58, 62–63, 115
Hurricane Ida, 25, 61, 108–9
Hurricane Irma, 2
Hurricane Katrina, 2–3, 25, 38, 40, 58, 60, 62, 92, 106; post-, 5, 39, 42–43, 63, 109–10
Hurricane Maria, 25, 60–61, 115
Hurricane Michael, 115
Hurricane Sandy, 1, 22–27, 37, 62, 66–68, 114. *See also* post-Sandy
Hurricane Sandy Rebuilding Task Force, U.S., 10–11, 40–41
hyperlocal organizing. *See specific topics*

identity/identities, 22, 68, 77, 101
Illinois, 27–28
improvisational disaster responses, 8–12, 22–26, 55–59
inclusion, 42–44, 78
income, 25–26, 76
indexes, survey, 4, 129–30
individuals. *See* citizens/individuals

inequalities, 2–3, 41–44, 53–54, 104, 108–9
informal, organizing, 27–30, 81, 101
information, 67–68, 80–81, 116, 122; ecosystems, 115, 118, 121. *See also* data
infrastructure, 34–35, 54, 67–78, 96, 105–6; organizational, 5, 35, 114; physical, 104, 108–9
institutionalization, 28–29, 59–62, 66, 75
institutions/institutional disaster response, 4, 36–38, 57–59; failure, 9–10, 38, 40, 61–63, 82–83, 114; frameworks, 41–44, 107; hyperlocal organizing and, 95–97; logics, 21, 28–29, 38, 89; Staten Island, 97–99. *See also specific institutions*
insurance, 25, 91, 98
Internews, 67–68, 115, 118, 123–24, 129
interorganizational communication, 5, 11, 25, 64–65, 68
interorganizational relationships (IORs), 11, 45, 93, 114, 116–17, 127; hyperlocal organizing and, 53–54, 64–69, 88
interviews, research, 120–24, 127
IORs. *See* interorganizational relationships
Ireland, 34–35
Ironbound Community Corporation, 97
Island of Jura, Scotland, 34–35, 116
The Islands Act of 2018, Scottish, 34
isolation, 9–10, 89

Japan, 8
JDT. *See* Jura Development Trust
Jim Crow era, 42–43
jobs. *See* employment
Joplin, Missouri, 20, 119
Jura Development Trust (JDT), 34–35
Jura Jottings (newsletters), 116

Karunarathne, Ananda Y., 7–8
Kendra, James, 9, 56
Kisselburgh, Lorraine G., 29
knowledge, 53, 89, 117; local, 10, 56–58, 100–101, 114
Kreps, Gary A., 36–38, 47, 94

Lai, Chih-Hui, 25
Lake Charles, Louisiana, 119
land, 34–35

Land Reform Act of 2003, Scottish, 34
landscapes, 62–63. *See also* organizational
    landscape
language, 22, 37–41, 44, *45*, 46, 128
laws, 34–35, 37. *See also specific laws*
leaders/leadership, 81, 89–91; community,
    18–19, 123; nonprofit, 92, 95–97;
    organizational, 68–69, 79, 122
libraries, 68
"lily pads" (temporary shelter), 62, 71n16
local, 26–27, 63–64, 68–69, 94, 96;
    knowledge, 10, 56–58, 100–101, 114
localization, 59–72
logistics, 18, 63–66, 114; institutional, 21,
    28–29, 38, 89
long-term disaster recovery, 4–6, 18–19, 21,
    59–62, 79–80, 110, 121; for Hurricane
    Sandy, 89–94, 114; hyperlocal
    organizing in, 87–88; for mid-Atlantic
    states, 101, 108–9, 127
Long-Term Recovery Groups (LTRGs)/
    Long-Term Recovery Organizations
    (LTROs), 4, 39, 47–48, 62–63, 93–96,
    99; face-to-face communication for,
    80–81
Louisiana, 10, 60, 61, 108–9. *See also* New
    Orleans, Louisiana
LTRGs/LTROs. *See* Long-Term Recovery
    Groups/Long-Term Recovery
    Organizations

macroprocesses, 88
Manhattan, New York, 55–58
maps/mapping, 62–63, 91, 106
marginalized populations, 36, 41–44, 97,
    104, 108–9, 114
maritime community, 9, 56, 59
Marticek, Sue, 4
mass communication, 66, 106
mayors, 69, 79, 96
measurability, 3, 60
media, 63, 95, 124; civic, 6, 64–68; social,
    77, 80–81
Mennonite Disaster Relief, 38–39
Meshnet Wireless, 106
messages/messaging, 17, 44, *45*, 46
methodology, reflexive, 117–19, 130
microprocesses, 88

microshelters, 23
mid-Atlantic states, 1, 101, 108–9, 114,
    127
middle class, 2–3, 108–9, 119
Middlesex County, New Jersey, 118
minimum-wage, 26, 28
Mintzberg, Henry, 75–76
misinformation, 65
missions, 7, 34, 47–48, 58–59, 95, 101
Missouri, 119
mitigation, disaster, 4, 96
Mobile, Alabama, 58
mobilization, 4, 8, 64–65, 96–97
Monmouth County, New Jersey, 95–96,
    98, 118
multi-stakeholder collaboration, 11, 47, 76
Municipal Business Administrators, 69
mutual aid, 61, 105, 115–16

Napoli, Phil, 115, 118
National Disaster Recovery Framework,
    FEMA, 38–41, 46, 98–99, 101
national nonprofits, 99–100
National Science Foundation, 115
natural resource management, 78–79
needs, 7, 19–20, 25–27, 63–64, 90–94
negative externality, 108
neighborhoods/neighborhood organizations,
    9, 62–63, 97, 114, 118
networks/networked, 20–21, 62–63, 105,
    129; civic, 22–26, 99; cross-sector, 7–8,
    36, 96; density, 69, 93–94; disaster
    recovery, 88, 93–94, 97; inequalities,
    53–54, 104; organizational, 7–9, 54,
    104, 106; recovery, 93, 97, 99; social
    impact, 6, 53–54; stakeholders, 7–8,
    63–64, 74–80, 103, 121
Newark, New Jersey, 97
New Jersey, 13, 55–58, 90–91, 114, 118–
    19, 121; VOAD, 10–11, 61, 97. *See also*
    coastal New Jersey; *specific cities*
New Jersey Organizing Project (NJOP), 95
New Orleans, Louisiana, 2–3, 61, 90,
    108–9, 119
New York, 9–12, 14, 56–58, 89, 91, 97;
    data collection in, 114–15, 123–24. *See*
    also specific boroughs
New York (boat), 56–57

New York Harbor, 8–9, 55–59, 118
9/11, 9, 55–59, 89, 116–17
NJOP. *See* New Jersey Organizing Project
nongovernmental stakeholders, 40–41
nonprofit organizations, 18, 35–36, 69,
    95–97, 99–100
Nordic countries/society, 77, 79, 83n1

Occupy Sandy, 8, 61–62, 64, 66–68, 89
Occupy Wall Street movement, 61, 67
Ocean County, New Jersey, 4, 60, 90,
    95, 123
Oceanport, New Jersey, 18–21, 23–24, 37,
    116–17
Oceanport Cares (nonprofit), 18–19
office of emergency management (OEM),
    35–36, 97, 99, 117
"organizational capital," 104, 114
organizational landscape, 6–7, 13, 20–21,
    45, 46–48, 116, 127
organizations/organizational, 10–11,
    17–18, 38–41, 107, 115–16, 121;
    backbone, 48, 100; coding of, 128–29;
    communication, 80; density, 119–20;
    ethics, 75, 77; infrastructure, 5, 35,
    114; landscapes, 33–35, 46–48;
    leaders, 68–69, 79, 122; networks,
    7–9, 54, 104, 106; organizing and,
    27–30; relationships, 53–54, 113–14;
    responsibilities, 62; roles of, 36–38,
    62, 129; social capital used by, 106;
    survivability, 13, 73–77; theory, 20–21;
    ties, 105, 109. *See also specific types of
    organizations*
organizing, 1–2, 13, 46, 66–67;
    communication as, 12, 17–27; emergent,
    28–29, 59–63, 88–89, 98–99, 113;
    informal, 27–30, 81, 101; processes,
    18–27, 103–4. *See also* self-organizing
organizing, emergent, 104
Orwell, George, 34
Otsuyama, Kensuke, 8
outcomes, disaster recovery, 38–41

Parliament, Scottish, 34–35
participants, research, 115, 120–24
participation, 6, 64–66, 68, 78

partnerships, 5, 34–35, 106
peer-peer communication, 66
perceptions, 2–3, 89, 100
Perrow, Charles, 76
phases/phased disaster recovery, 3–5,
    36–38, 106
philanthropy, 11, 91
phone, communication by, 81
physical infrastructure, 104, 108–9
pilots, New York Harbor, 56–58
places (physical locations), 22–27, 63–64,
    67–69, 77
plantation economies, 42–43
plural sector, 7–10, 37–39, 46–48, 74–76,
    87, 97, 107, 122
police, 9, 99
policy/policies, public, 38–43, 93, 96–97,
    108; institutional messaging and, 44,
    45, 46; Scottish, 33–35. *See also* federal
    disaster response/policies; *specific policies*
politics/political life, 3, 61, 103, 107
"pop-up" organizations, 11–12, 22, 61–62,
    89, 98–100
Port of New York and New Jersey, 55
post-disaster/post-disaster recovery. *See
    specific topics*
Post-Katrina Emergency Reform Act of
    2006, U.S., 40
Post Office, U.S., 68
post-Sandy, 4–5, 11–13, 22–26, 39; coastal
    New Jersey, 18–21, 89–101; Staten
    Island, 77–78, 89–101
power, 6, 20–21, 53, 75, 79, 106, 109
power (energy), 34–35, 67–68, 108–9
preparedness, disaster, 4, 41–44
presidential election (2020), U.S., 65
Presidential Executive Order 13985, U.S.,
    42
primary stakeholders, 76–77
private sector, 7, 10, 35–36, 46, 74–75
problem-solving, 79, 87–88
process coding, 128
processes, 17–27, 43–44, 64–66, 87–89,
    105, 108; communicative management,
    77–83, 110; long-term recovery, 60, 93;
    organizing, 18–27, 103–4; relational, 6,
    17–18, 105–6; research, 113–17

Promontory Point swimmers, 27–30, 81
psychological resilience, 104
public infrastructure, 96
public sector, 6, 35–36, 46, 74–75, 107, 122
Puerto Rico, 2, 61

qualitative data, 127–28
Quarantelli, Enrico L., 2–3
questions, 81–82, 122–24

race/racial, 2–3, 42–44, 97, 108
radio, 56, 106
RDT. *See* resource dependency theory
rebuilding, 25, 60, 81, 93–97
Reconstruction, Rehabilitation, and Mitigation Program (RREM), New Jersey, 91
recovery, disaster, 35–41, 87; networks of, 92, 97, 99; as phased, 36–38, 106. *See also* long-term disaster recovery
Recovery Support Functions (RSFs), FEMA, 38–41, 46–48, 98–99
Red Cross, American, 8, 22, 29, 37–40, 100
reflexive methodology, 117–19, 130
reform, policy, 96–99
regional, 91, 92. *See also* mid-Atlantic states
relational process, 6, 17–18, 105–6
relationships, 13, 101; cross-sector, 12, 19, 54; organizational, 53–54, 113–14; stakeholder, 59, 109. *See also* interorganizational relationships (IORs)
religious faith, 18–19, 75
remixing, 66–67, 82, 109
renewable energy (power), 34–35
representation, 79, 97
research, 41–42, 53–54, 113, 120; data collection in, 114–17, 122–24; reflexive methodology in, 117–19, 130
researchers, 113–17
residents. *See* citizens/individuals
resilience, 19, 40, 53–54, 103–6, 108, 115
resource dependency theory (RDT), 20–21
resources, 20–21, 43–44, 78–79, 97, 99–101, 105, 108
responsibilities, 22, 61–62, 76–78, 87–95; of FEMA, 40, 43–44, 99–100

restaurants, 26–27
Revenue Cutter Service, Department of Treasury, 58
Rhenman, Eric, 79
rights, 21, 34–35
Rockefeller Foundation, 115
roles, 2, 36–38, 40, 46–47, 91–100; of Coast Guard, 57–58; of communication, 17–18, 79–80, 105–6; of communities, 77–83; of hyperlocal organizing, 100–101, 114; of information, 67–68; of National VOAD, 46–48; of organizations, 36–38, 62, 129; of researcher, 115–17
RREM. *See* Reconstruction, Rehabilitation, and Mitigation Program, New Jersey
RSF. *See* Recovery Support Functions
Rubin, Claire, 5–6
Rutgers Eagleton Institute of Politics, 99, 118, 123–24, 129

safety, 4, 57–58
Salvation Army, 22, 37–39
saturation, theoretical, 121
SBP (nonprofit, formerly the "St. Bernard Project"), 5, 19, 60, 89–91
schools, public, 23, 68
Scotland/Scottish/Jura Isle, 33–35, 83n1, 116
Sea Bright, New Jersey, 19, 24, 27, 90
Sea Bright Resource Center, 27
Sea Bright Rising (hyperlocal organization), 27
secondary stakeholders, 76–77
second wave interviews, 122–24
segregation, 108
self-organizing, 27–30, 55–58, 61, 89
sensemaking, 30, 56, 100, 106
sequential interviewing, 120–24
shared goals, 22, 27–28, 30, 82–83
Shaw, Rajib, 8
shelters, 4, 22–24, 98, 116–17
Shoal, John, 18
ShopRite (regional supermarket), 37
short-term disaster recovery, 4, 60, 93, 100–101
Shumate, Michelle, 54

SI COAD. *See* Staten Island Coalition of
    Organizations Active in Disaster
SILTRO. *See* Staten Island Long-Term
    Recovery Organization
SINFPA. *See* Staten Island Not For Profit
    Association
sites, research, 114–17. *See also* place
    (physical locations)
slavery, 42–44
Small, Mario Luis, 54, 104, 114
Smith, Adam, 75
social capital, 7–8, 53–54, 88, 103–6, 114
social enterprises, 33–35
social impact networks, 6, 53–54
social media, 28, 77, 80–81
social resilience, 104–10
social ties, 54, 89, 105–8
social welfare, 107–8
spontaneous volunteering, 13, 56–58, 88
Sri Lanka, 7–8
Stafford Act, U.S., 38–39, *45*, 101, 110
stakeholders, 8, 17, 40–41, 58–59, 87–88,
    108; engagement of, 78–79, 82, 96–97;
    networked, 7–8, 63–64, 75–80, 103,
    121; theory, 6–7, 13, 21, 74–83
Staten Island, New York, 19–20, 55,
    66–68, 97–100, 115, 118; interviews
    from, 121, 123–24; post-Sandy, 77–78,
    89–101
Staten Island Coalition of Organizations
    Active in Disaster (SI COAD), 97–99
Staten Island Long-Term Recovery
    Organization (SILTRO), 67, 69, 89,
    97–100
Staten Island Not For Profit Association
    (SINFPA), 97–98
St. Bernard Parish, 3, 10, 19, 60
strategic management theory, 76–77
supermarkets, 23–24, 37
supply chain, 10, 36, 55
survey, 34, 99–100, 123–24, 129–30
survivability/survival, 21; community, 7,
    25–26, 73–77, 100, 105; organizational,
    13, 73–77
survivors, 9–11, 55–58
swimmers, Promontory Point, 27–30, 81

technology/technologies, 62–68, 106

Texas, 61–63, 90, 115–16, 119
theory/theories, 1–2, 6, 13, 20–21;
    construction of, 113–14, 121. *See also*
    specific theories
"third spaces," 22, 54
ties, 129–30; associational, 13, 103–4,
    107; communal, 13, 103–4, 107;
    organizational, 105, 109; social, 54, 89,
    105–8
time-based frameworks, 3–5, 106, 114–15,
    120–24
Title III, Stafford Act, 38–39
Tocqueville, Alexis de, 68, 107
tornadoes, 109
trauma, 103, 117
trust, 106, 124
tsunami, 8
2022-2026 Strategic Plan, FEMA, 41–44
Type 1 disaster responses, 36–37
Type 2 disaster responses, 37, 47
Type 3 disaster responses, 37, 47–48
Type 4 disaster responses, 37–38
typhoons, 1

UK Community Energy sector survey
    (2021), 34
unemployment, 25
unions (labor), 77, 91
United Kingdom, 34, 83n1
United Methodists of Greater New Jersey,
    18–19
United States (U.S.), 1–2, 13, *45*, 55, 58,
    68, 91, 103–4; faith-based organizations
    in, 39; federal assistance, 109; slavery in,
    42–44; township governance in, 107;
    voluntary associations in, 46, 109. *See*
    also specific laws
University of Colorado Boulder, 115

virtual spaces, 22, 77
VOAD, National (National Voluntary
    Organizations Active in Disaster), 4,
    13, 38–40, 46–48, 62–63, 100; of New
    Jersey, 10–11, 61, 97
voluntary associations, 13, 46, 75, 107, 109
volunteering/volunteer, 9, 18–19, 27,
    60–63, 99, 103, 117; firehouses, 8, 23,
    91; spontaneous, 13, 56–58, 88, 98, 104

Wachtendorf, Tricia, 9, 56
wages, 25–26, 76. *See also* income
wealth, 3, 108, 119
Wegmans (supermarket), 23–24
well-being, 6, 21, 54, 105–6
Wellstone, Paul, 107
Western society, 75–77, 79
white people, 2–3
wildfires, 1–2

Wilhoit, Elizabeth D., 29
Wilson Carey McWilliams, 75
Winter Storm Uri, 61, 116
Wollman, Jeff, 9
Wollman, Steven, 56
Woody's (restaurant), 27
working class, 3, 108
World Trade Center, 9–12, 55
World War II, 56

About the Author

Jack L. Harris is a visiting assistant professor of communication and summer internship director at the University of Illinois Urbana-Champaign. He is an expert on long-term recovery after disaster, community collaborations, communicative resilience, and disaster communication. In addition to his academic research, he has held volunteer leadership roles in disaster recovery and planning in coastal New Jersey.

www.ingramcontent.com/pod-product-compliance
Lightning Source LLC
Chambersburg PA
CBHW022321280326
41932CB00010B/1177

* 9 7 8 1 6 6 6 9 2 7 2 5 2 *